EXISTENTIAL FLOURISHING

This innovative volume argues that flourishing is achieved when individuals successfully balance their responsiveness to three kinds of normative claim: self-fulfilment, moral responsibility, and intersubjective answerability. Applying underutilized resources in existential phenomenology, Irene McMullin reconceives practical reason, addresses traditional problems in virtue ethics, and analyzes four virtues: justice, patience, modesty, and courage. Her central argument is that there is an irreducible normative plurality arising from the different practical perspectives we can adopt – the first-, second-, and third-person stances – which each presents us with different kinds of normative claim. Flourishing is human excellence within each of these normative domains, achieved in such a way that success in one does not compromise success in another. The individual virtues are solutions to specific existential challenges we face in attempting to do so. This book will be important for anyone working in the fields of moral theory, existential phenomenology, and virtue ethics.

IRENE MCMULLIN is Senior Lecturer in Philosophy at the University of Essex. She is the author of *Time and the Shared World* (2013) and numerous articles in journals including *Philosophical Review*, *European Journal of Philosophy*, *Kantian Review*, and *Philosophical Topics*.

EXISTENTIAL FLOURISHING

A Phenomenology of the Virtues

IRENE MCMULLIN
University of Essex

CAMBRIDGE
UNIVERSITY PRESS

University Printing House, Cambridge CB2 8BS, United Kingdom

One Liberty Plaza, 20th Floor, New York, NY 10006, USA

477 Williamstown Road, Port Melbourne, VIC 3207, Australia

314–321, 3rd Floor, Plot 3, Splendor Forum, Jasola District Centre, New Delhi – 110025, India

79 Anson Road, #06–04/06, Singapore 079906

Cambridge University Press is part of the University of Cambridge.

It furthers the University's mission by disseminating knowledge in the pursuit of education, learning, and research at the highest international levels of excellence.

www.cambridge.org
Information on this title: www.cambridge.org/9781108471664
DOI: 10.1017/9781108617260

© Irene McMullin 2019

This publication is in copyright. Subject to statutory exception and to the provisions of relevant collective licensing agreements, no reproduction of any part may take place without the written permission of Cambridge University Press.

First published 2019

Printed and bound in Great Britain by Clays Ltd, Elcograf S.p.A.

A catalogue record for this publication is available from the British Library.

Library of Congress Cataloging-in-Publication Data
NAMES: McMullin, Irene, author.
TITLE: Existential flourishing : a phenomenology of the virtues / Irene McMullin.
DESCRIPTION: New York : Cambridge University Press, 2018. | Includes bibliographical references and index.
IDENTIFIERS: LCCN 2018029889 | ISBN 9781108471664 (hardback : alk. paper)
SUBJECTS: LCSH: Normativity (Ethics) | Success. | Existential phenomenology. | Ethics. | Virtues.
CLASSIFICATION: LCC BJ1458.3 .M37 2018 | DDC 179/.9–DC23
LC record available at https://lccn.loc.gov/2018029889

ISBN 978-1-108-47166-4 Hardback

Cambridge University Press has no responsibility for the persistence or accuracy of URLs for external or third-party internet websites referred to in this publication and does not guarantee that any content on such websites is, or will remain, accurate or appropriate.

To Mary, Lucy, and Matthew with love

To Mary, Lucy and Matthew with love

Contents

Acknowledgments		*page* viii
Introduction		1
1	What Is Flourishing?	12
2	Three Domains of Reason	40
3	Justice, the Virtues, and Existential Problem-Solving	68
4	Unity, Comparison, Constraint	86
5	Called to Be Oneself: Role Models and the Project of Becoming Virtuous	107
6	Corrupting the Youth	129
7	Patience	152
8	Modesty	178
9	Courage	202
Conclusion		223
Bibliography		227
Index		241

Acknowledgments

My thinking on this topic first began almost twenty years ago and I have received invaluable support and feedback from family, friends, and colleagues in the years since. I am indebted to my teachers at Rice University – especially Steven Crowell – for giving me the philosophical tools necessary for completing such a project. Early work on the book occurred while I was teaching at the University of Arkansas, Fayetteville, and I am grateful for the support and encouragement I received there. The majority of the book was written since arriving at the University of Essex in 2013. It would not have been possible without the extraordinary intellectual community I found here. I am deeply indebted to David Batho, Matthew Burch, Peter Dews, Matteo Falomi, Lorna Finlayson, Fabian Freyenhagen, Steve Gormley, Marie Guillot, Béatrice Han-Pile, Fiona Hughes, Timo Jütten, Yannig Luthra, Wayne Martin, Alexandra Popescu, Jörg Schaub, Ellisif Wasmuth, Dan Watts, and Rosie Worsdale for their support, philosophical conversation, and feedback, especially at the 'mini-course' I was invited to give in 2015. It is a privilege to be part of such a wonderful group of philosophers and friends. I am also thankful for the many rewarding and thought-provoking conversations I have had with my PhD students – Darshan Cowles and Jakub Kowalewski – over the years.

I am grateful to all the audiences who sat through talks on related material at the Universities of Oslo, Bristol, Dublin, Seattle, Oxford, and Warwick – along with the International Society for Phenomenological Studies conference participants. The questions, challenges, and recommendations that arose there have been invaluable.

Special thanks go to Alexandra Popescu for her incredible work in preparing the manuscript and index for publication.

I also owe a debt of gratitude to my wonderful family: Mom, Jim, Heather, Neil, Laura, Mike, Amanda, Pip, Anita, Fred, Eleanor, and clan Burch: thank you for constantly serving as my role models, cheerleaders, and interlocutors.

My deepest thanks of all go to Matt, Lucy, and Mary. Every day is better because you are there to share it with me.

Introduction

The aim of this book is to bring together virtue ethics and existential phenomenology to produce a phenomenologically sensitive form of virtue ethics. In doing so it resists the tendency in moral theory toward what existentialists call bad faith – namely, a tendency to conceptualize one's condition in terms of a false dichotomy and fluctuate between self-interpretations manifesting one or the other half of the dichotomy. We see this tendency in virtue ethics when flourishing is characterized as either a private state of the subject or an objective state of the person conceptualized as a worldly thing. In contrast, this book insists that excellent human lives are characterized by a kind of self-world fit at odds with such views – which either fail to demonstrate the essential dependence of the self on the world and the others who share it or fail to accommodate the lived normative responsiveness that defines us in our striving to be in the world well.

For many, the appeal of the revival of virtue ethics has been its insistence that we shift our focus from assessing isolated acts or act types to evaluating the shape and texture of lives as a whole. This shift has largely been motivated by the recognition that the meaning and motivation of individual acts cannot be understood in isolation from the context of the lives in which they occur. As a result, the suggestion is that we should be examining the extent to which a person is succeeding or failing at realizing an ideal of human excellence more globally understood.

Many recent virtue ethical attempts to define this human ideal – flourishing – have done so by relying on a naturalism that grounds moral theory in science-inspired analyses of characteristic human traits. While this approach has its merits, it can also come at the cost of both depersonalizing ethics and failing to account for its normativity. By conceiving of the moral agent simply as an instantiation of a natural kind, the individuation of the self in its struggle to be the best version of itself is obscured, as is the *ought* that underwrites ostensibly normatively neutral accounts of the characteristic human behaviours constitutive of human nature. On the other hand, attempts to define human excellence with reference only to the lived experience of the agent and her personal satisfaction levels risk isolating the agent from the worldly context of meaning in terms of which those satisfactions find content, expression, and some measure of objective legitimacy. Viewing the self as a theatre of representations and pleasures that can be privately organized in an enjoyable or efficacious way loses the link to the world wherein the legitimacy of those thoughts and feelings is tested. On such an account, it would be possible to flourish in solipsistic isolation – a conclusion at odds with many of our intuitions about what a good human life looks like.

This book addresses these problems by making use of resources from the existential phenomenological tradition to provide an account of human flourishing that navigates a middle path between these two extremes. It also aims to provide phenomenological descriptions of what it is like to experience the normative claim particular to different virtues – descriptions that virtue ethical accounts have largely failed to supply to date. My approach in this regard is not characterized by simple fidelity to the existential phenomenological tradition but rather by creative appropriation of its best methods and arguments. I am committed to the idea that we can enrich our understanding of the issues by bringing this tradition into conversation with virtue ethics. When we do so, we recognize that the existential tradition affords us the following insights:

1. A recognition that to be human is to be consumed with the deeply personal question 'What does it mean for *me* to be?' and that flourishing cannot be understood without addressing this first-personal dimension of experience – this sense that each of us is at stake in our choices.
2. An understanding that we can answer this question only in dialogue with the world and the third-person normative categories it provides for defining our struggle to be who we are – which includes but is not limited to those categories used to specify a scientifically grounded account of human nature.
3. An acknowledgment that the immediate normative claims that other individuals make on us are irreducible to either first- or third-person categories but bear a distinctive kind of authority by which we are also bound in our struggle to be in the world well.
4. A recognition that the task of living well is necessarily fraught with an open-ended indeterminacy and irresolvable normative tension

Introduction

between these three types of claim, a fact we must acknow
and accept.
5. A commitment to the idea that it is in terms of the question of who
one wishes to be in the world that one does the negotiation work
necessary for navigating this plural normative terrain. Namely, each of
us experiences herself as tasked with making her life a well-balanced
unity in the face of this normative complexity.

A central argument of this book, then, is that there is no single normative perspective through which we understand and manage our relationship to self, other, and world. There is, on the contrary, an irreducible normative plurality intrinsic to the plurality of perspectives that we can adopt on the world – first-person, second-person, and third-person stances – all of which make claims on us that we understand ourselves as having reason to meet.

From the first-person perspective, the agent is claimed by the success of her own individual agency – she is concerned to be efficacious and autonomous and to realize the unique configuration of abilities and preferences to which she is born. But from the second-person perspective, an agent experiences herself as claimed by the specific others with whom she shares her life. She acknowledges their authority to make binding claims on her. And from the third-person perspective, she recognizes demands that arise from her membership in the human community and its commitment to intersubjective projects aimed at understanding and establishing a shared world. Each of the perspectives offers us a set of distinct reasons that cannot be reduced to or translated into the others.

A flourishing life requires us to both respond well to these distinct normative terrains and negotiate the tensions that might arise between them. Each domain has its own internal standard for assessing what counts as a legitimate claim within it. Determining which claims we have reason to act on in each circumstance will depend both on the normative structure intrinsic to each domain and the demand to balance the claims arising from these normative domains against each other such that one's life as a whole embodies a responsiveness to all three types of claim.

This condition should be entirely familiar from the experience of our daily lives. While walking through the city you observe a man selling homemade plastic crafts and you feel claimed by competing demands: the sense of immediate obligation toward him in his poverty and enterprise, the urge to use that money to satisfy one's own preferences instead, and the belief that the endless consumption of useless plastic items – let alone the endorsement of individual charity instead of structural solutions to poverty – will not create a world in which the needs of all are best met. These classes of normative claim cannot be reduced to each other or to a non-normative natural state. Nor is there a clear hierarchy among them. The consequence is that there is a fundamental and irresolvable tension characterizing human life; we are tasked with negotiating competing claims with no recourse to an overarching or ultimate metric in terms of which these conflicts can be neatly adjudicated. Understanding flourishing means acknowledging this lived indeterminacy and tension rather than dissolving it via a neat theoretical solution. Flourishing requires an ongoing negotiation of these competing types of legitimate claim in order to achieve a kind of proportionality – a fragile and shifting balance – between the different normative terrains. Flourishing is best defined as human excellence within each of these domains (self-fulfilment, moral responsibility, and responsiveness to intersubjective norms) but achieved in such a way that success in one domain does not compromise success in another. As we will see in Chapter 3, the task of negotiating these competing normative domains ultimately falls under the purview of the virtue of justice, since justice is the stance according to which one gives competing legitimate claims their due. In Chapter 4 we will discuss the role that *phronēsis* plays in this negotiation work. And in later chapters we will see that each specific virtue is best understood as such skilful negotiation work in the face of different kinds of challenging circumstance innate to the human condition.

The difficulty of performing this negotiation work helps explain problems that arise within the virtue ethical literature itself. One such difficulty is the so-called action-guidingness issue, according to which virtue ethics supposedly does not offer sufficient guidance for answering what one ought to do – at least compared with deontology or utilitarianism. But on my account both deontology and utilitarianism succeed in offering such guidance primarily because they tend to operate almost exclusively in terms of the norms of a single stance – a stance according to which all first-person and second-person claims can be translated into a single third-personally available universal standard, whether it be utility or rational duty.

This is not to oversimplify these positions, however. Kantian deontology prioritizes the third-person universality of a reason that is understood to be identically present in all agents, but it attempts to accommodate the other normative perspectives through the notions of respect for others (the second-person dimension) and respect for self (the first-person dimension). Similarly, utilitarianism prioritizes the third-person norm of universal utility, but it attempts to accommodate the other perspectives through the fact that one's own utility does not automatically trump the other person's (the second-person dimension) and the fact that the nature of its guiding norm – *satisfaction* – includes a fundamental reference to the first-personal domain. But in both cases the intention – an intention that is understood as realizable – is to provide a decision procedure that stipulates adopting a neutral third-person stance that purportedly captures the normative force or authority of the other two normative domains.

Indeed, virtue ethical accounts themselves fail to understand the nature of flourishing when they insist that such messiness can be avoided – by claiming, for example, that the fully virtuous person would never experience virtuous action as a sacrifice.[1] Failing to recognize the compromise among perspectives *as* compromise – i.e., as a condition in which legitimate claims sometimes cannot be met fully – is a failure to acknowledge the legitimacy of the claims. But by shifting our emphasis from specific acts to lives as a whole we can overcome this difficulty to some degree, since each agent will be assessed on the extent to which her life embodies a general respect for the different kinds of normative claim that she is tasked with meeting, not necessarily on the extent to which she does so in each particular act. However, we will see in Chapter 4 that certain deontic constraints must be operative – lowest common denominators below which the agent cannot go if she is to count as meeting the minimal requirements of each normative domain. Nevertheless, these constraints are both minimal and specific to the domains in question – and thus incapable of dissolving all possibilities of conflict. I will argue in Chapters 5 and 6 that ultimately we must look to specific virtuous lives as exemplars of the kind of perspectival balancing that is at stake in flourishing. There is no simple decision procedure or algorithm for determining what one ought to do or how one ought to be in every situation. But this is the truth of our moral predicament, not a flaw in our moral theory.

An existentialism-informed virtue ethics is a natural fit for accommodating this irrevocable tension at the heart of human life. It acknowledges that the messiness and complexity involved in negotiating such a normative plurality cannot be avoided. Broadly understood, existentialism analyzes the nature of human existence – understanding it above all in terms

---

[1] See McDowell 1980 and Phillips 1965.

of the fact that human beings take their existence to be at issue for them, relating to it in terms of questions of success and failure. Human existence is fundamentally oriented to questions of better and worse, and each of us experiences ourself as being at stake in how we navigate such normative demands. We care about doing what we have reason to do, and since practical reasons arise from incommensurable domains of value in human life, this means we care about knowing how to navigate this irrevocable tension well.

Phenomenology is the method regularly endorsed by thinkers of this existentialist tradition – largely because it explicitly attempts to embody this normative plurality in its methodology.[2] Phenomenology is a method committed to uncovering universal truths about the structure of meaning (third-personal categories) through descriptive analyses of one's first-person experience. These descriptions are aimed at evoking in others a corresponding grasp of that experience – a second-personal stance that recognizes others as occupants of their own first-person domain of experience. Though this characterization of phenomenology in many ways applies to philosophy in general, phenomenology understands itself as tasked with negotiating the plurality and tension that existentialism describes: it analyzes how objects both immanent and transcendent to first-person experience – the self, the world, and the others in it – are structured within that experience such that they accomplish their meaning *as* what they are for the agent engaged in her struggle to be. As such, it bears within its methodology an explicit acknowledgment of the plurality of perspectives with which it is operating: A good phenomenological analysis is aimed at examining and describing the nature of one's own first-person experience in such a way that it provokes in others similar first-personal self-grasping intuitions that can serve to confirm or disconfirm one's understanding of the structures of intelligibility that govern the possibility of that meaningful experience. And, importantly for my claim that phenomenology strives to embody methodological variations of all three normative stances, Husserl insisted that first-person reflection on the field of meaningful experiences could yield universal structural necessities. The most fundamental meaning structure of this kind, according to Husserl, is the fact that all consciousness is characterized by intentionality. Namely, consciousness is always consciousness *of* something; it is always

---

[2] Though we sometimes see the expression 'phenomenology' used to refer simply to the 'what it is like' nature of experience, here I use it in the sense developed by Edmund Husserl and his critical admirers in the early twentieth century. For a good introduction to this tradition, see Crowell 2013.

directed toward some meaningful object. This relationship is therefore composed of two *relata*: the act by which the meaningful appearance comes to manifestation and the object in its appearing. Phenomenology studies the correlation of these two elements, i.e., the dynamic interplay between the experiencer and the experienced such that meaning arises. Though it is possible to tease them apart in analysis, these two 'sides' of the meaning experience belong together inseparably (Husserl 1999, 39/77). Phenomenology's insistence on the importance of examining all meanings from the perspective of lived experience is motivated by its recognition of this necessary interplay between self and world.

Heidegger famously builds on Husserl's analyses of intentionality, critiquing the philosophical tendency to conceptualize lived experience through the lens of a kind of subject/object dichotomy that artificially separates the self from the world. He insists that being true to the nature of lived experience requires us to recognize that we are not typically 'subjects' grasping 'objects', but rather agents immersed in the world in a way that belies such a divide. Indeed, Heidegger more explicitly links phenomenology with existentialist themes by insisting that experiencing and analyzing meaning in this way depends on a normatively governed striving to be who one is in the world.

As will become evident, this existential-phenomenological approach is at work throughout the book. We see it in particular in my application of Heidegger's challenge to views of flourishing that isolate a subjective inner life from an objective external world, in my insistence that the dynamic correlation between experiencer and experienced – between agent and world – requires us to think differently about what kind of agents we are in our striving to flourish. Further, when we attend carefully to the phenomena we are forced to reject moral theories that model praxis on abstract knowledge or that prioritize one normative domain to the exclusion of others – whether that reductionist agenda is understood in terms of individual desire-satisfaction or in terms of third-personally conceived realizations of objective values or human nature. Genuinely understanding what a good human life is requires us to acknowledge the complex normative terrain and perspectival manifold that characterizes the experience of human life as it is lived – not to look for an artificial simplicity that can be applied to it from without. Succumbing to that temptation is a common human tendency since it offers clarity and direction to those yearning for it. But doing so involves bad faith: it is a failure to face up to the paradox and complexity of being subjects who are also worldly objects that can conceptualize themselves as such.

As we will see, this existential-phenomenological approach is in many ways a natural fit with a neo-Aristotelian virtue ethics insofar as the latter emphasizes the necessity of understanding agents as a whole: our striving for an excellence that manifests as both subjective pleasure and worldly achievement and the practical reason that allows us to navigate the normative questions intrinsic to a life that is always understood as governed by questions of success and failure. As I will show, humanity's characteristic activity in this regard is indeed 'an activity of the soul in accordance with reason',[3] but in what follows I will argue that 'reason' must be understood such that it accommodates the normative plurality of perspectives through which the world shows up as meaningful in the way that I have specified above. As such, defining reason as deliberation about how best to realize first-person preferences or conform to third-person categories of universalizability or scientific objectivity is too narrow. Reason must instead be understood in terms of a person's capacity to see the world not merely from the constraints of her own projects, but also in terms of the individual others we encounter and the intersubjectively determined standards established by the human community for sharing the world. These domains all provide flourishing agents with reasons – considerations that count in favour of an action or belief – and there is no ultimate perspective from which the different classes of reason can be definitively ordered. As a result, flourishing requires that one negotiate the complexity and tension that is characteristic of a life experienced from multiple perspectives and governed by the different demands that those perspectives reveal.

Chapter Breakdown

In Chapter 1, 'What Is Flourishing?', I defend the virtue ethical claim that the ultimate objects of moral assessment are lives, not actions, and I challenge both subjectivist and objectivist models of what an excellent or flourishing human life looks like, arguing that both approaches obscure the complexity of creatures who exist simultaneously as experiencing subjects and worldly objects. In contrast, I argue that practical rationality must be understood as the way in which agents enact their commitment to the project of being in the world well: a condition that overcomes the false

---

[3] Aristotle 2000: I.7.1098a10–11. All references to Aristotle 2000 – the *Nichomachean Ethics* – will henceforth be referenced in the text as *NE* followed by book, section, and line number.

subject/object dichotomy with which other accounts of flourishing tend to operate.

Chapter 2, 'Three Domains of Reason', builds on the claim that the right way to understand flourishing is in terms of different possibilities of self-world fit that arise from the three normative domains to which flourishing agents are appropriately responsive: first-person claims of the self, second-person claims of the other, and third-person claims of the shared world. This chapter examines each of these normative domains and the standards internal to them.

In Chapter 3, 'Justice, the Virtues, and Existential Problem-Solving', I address the question of how to integrate the different normative perspectives within one's life. This chapter also discusses what virtues are and how they relate to flourishing. I argue that they are problem-solving stances that overcome recurring existential problems that undermine our ability to flourish. I examine the virtue of justice in particular, endorsing the ancient claim that justice can serve as a stand-in for all the virtues, since its purview is the appropriate balancing of the three normative domains.

Chapter 4, 'Unity, Comparison, Constraint', examines the relationship between the virtues and defends a version of the ancient 'unity of the virtues' thesis. Here I also consider how practical wisdom allows us to compare claims arising from the incommensurable normative terrains and reach a decision on what to do. I also respond to the objection that a virtue ethical account of this kind has no room for deontological constraints. To the contrary, I argue that there are minimal requirements governing what counts as responding to each of the three different normative domains.

Chapter 5, 'Called to Be Oneself: Role Models and the Project of Becoming Virtuous', examines the claim that virtuous agents are the ultimate criterion of right action. I present an account of role models and moral development that echoes the tripartite structure of norm-governed agency developed in Chapters 1 and 2 by arguing that the three key modes of moral development — imitation, habituation, and critical comparison — are shown to particularly rely on and enable the second-person, first-person, and third-person normative stances, respectively.

By making moral agency dependent on habituation and the imitation of exemplars, this view is open to a major objection: namely, that there seem to be no protections against bad exemplars who model the wrong kinds of life and thereby pervert one's moral agency. Chapter 6, 'Corrupting the Youth', addresses this worry by demonstrating the role that the third-person perspective plays in introducing critical distance between the agent and her exemplar. It also considers the role that deliberation and moral perception play in the flourishing agent's life.

Chapter 7, 'Patience', examines the way in which patience is a response to the challenge posed by temporal finitude. It discusses how this finitude manifests as both temporal scarcity and in terms of the fact that the project of human self-becoming is dispersed in time such that it necessarily resists completion and determinacy.

Chapter 8, 'Modesty', argues that modesty is a stance the virtuous agent adopts in the face of differences in accomplishment or status that might be experienced as painful to others. Modesty requires one to engage in pain-alleviating behaviour aimed at helping others cope with those differences and involves an appropriate understanding of the degree to which public measures of success ought to be taken as definitive of one's identity and value.

Chapter 9, 'Courage', examines the specific virtuousness of courage and, in particular, the extent to which we can accept Aristotle's claim that this virtue applies only when one faces death in battle. Building on Aristotle's claim, I argue that courage must be understood as arising in conditions of crisis where one's way of being is at stake. Courage enables one to choose one's better self – as measured by first-, second-, or third-person norms of assessment – in situations where one's identity is on the line.

A Note on the Virtues

The four virtues chosen for extended examination in the book – justice, modesty, patience, and courage – are meant to be illustrative, not exhaustive, since a full enumeration of how many (and which) virtues there are would require a complete taxonomy of the human condition and the challenges that arise therefrom. However, I have not chosen them at random. As we will see in Chapter 3, justice is a particularly central virtue insofar as it is both a specific virtue and a name for virtuousness as such. It is therefore essential to my account. The remaining three virtues were chosen not because they too have such a central status, but because each of the three tends to be interpreted primarily in terms of one of the three normative perspectives. For example, patience tends to be viewed primarily as an accommodating passivity in the face of another person's needs (a primarily second-person stance), while in contrast courage is typically characterized as a heroic virtue involving a kind of active self-assertion (a primarily first-person stance). Modesty, on the other hand (if recognized as a virtue at all), is regularly understood as involving an individual's attitudes toward third-person claims: public standards of success and questions of social cohesion. Examining these three virtues thereby allows me to show that contrary to what many believe, all three virtues are in fact characterized by responsivity to the tripartite condition of normative plurality at the heart of my account. Other candidates for virtue – generosity, fortitude, etc. – can also be examined using this framework, though I have not done so in detail here.

CHAPTER 1
What Is Flourishing?

Ethics is typically taken to be a discipline dedicated to the task of answering certain questions about what we ought to do and how we ought to be in the world. How to best approach answering those questions has variously focused on the structure or consequences of specific actions – as in deontology and consequentialism – or on the agent's character and the shape of her life as a whole, as in virtue ethics. Despite this difference, much of the recent discussion of virtue ethics has focused on whether it can serve as a genuine rival to deontology and utilitarianism by questioning whether it can be action-guiding in the same way that the norms of utility maximization or duty can be. Indeed, one trend has been to read 'virtue theory' merely as a branch of deontology or utilitarianism, the claim being that the virtues simply express character orientations necessary for maximizing utility or acting in accord with duty.[1]

Though these discussions have been fruitful, they can nevertheless obscure the defining feature of virtue ethics – namely, the fact that it is primarily an account of what excellent lives look like as a whole, and – further – not merely an account of what *morally* excellent lives look like.[2] The virtue ethical focus is not merely on answering the question 'What ought I to do?' but on the question 'What must be the case if human beings are to live good lives?' By focusing only on specific acts, the general context of human agency can be neglected: the complex set of beliefs, affective orientations, and behavioural tendencies from which specific acts arise (one's character[3]); the temporal spread of an agent's plans and identities across a lifetime; and the conditions of moral luck that enable or inhibit that agency – good parents, a virtue-promoting political environment, and other pieces of luck such as health.

---

[1] See, for example, Crisp 2015.
[2] See Annas 1995a.
[3] See Swanton 2003.

But what exactly is at stake in these different evaluative orientations toward 'being' versus 'doing', as it is sometimes put? Why should we take an agent's life and character to be the most basic objects of moral assessment, as virtue ethics claims we ought? George Sher examines this issue in 'Ethics, Character, and Action' (1998), where he points out that much of the debate on this issue tends to simply presuppose and reiterate the general metaethical orientation for which each camp is arguing. Thus virtue ethicists accuse action-based accounts of being 'unacceptably abstract or impersonal' or failing to 'do justice to the immense complexity of human affairs' (Sher 1998, 1). Further, they fail to recognize the close link between stable traits and identity. In other words, they accuse duty-based accounts of focusing on acts instead of character, which is precisely the issue in question. Similarly, duty theorists 'complain that accounts of the virtues provide no concrete guide to action', while the moral significance of control seems to demand an emphasis on actions rather than traits (Sher 1998, 1, 7). So the other approaches essentially accuse virtue ethicists of focusing on character instead of acts; that is, they accuse them of being virtue ethicists. In both cases features taken as independent evidence for the legitimacy of focusing on character or act as the appropriate object of moral evaluation simply presuppose it.

What, then, is the relationship between action and character, and does this relationship give us reason to grant one priority? On one reading, action has a kind of conceptual priority over character since it is only through what one does (or does not do) that a person's character could be known or understood. Thus the idea of character is conceptually dependent on certain act types. But on another reading, character has explanatory priority over action, since an action is more easily understood and categorized if we know that it arose out of a certain kind of character.[4] How are we to adjudicate between these modes of priority and to which approach ought we to grant *evaluative* priority?

In response to this impasse, Sher and others have suggested that we should question whether there is a problem with the unexamined assumption underlying both approaches: namely, the assumption that the task of ethics is to uncover the moral objects that we are in the business of evaluating. This assumption is problematic because it shifts our focus from practice to theory, presupposing that we can simply reveal what the conceptual categories are for moral classification, at which point it should be fairly obvious how to actually apply them in our lives. As Korsgaard points out, there is an unacknowledged tendency in ethical theory to wrongly think of

---

[4] Sher 1998, 4–6. See also Watson 2003, 262.

morality on the model of knowledge application, when it should be understood as a 'practical enterprise, an enterprise of working out the solutions to problems, not a mysteriously non-empirical theoretical enterprise aimed at identifying normative facts that are somehow part of the external world' (2008, 23). In attempting to determine evaluative priority we are not focused (primarily) on any kind of explicit categorization activity – especially of other people – but rather on the agent's ongoing assessment of how best to enact and direct her own practical engagement with the world. If we recognize that ethics is fundamentally a *practical* discipline in this way, what implications will that have for deciding whether to prioritize action over character in our struggle to answer the practical problems posed by life?

Sher argues that the practical orientation points us in the direction of action – i.e. knowing what to *do*. But in his framing of how to understand this practical reorientation he himself grants action an unargued-for priority in the very way that he critiques others for doing. Note his claim, for example, that:

> When we inquire about how to live, our aim is obviously to live that way; and living, in this sense, is unavoidably something we do. Moreover, although our lives are spread over many years, we live them one moment – and (roughly) one action – at a time. (1998, 16)

But it is far from clear that either of these claims is unambiguously true. Is living something we do, or something we are? And even if it *is* something we 'do', is it really the case that this 'doing' involves living one moment or one action at a time – in other words, that life is a series of discrete actions? The phenomenology of agency and temporality appears to be at odds with both of these claims.

The first claim – that life is what we *do* – seems to illegitimately sideline the beliefs, affective orientations, and relationships that are constitutive of our way of living but are not really something that we *do*. Indeed, this is precisely why virtue ethics insists that the virtues of character cannot be understood simply as standing dispositions to act in this or that way, but must also include the affective and intellectual stances that we take toward the world and which underpin our actions.[5] The practical project of a life well lived is concerned not just with what acts we are directly responsible for choosing at each moment but with the entire terrain of who we are and who we are striving to be. And the affective and cognitive stances constitutive of character are not the products of momentary choice but are,

---

[5] See Annas 1995a (especially ch. 1) and Solomon 1988, 428–429.

rather, the result of a lifetime of habituation into ways of seeing, feeling, and doing. Thus the claim that we live one moment or one action at a time is problematic, especially when we consider that the nature of temporality as it is lived – as opposed to how it is theorized in, say, Newtonian physics – is such that each moment cannot accurately be characterized as a discrete and interchangeable 'now' separated off from the others.[6]

If we are to take seriously the primacy of the practical stance in ethics we must take seriously the perspective from which it is lived: the first-person experience of the agent engaged in the task of living well. And from such a perspective, past, present, and future cannot be grasped adequately by theorizing them as occupying particular regions of some linear sequence of undifferentiated moments observable from without. From the perspective of practical agency, each 'now' is weighted with a past and directed toward a future. We experience ourselves as temporally dispersed beings oriented toward overarching goals and continuing practical identities, not as collections of temporally discrete acts that can be isolated from the flow of the life in which they find meaning. Each moment has the meaning that it does for my practical agency (and those other practical agents with whom I interact) only on the basis of a past that shapes the way the world shows up for me and a future that gives direction to my striving. Understood in this way, the suggestion that the practical stance in ethics should focus its attention on discrete moments of action seems highly problematic.

This problem is sharpened if we return to the suggestion that action has conceptual priority over character, namely, that the concept of character presupposes that of action, while the reverse does not hold. Sher supports this view by specifying three conditions necessary for something to be an 'action':

> When we describe someone as (physically) acting, we always imply that (1) his body moves in certain ways, that (2) those movements are in some sense initiated by him, and that (3) he initiates them with some intention or to achieve some purpose. (1998, 5)

Sher argues that none of these three conditions has implications for prioritizing character, since he reads character traits as constant

---

[6] This is a point made famous by Martin Heidegger, who – inspired by Husserl and Bergson – argues for the necessity of getting an ontologically correct understanding of lived time if we are to understand what we are. For Heidegger, lived time is characterized by projecting into a future whose possibilities are defined by the past, not in terms of discrete 'now' points. A full discussion of phenomenological accounts of temporal agency is beyond the scope of this discussion. For my own interpretation of Heidegger's account, see McMullin 2013.

dispositions to performing specific kinds of action despite varying circumstances. But notice that this way of conceiving of a character trait has already smuggled in the prioritization of action, since it reads traits as dispositions to perform action types that are specified in advance. In other words, the action type is itself what defines the character trait. This approach is typical of what Daniel C. Russell calls 'dispositionism', which treats personality as relatively independent from situation and specifies personality traits on the basis of nominally or externally attributed dispositions toward stereotypical behaviour associated with those traits.[7] But if we reject such a conception of character, reading it, instead, as modes of responsivity to varying circumstances in light of unifying goals and reasons – as Russell's account encourages us to do – then it is not so clear that we can simply prioritize action over character, since character is no longer definable simply in terms of action types.

Think further about what is implied under conjunct (3). What does the intentional structure of action tell us about the agent who performs it? Sher's account seems to operate with the supposition that discrete actions can in some sense be taken to be intrinsically meaningful insofar as they need not appeal to something outside themselves in order to explain the intentionality that establishes their meaning as the kind of action that they are. But one might question this supposition by pointing out that individual acts are meaningful via intentions that are themselves meaningful only in light of the overarching agency of which they are a part. This contrast turns on our understanding of the second part of Sher's third conjunct: namely, the claim that actions are initiated to achieve some purpose. For an action to be an action – as opposed to a meaningless movement – it must be governed by a norm specifying what it is trying to be or do, and that norm must be present to the agent as such on some level, though typically not in the form of an explicit belief. It must be 'initiated with some intention', as Sher puts it.[8] In other words, for something to be an

---

[7] Russell 2009, 239–331. Understood in this way, the virtues have been the target of situationist criticisms. See Doris 2002. Russell demonstrates the manner in which situationism and virtue ethics can be read as mutually supportive, rather than at odds, so long as virtues are understood as cognitive-affective repertoires responsive to the way that well-functioning practical reason allows the situation to be construed. See also Kamtekar 2004 for another virtue ethical response to situationism that challenges the way that it reads virtues/character traits as broad-based behavioural tendencies.

[8] Annas supports this reading, arguing, 'We may do some things which are pointless or spontaneous, but these are not clear examples of actions or choices' (1995a, 30). Alisdair MacIntyre makes a similar point in *After Virtue* (1984, 209), taking this to be reason to endorse a narrative account of the self. I am not arguing for such a narrativist view here, though I agree that literature is an essential tool in moral discourse and education. See also Kawall 2009, 9; Stocker 1976.

action, there must be an intention in action that helps to specify the action as a particular kind available for assessment as such a kind. For example, am I brushing my teeth or engaged in performance art? Without these norms in place it would be impossible to make this determination. Though something as simple as brushing one's teeth appears to be a discrete and isolable action that can be considered in the way that the action-based approaches endorse, the claim to independence falls flat when we examine the nature and origin of the standards governing whether an act succeeds at being the action it purports to be. In other words, what I am trying to do when I brush my teeth is not simply move the bristles around on my pearly whites but rather move them around in a way that is conducive to maintaining a condition of oral health. Trying to realize that end is ultimately what gives my action the meaning that allows us to assess its success or failure *as* being the action that it is – as opposed to, say, an act of political protest. It also gives a variety of actions a kind of unity insofar as they all express this overarching agenda. Though having my tooth drilled at the dentist and flossing every evening are very different action tendencies, they are unified by the overarching aim of a healthy life of which the specific acts are constitutive embodiments. This point becomes only more obvious when the action is not tooth-brushing but something like courage, i.e. a complex cluster of behaviour, motivation, affect, and consequence whose meaning as an 'act of courage' is determined by the intentional framework in which it occurs.

Of course, a common objection to the virtue ethical emphasis on excellent human lives is that virtuous agents can in fact be recognized as such only on the basis of their tendency to maximize the good or to perform right actions.[9] But though it may be true that we typically come to *recognize* excellent agents by way of their excellent actions, this epistemic priority does not commit us to granting actions explanatory or evaluative priority.[10] So while it is true that virtuous actions are a useful guide for recognizing virtuous people, the virtue ethical claim is that some actions are taken to be virtuous only on the basis of the idea that they exemplify a certain underlying pattern of being and set of

---

[9] See Kawall 2009.
[10] 'To see this, compare the case of a disease and its symptoms. Clearly, we often identify the presence of a disease through its symptoms, yet we would not claim that these symptoms cause or explain the presence of the disease. And when we examine our concepts of disease and symptom, we best explain the notion of a symptom in terms of the more basic concept of a disease – even if we have better epistemic access to the presence of actual symptoms than to the presence of the more fundamental disease' (Kawall 2009, 3).

commitments, even if we might primarily identify particular people *as* virtuous through their actions.

Of course, one could grant all this but deny that these intentional orientations depend on 'character traits' understood as robust dispositions to certain specific behavioural patterns.[11] But as we have seen, virtue ethics need not operate with that dispositionalist account of character. If we understand character, rather, as patterns of striving to be in certain ways – ways of being that cannot be defined in terms of action types specifiable in isolation from the commitments that make them what they are – it becomes less problematic.

Thinking of character in terms of situation-responsive patterns of striving to be in the world in certain ways allows us to recognize that our intentional orientations are only rarely toward one-off future states that the action does or does not succeed in bringing about. In other words, specific actions are not typically aimed solely at realizing discrete results. Though brushing my teeth now means I want to produce clean teeth now, ultimately that activity is part of the overarching intention to maintain health throughout my life, and its meaning hinges on the norms established by that intention. For example, if my interest were simply in having clean-*feeling* teeth in the immediate future, chewing mint gum would be just as good as brushing my teeth. But since I am aimed at maintaining a level of health across a lifetime, the intention underwriting the meaning of my tooth-brushing now extends beyond this discrete activity. Ultimately the norms governing specific actions must be understood as intrinsic to the activity of trying to *be* in a certain way. Character traits are simply names for these patterns of striving, and specific actions embody that striving to greater and lesser degrees, depending on the circumstance.

> Unlike trying to do something, trying to be something is not assessed in terms of what it (futurally) brings about, but in light of what it (ongoingly) is. In exercising the skills involved in revising my paper, for instance, I aim futurally at a revised paper; revising my paper is what I am trying to do. But exercising such skills is not, in turn, futural; it is a way of being a writer, and

---

[11] For example, Sher specifies that he is assuming 'that we can specify what someone does exclusively in terms of his movements, intentions, and other facts about him which do not commit us to any view of his character. Against this, it could be argued that a full specification of any given action requires reference to feelings and thoughts that *do* have implications about the agent's character. However, as long as a bare-bones description of someone's action which makes no reference to his character is possible, while a bare-bones description of his character which makes no reference to his actions is not, a version of the claim that action is conceptually prior will remain intact' (Sher 1998, 5 n. 13).

What Is Flourishing?

it is precisely in exercising the skill – not in projecting its future fulfillment – that the intention-in-action is constituted. (Crowell 2013, 11)

Thus the normative framework within which actions are meaningful *as* actions must be understood in terms of an agent striving to *be* something – with all of the relevant affective and intellectual orientations involved in that state of being – rather than simply as a striving to *do*.[12]

As we will see throughout the book, I will argue that the virtues are to be understood as problem-solving abilities or skills that help us in this project of striving to be. It is therefore important at the outset that we properly understand the interpretation of 'skill' that I will be using in terms of the above discussion. Doing so will allow us to avoid many of the problems associated with the skill model of virtue. Critics of that model have focused on the way that 'skill' has been characterized by some influential proponents in formal and relatively intellectualist terms along the lines of playing bridge.[13] In keeping with this, skilled action is viewed as governed by articulable, precise rules and practiced and adopted by choice, typically by mature people who have an antecedent interest in and liking of those activities.[14] Understood as such, it is unsurprising that critics reject this view as an inappropriate model of virtuous action. But on my account this interpretation speaks to only a small subset of what I mean by skill. Skillful action is best understood as a norm-governed but pre-theoretical form of fluid response to the environment and its affordances – a responsivity that is only sometimes deliberately chosen. It is future-directed striving embedded in structures of significance that govern the success and failure conditions to which the skillful agent is responsive. Skill should therefore be understood in terms of a continuum – with the unthinking and unchosen skills we learn as infants (such as sensory-motor skills, eating, walking, etc.) at one end of the continuum, all the way up to highly codified and deliberate skills such as bridge-playing or astrophysics at the

---

[12] Here there are important overlaps with Korsgaard's account of practical identity (1996), though I agree with Michael Bratman in rejecting the idea that a practical identity 'explicitly includes in its content the very idea that it is a conception of one's identity' (2007, 41). My account focuses on normatively governed abilities to be – what Heidegger calls *Seinkönnen* – only some of which will be evident to the agent as such.

[13] For example, Annas 2003 and 2011 argues that a skill involves teachability, unifying principles, and the ability to give an account. For this reason, she claims that Aristotle is one of the few philosophers who *rejects* the skill model of virtue. In contrast, Stitcher 2007 argues that Aristotle is indeed offering a skill model of virtue, but one that is at odds with the strongly intellectualist Socratic model of skill that Annas champions. See Angier 2012 and 2015a for discussion of problems with many versions of the skill model of virtue.

[14] I am grateful to an anonymous reviewer for this formulation of the view.

other. Understanding the nature of skill solely in terms of the latter end of the continuum misunderstands the whole and overlooks how deeply such norm-governed striving runs through the entire human condition. To compare the virtues to skills, then, is on my account simply to highlight the fact that they are specific norm-governed modes of seeing, feeling, and doing that embody and realize an agent's project of trying to be in the world in a way that is responsive to the different normative sources that make a claim on her. They are, as Heidegger would put it, abilities to be – or *Seinkönnen* – by which we act into possibilities we recognize the world to be offering us in light of an implicit understanding of their success and failure conditions and our care to respond to these well. Though such abilities are sometimes deliberately chosen and governed by articulable rules, generally they are not.[15] It is important not to get too fixated on the idea of a skill as being a highly specific and formalized set of behaviours, then, but rather understand it in terms of patterns of responsive coping governed by an orientation toward the better and worse.

Of course, one might object that with this talk of skillful striving and abilities to be in the world I myself have simply presupposed the virtue ethical normative orientation in the way that Sher diagnosed. After all, I have presupposed that we must conceive of the practical project of ethics as primarily focused on helping us solve the problem of how to live good *lives* and thus viewing actions in terms of their contribution to realizing the projects and patterns of being that comprise those lives. On that reading, we cannot treat the intentional context of action as irrelevant to those assessments. But one might endorse an alternative conception of the kind of practical purpose our ethical theories are meant to serve. Namely, one might suggest that the purpose of moral theory is to specify what acts are and are not acceptable – its purpose being to set the minimal standard of behaviour to be expected of people, *not* to help individuals reflect on and live excellent lives. If so, then it seems that action may indeed have a kind of evaluative priority, since we are concerned in this latter approach primarily with what agents do, not with who and how they are. And in the service of this practical orientation toward behaviour, one might argue, we can and should abstract from the context of agency to list action types that are and are not permitted.

But such an approach does not address the deeper question about *why* we should be interested in what is permitted of us. If ethics is a practical affair, then the question of what is permitted must arise in an agent's life as

---

[15] See Heidegger 1985, §31.

a problem to be solved – not simply as a theoretical puzzle to be analyzed. And when we remember this fact, it seems clear that conceiving of ethics in terms of the 'what is permitted?' problematic adopts an implicitly *political* conception of ethics insofar as it is aimed at solving the problem of what minimal rules of conduct are necessary for group functioning. In other words, it takes the specification of behavioural rules to be the fundamental practical problem that human beings understand themselves to be faced with. On my reading, on the contrary, the task of specifying minimal standards of behaviour – indeed, the very problem of how best to enable group functioning, whether through specific rules or otherwise, is itself meaningful only insofar as we are interested in living good lives. On this reading, ethics is the name of the discipline aimed at helping people answer this practical problem. Lives have evaluative priority over actions, I believe, because ethics is to be understood as the practical project of figuring out how to live well and be good, not simply the project of avoiding actions that are bad enough to prevent communities from functioning.[16]

However, the ultimate lesson of our engagement with Sher's rewarding discussion should be that trying to carve one area off from the other is an artificial and misleading endeavour that ought to be challenged – though if one *must* choose, then it is humanity's striving to be a certain way that is the ultimate object of evaluation, since all actions only are what they are in light of that striving, and the purpose of ethics is to help us do it well.[17] One cannot offer a bare-bones description of someone's action without reference to her character because her character entails a commitment to who she is trying to be, and such trying – comprised of goals and motivations, modes of feeling and believing and responding to the world over time – is constitutive of the meaning of any particular action she undertakes. 'Character' is the closest name we have for the direction and tenor of an agent's striving – that set of cognitive, affective, evaluative, and behavioural orientations that comprise a person's temporally extended agency, a set that must be considered as an organic whole if we are to get an adequate grasp of how well agents are faring in that striving.

---

[16] I am grateful to Fabian Freyenhagen for his helpful suggestions here.
[17] Nussbaum holds a similar view: 'Moral philosophy should focus not only on isolated acts of choice, but also, and more importantly, on the whole course of the agent's moral life, its patterns of commitment, conduct, and also passion' (1999, 170). Indeed, she argues that it is just Anglo-American moral philosophy from the 1950s to 1970s that ignored these points and in doing so, neglected its own history.

The Good Life

At this point we must turn to the question of what exactly we are striving to be. Though it is in some sense obvious that we are striving to be healthy when we go to the gym or eat kale, a great deal of the literature on virtue ethics has addressed itself to asking what we are striving to be when we cultivate character traits typically known as the virtues, such as courage, modesty, and justice. By all accounts the answer is *eudaimonia* – namely, 'excellent' or 'happy' or *flourishing* – though all of these terms have a tendency to reify the active nature of what they are attempting to designate. Simply put, it is human life ongoingly lived well.[18] Though the relationship between the virtues and flourishing is sometimes given an instrumental reading – namely, the virtues are those characteristic stances necessary to bring about flourishing understood as a state separate from the virtues themselves – they are more typically understood as *constitutive* of flourishing in the way that was discussed above. Namely, one engages in practices of excellent living (the virtues) in order to live excellently (flourish) just as one engages in practices of good writing in order to be a good writer. The practices are constitutive of the identity that one is striving to embody. They are successful as such practices insofar as they do in fact embody that way to be in the world.

What does human life lived well look like? Unsurprisingly, there is an enormous literature dedicated to this question – much of it falling under the auspices of questions about either 'flourishing' or 'well-being'. These two different terms track the general tendency to take one of two approaches to the question of the human good, which are sometimes referred to as 'objectivist' and 'subjectivist' theories, respectively.[19] By briefly analyzing these two different approaches, we will see that there are difficulties with both orientations – difficulties that arise from a failure to accurately conceptualize the self that is engaged in this project of striving to be.

---

[18] See Annas 1995a on the translation – despite designating the highest of all human goods, the goal is an activity, not a state. This is in keeping with Aristotle's claim in Book X of the *Nicomachean Ethics* that *eudaimonia* is an activity and not a state (X.6.1176a–b). Thus J. L. Ackrill points out that *Eudaimonia* 'is doing well (*Eupraxia*), not the result of doing well; a life, not the reward of a life' (1980, 24). See also Baril 2014.

[19] See Annas 2011; Haybron 2008; McGregor and Little 1998; Waterman 1993; and Zagzebski 2006.

Subjectivist Accounts of the Good

Subjectivist theories of the good human life are those that make welfare depend on some mental state, where 'mental state' is taken to encompass both cognitive beliefs about life satisfaction and affective experiences of pleasure and fulfillment.[20] As Arneson puts it, for accounts of this kind, 'what is good for each person is entirely determined by that very person's evaluative perspective. Call this the claim of agent sovereignty' (1999, 116). In other words, on the subjectivist account what is good for people – what counts as their flourishing – is what they decide or believe it is. The key intuition for this view is that any account of human well-being must display a deep connection with each individual agent's particular desires, interests, and projects. As Daniel Haybron puts it, 'My welfare must not be alien to me, a value that floats down from some Platonic realm and, remora-like, affixes itself to me with little regard to the particulars of my constitution' (2007, 2–3). Rather, what I value, what I choose, the projects in which I am engaged must arise out of the particularity of who I am and be recognized from the perspective of the agent herself as satisfying the preferences of that particularity.

One benefit of subjectivist accounts is that they can accommodate the modern sense that visions of the good life are legitimately plural. Each person chooses for *herself* what is valuable in her life, and the goodness of achieving it lies in the positive experience achieved by the satisfaction of the preference, not in the content of the preference itself. Thus on subjectivist accounts all candidates for the good – all possible reasons for action – are assessed in light of a standard internal to individual agents.

The simplest form of this subjectivist approach is hedonism, which simply equates flourishing with feeling pleasure. Few endorse this view in its most basic form since it commits one to the counterintuitive implication that nothing can matter to me except the pleasurable quality of my experience.[21] Nozick's famous 'experience machine' objection makes short work of this view, since it forces us to question whether a subject who is completely passive and isolated from the world – a subject living a kind of illusion – can be understood as flourishing, no matter how enjoyable that subject's experiences might be. Doubt about the ability and authority of agents to truly assess the value of the pleasures they experience is further

---

[20] Sumner 1996, 82. For research in psychology on this, see Diener et al. 1999, 277; Myers and Diener 1995, 11; Ryan and Deci 2000, 144.
[21] See Arneson 1999, 114 and Nozick 1974, 42–43.

evident in Mill's attempt to reconceive utilitarianism after Bentham's version of that theory was derided as a 'pig philosophy' blind to distinctions between the quality of preferences being satisfied – distinctions that individuals *ought* to respect.[22] The problem with subjective accounts of flourishing, in other words, is that they collapse into mere ungrounded preference and so run afoul of our intuitions regarding the objectivity and publicity of claims about what can count as a genuinely good human life.

In response to such worries, most subjectivist accounts attempt to complicate simple hedonism by placing certain kinds of objective constraints on when to accept the attitudes an agent has toward her well-being as accurate measures of that well-being.[23] We can think of these as moderate subjectivist approaches, or hybrid accounts that attempt to graft on objective protections against the worst implications of subjectivism. For example, Mill's version of utilitarianism makes a nod to objectivism in the form of a panel of expert judges that can essentially tell you when your assessments of first-person subjective experience are wrong[24] because, for example, you hold false beliefs or you have a defective capacity for desire or evaluation.[25]

Perhaps the most vocal recent champion of such an endeavour is Wayne Sumner, who acknowledges the worry about distorted preferences and 'false' desires by developing a theory of 'authentic' desires. The idea is that if agents are acting with distorted evaluative capacities or false information, then their attitudes about well-being are not truly their own and cannot be taken as accurate assessments of that well-being. An agent is *in fact* such an ultimate authority only if he did not develop his evaluative capacities in a life context that eroded that individual's capacity for the critical evaluation of his own beliefs.[26] In the case of deliberated desire versions of

---

[22] Mill addresses the worry that utilitarianism is a doctrine worthy only of swine in chapter 2 of *Utilitarianism*.

[23] See Brandt 1996 and Railton 1986.

[24] Mark LeBar argues that subjectivist accounts cannot explain the origin and function of such objectivist intuitions (2004). Some have argued that the needed 'objectivity' lies in the *observer's* assessment of the goodness of the life as opposed to the agent's own self-assessment. See, for example Scanlon 1993, 188. But this is considered a kind of subjectivism because one's well-being is still being understood as a function of an attitude held (whether mine or the other's) – as opposed to a condition obtaining in the world.

[25] See LeBar 2004, 196–197. There is a great deal of literature on the issue of distorted preferences. See, for example, Sen 1987, who claims that 'the hopelessly deprived lack the courage to desire much, and their deprivations are muted and deadened in the scale of desire-fulfillment' (46).

[26] The sources of such erosion may also be internal to the agent – such as tendencies to self-deception or laziness that result in a failure to cultivate the capacity for authentic choice. I am grateful to an anonymous reviewer for flagging this point.

subjectivism, that standard is some kind of long-term or 'deep' desire. What matters in assessing good lives is that the agent takes part in legitimate processes of preference endorsement or vetting of desires.[27] Thus what makes the object good is still the fact that it satisfies my desire – it is still a subjectivist theory – but the desire is no mere passing whim but a sustaining passion that has been endorsed in a certain way (Haybron 2007).

Of course, the problem then arises regarding how to specify *when* an agent's evaluative capacities are operating authentically without appealing to an objective account of human nature or agency that specifies the necessary conditions for an attitude to count as being 'my own'.[28] In other words, the idea of well-functioning evaluative capacities seems to rest on an objective account of human nature that is at odds with the subjectivist impulse with which such accounts began. How is one to specify which procedural constraints can differentiate legitimate from illegitimate desires without straying so far afield from the original intuition of the subjectivist approach as to become something entirely other?

Objectivist Accounts of the Good

The difficulty that subjectivist accounts have in critiquing the happiness of the deluded or perverse is what motivates objectivist accounts of flourishing, which make well-being dependent on states of the world, not states of mind or agency. According to objectivist accounts, the concept of well-being tracks the healthy social, physical, and psychological human life understood in a way that is not determined (primarily) on the basis of first-person experience. Arguments in favour of this kind of approach point to ways that our practices support this objectivist reading. For example, we typically believe that our value judgments can be subject to legitimate criticism by others, that we can communicate to others why they *ought* to endorse our valuings, that we are capable of transmitting value assessments across generations through practices and institutions, and so on. Namely, the suggestion is that our practices give us reason to believe that our conceptions of the good life are more public and objective than the subjectivist account acknowledges.[29] This prompts some to claim that

---

[27] For other examples, see Brandt 1998, especially part I; Griffin 1986, 7–39; Rawls 1999, sections 60–64. For helpful discussion, see Friedman 1986 and Velleman 1988.
[28] LeBar 2004 argues that objective constraints on subjectivist approaches presuppose 'a theory of what persons truly are or ought to be – a normative theory of persons' (200–201).
[29] For further discussion, see Foot 2002, 96–109.

there must be universal forms of human striving whose goodness transcends cultural and individual differences and which allow us to assess individuals on the basis of their success in realizing them, regardless of the quality of their lived experience in doing so.[30]

One such approach to this demand is to come up with an objective list of all of the properties necessary for a good human life. The most prevalent version of this approach is a naturalism that grounds the list in an account of human nature. Such an account purports to demonstrate why the entries on it are not arbitrarily chosen but are in some sense scientifically grounded. This has the appeal of linking moral claims – which are typically viewed as requiring justification – with scientific claims – which are not.[31] We can see this approach when we consider Aristotle's claim that to flourish is to perform the human *ergon* – its function or characteristic activity – well. Aristotle attempts to motivate his view by noting that other things have characteristic activities and arguing that the human being as a whole must therefore have a comparable function (*NE*, I.7). On this view, we can clearly recognize how to assess lives and actions – namely, in terms of the function that gives them meaning as what they are.

In virtue ethics this function argument is typically given a naturalist interpretation wherein a broadly scientifically based account of human nature is taken to be the foundation for our understanding of the human 'function'. We look to characteristic human behaviours and dispositions constitutive of the kinds of things that we are – which we can observe like any other natural thing. Those that are realizations of human nature will be called good or virtuous, and those that are distortions or perversions of it will be called evil. As Philippa Foot argues, we should not assume that the term 'good' suddenly takes on a radically different meaning when applied to human lives. When we call something a good cactus or a good knife we mean that we're evaluating them 'qua specimens of their kind'.[32] When we call a human being good, we should think in the same way: moral evaluation is essentially just evaluation of humans as specimens of their kind. Thus there is something defective in a human being lacking justice or charity just as there is something defective about an antisocial bee.

---

[30] See Drummond 2002, 33–39.
[31] See Zagzebski 2006, 53–54.
[32] See Foot 2002, 132–147. As Rasmussen puts it, activities constitutive of flourishing are 'those that both express and produce in a human being an actualization of potentialities that are specific to its natural kind' (1999, 4).

This so-called function argument has been the object of a great deal of criticism. The language of 'function' seems to assume that human flourishing is equivalent to fulfilling our 'purpose' by developing some innate human nature or ability – the trouble being that this seems to commit us to a debunked teleological metaphysics.[33] But as Korsgaard points out, humanity's 'function' or 'ergon' need not be read in terms of some type of metaphysical *telos* – rather, 'function' is better conceptualized as 'characteristic activity' constitutive of the things that we are – in keeping with Crisp's updated translation of that term.[34] This has the benefit of avoiding static or thing-like characterizations of self, since the idea of characteristic activity involves a notion of accomplishment; it is an ongoing project for which the agent is responsible.

So the question then becomes: What does humanity as a species characteristically do, and how is it built such that it can do it? We can talk about those questions without having to believe that human beings have some kind of higher (perhaps God-given) purpose that they are trying to serve through these characteristic activities. What we are attempting to discover when we analyze humanity's 'function', then, are those basic structures of our being that allow us to be the kinds of things that we are – regardless of how or why these structures came into being, metaphysically speaking (Korsgaard 2008, 137–140). A good cactus or a good human is one whose parts and activities enable its characteristic way of life. Understood as such, flourishing is defined in purely objective terms; human lives can be assessed for excellence on an objective scale that is observable from the outside.

The problem, however, is that making our *eudaimonia* assessments dependent on objective states of the world – not the attitudes of the agent

---

[33] Another tradition in ethical theory – the natural law tradition – defines nature in terms of such a teleological metaphysics. For this tradition 'nature is thoroughly normative, being the arena of a host of rational ends, which are inextricably embedded in its myriad workings. And it is this teleological conception of nature – according to which description and prescription, "fact" and "value" are deeply intertwined, and never finally separable – that will be the hallmark of natural law ethics hereafter' (Angier 2015b, 54). As we will see in the next section, my account is consistent with the natural law tradition's claim that being human involves an orientation toward seeking certain goods – and developing the virtues that allow us to realize them – but unlike that tradition, it takes no stand on how we became this way. Typically, natural law theory holds that the natural law is grounded in an eternal divine law that is the source of its normative force – though one need not know or believe this to be claimed by its constraints. Since phenomenology brackets metaphysical commitments in the interest of simply describing meaningful experience and uncovering the transcendental conditions that enable it, the natural law tradition's approach is largely orthogonal to my own. For further discussion, see Chappell and Oderberg 2004; Haldane 2009; Kainz 2004.

[34] See Korsgaard 2008, 134–135; 2009, 37–40.

herself – means that it is perfectly possible for an agent to despise or feel alienated from something that, objectively speaking, is constitutive of her well-being. Critics object that this allows for characterizing situations as instances of 'flourishing' regardless of whether it *feels* like flourishing to the agent involved. Thus learning to play chess is counted as an event of greater flourishing than watching television, since the former involves social interaction, greater intellectual challenges, capacity for growth, etc. – a judgment we can make regardless of the misery experienced by the chess student.[35] Such approaches appear to neglect the first-person lived experience of the person doing the flourishing. While subjectivist accounts appeared to be too internal, objectivist accounts appear to be too *external*.

Hursthouse has attempted to avoid this difficulty by defining humanity's characteristic way of life in terms of what she specifies as the four goals of all higher animals: individual and species survival, group functioning, and enjoyment.[36] Note that on this list a certain level of subjective enjoyment is a necessary constituent of flourishing. Thus she accommodates the subjective dimension – the quality of lived experience – within the objectivist approach: producing a hybrid or compromise view akin to the subjectivist attempt to accommodate objectivity through the idea of 'authentic' desires.

When we apply this list of criteria to humans, we recognize the virtues as those character traits conducive to humanity functioning well in these four domains. Taken together, Hursthouse argues, we can use these goals to assess individual lives and the actions and dispositions of the individuals who lead them. Thus the virtue of charity can be understood as directly serving the goals of species continuance and the good functioning of the social group, and this in turn indirectly serves the goals of survival and enjoyment.

Note that though positive subjective experience is a feature on the list of ends constitutive of the human good, it is taken to be an *objective* fact that subjectively positive experiences are constitutive of the good life for all human beings, and this class of experiences can accommodate a wide variety of idiosyncratic preferences that many individuals would not necessarily count as positive. In other words, the objectivist approach to the

---

[35] See Haybron 2007, 9 and Sumner 1996, 24 for examples.
[36] See Hursthouse 1999, 197–202. See also Foot 2001 and 2003, 189–208 for a more sustained defence of the idea that moral assessments are continuous with assessments of plants and animals as defective or excellent examples of their kind.

human good specifies as an objective fact of human flourishing that a certain level of subjective happiness is a necessary constituent thereof, while recognizing that the actual content of that subjective happiness will vary between persons. Thus an element of individuality is maintained: individuals are not simply interchangeable tokens instantiating universal and generic goods.[37] Rather, it is only when the individual's particular talents, desires, and potentialities are brought to worldly expression and experienced first-personally as such that *eudaimonia* is possible for her.

Though naturalistic approaches have what some consider to be the attractive result of being continuous with the scientific worldview such that ethics essentially becomes a branch of zoology, they sometimes do so by obscuring the normative dimension central to the meaning of ethics. Namely, they have a difficult time answering how nature gets its normative grip on us. Why *ought* we pursue the ends laid down by nature? It takes for granted the idea that it is *good* to realize such a human nature.[38] Further, how do we decide what *counts* as normal functioning or characteristic activity? As critics working on philosophies of gender, race, and disability have pointed out, the notion of 'normal' functioning is rarely neutral but has tended to marginalize significant portions of the human population.[39] Further, if we're concerned with what is distinctively and characteristically human, why aren't making fire, 'having sexual intercourse without regard to season; despoiling the environment and upsetting the balance of nature; or killing things for fun' taken to be the activities that we ought to pursue? (Williams 1972, 59). Why isn't someone a defective human if they fight to save the environment, for example, since virtually every other human (at least in modernity) has been characteristically bent on its exploitation? Of course, one could respond that despoiling the environment is *really* just a poorly executed effort to promote individual and species survival or enjoyment. But in making this claim one is required to adopt a stance whereby some characteristic human activities are interpreted in light of others. Some characteristic activities are taken to be central 'oughts' while others are viewed as merely being better and worse instantiations of those central normative imperatives supposedly given to us as such by human nature. But once we adopt such an evaluative stance, we have in effect left naturalism behind. No longer are the categories at work characterizable as

---

[37] See Rasmussen 1999, 6.
[38] See Hurka 1999, 47. See Foot 2001 for a response to this objection.
[39] See, for example, Amundson 2000; Carel 2016; Freeland 2010.

purely objective since they are shaped by the presuppositions and preferences of the theorists who decide what is to count as part of human nature.

The adoption of an (unnatural) evaluative stance in deciding which activities are characteristic of human nature is further evident in the fact that such approaches often take an overly optimistic view in their specification of what makes for a characteristically human life. As Haybron puts it: 'Is humanitarian concern for strangers really necessary for a full or rich, or even a characteristically, human life? History offers little reason for optimism on this count' (2007, 6). We tend to believe that respect for the dignity of all others is central to our moral concerns, but it would require a stretch to turn our animalistic interest in the good functioning of our social group into the disinterested altruism that many take to be the mark of human morality. Indeed, by simply specifying 'enjoyment' as one of the goals that we naturally pursue, we have imported the problem with the subjectivist view into the objectivist view – namely, how to distinguish higher- and lower-order enjoyments in such a way that the pursuit of the former can be viewed as a characteristic activity, thereby grounding our assessment of better and worse lives.

In general, then, the naturalist approach pretends to an objectivity that can be read off nature when in fact it is operating with a normatively loaded vision of the 'natural' that is not available from an evaluatively neutral standpoint.

Neither Subjective nor Objective: Reconceptualizing the Self

Such difficulties lead some to wonder whether objectivist accounts of *eudaimonia* and subjectivist theories of well-being are even investigating the same things. Thus Haybron suggests that when Julia Annas claims that the fundamental question is 'How ought I to live?' (1995a, 27), she is asking us to take up a perspective from which we are asking about our ultimate priorities or goals, which is *not* the same thing as asking about what would make us happy. If modern theories of well-being are not asking the question of what it means to live well, then subjectivist and objectivist accounts are speaking past each other, despite using much of the same terminology. This difficulty is evident in the fact that most subjectivist accounts would endorse the idea that a terrible person is capable of flourishing. Indeed, they would argue that eudaimonists are simply equivocating by treating 'flourishing' as meaning two fundamentally different things: both the good life (an objective good we ought to pursue and which can be recognized from without) *and* well-being (a subjective good

What Is Flourishing? 31

we want to enjoy and which can be recognized only from within). Most Aristotelians try to capture both aspects within a single concept by denying that there is in fact a distinction; namely, they claim that well-being *just is* leading an objectively good life.[40] Thus we can understand all the effort expended to show why things like justice are *in fact* good for the bearer of that virtue – i.e. ultimately lead to greater experiences of satisfaction – even if it may *appear* to be extremely individually costly to act on.

What we have seen, then, is that there is a conflict regarding whether flourishing should be assessed in terms of what could be called an 'internal' or 'external' perspective. When the latter is adopted and the worldly objective aspect is being emphasized, human beings are taken to be objectively present scientifically observable objects. On this approach, the individual's lived experience is taken to be a feature of a particular kind of object – a feature that should be acknowledged, but one that does not fundamentally change the task of assessment. Human beings are *really* just objects that can be assessed by observing them as a species and breaking up their observable behaviours into discrete actions that are or are not shared by other members of that species. They can be assessed from the outside as we do all other objects.

But when the internal stance is adopted, it is claimed that human lives are *really* about the individual's lived experience – with only secondary or derivative reference to their status as objects in a public world. Agents are taken to be in some important sense separable from the nature to which they belong. The real game is in the subjective experiences of pleasure or operations of personal agency that are taken to be our true object and thus the appropriate standard for measuring our success at living well.

The problem is that this disjunctive approach to human life artificially emphasizes one or the other aspect of what is in fact a complex unity. People strive to both *feel* good and *be* good and they typically view these as being impossible to fully separate. Indeed, their efforts are typically aimed at structuring their lives such that these things are not in tension but mutually supportive. The more complex and compelling the versions of subjectivism or objectivism on the table – and the rough sketch of these approaches given here is not meant to deny the sophistication of many such accounts – the more likely they are to attempt to overcome or

---

[40] 'The eudaimonist can hit the jackpot ... if she can defend the Aristotelian view that flourishing in the biological sense and happiness in the psychological sense are components of the very same state or property of the person's life' (Zagzebski 2006, 55). See Foot 2001, 94 and Hursthouse 1999, 172. See Snow 2008 for empirical support for this view.

downplay this dichotomy. In light of this, it is perhaps time to reject it from the outset: namely, the view that it is *either* internal experiences *or* objective categories that we must prioritize in assessing how to live well. Rather, we must recognize that the self that is at stake in the practical project of ethics cannot be understood primarily as a 'subject' with private access to an isolable inner domain nor as an 'object' that can be described in anonymous object-appropriate terms. This dichotomy is a distortion. Human beings live in the world such that we are embedded, enabled, and constrained by it in ways that resist this isolation of the 'internal' from the 'external'. To be a self is to be in the grip of the world, and the task of flourishing is to find a good fit for one's striving within the possibilities and limitations given by it.

Understood in this sense, 'world' does not mean the collection of material stuff with which I am physically engaged, but rather the articulated context of meaning in terms of which I understand who and what I can be. This is the way in which the 'external' world primarily shows up for the practical agent, and it is only by secondarily adopting an abstract theoretical stance on these practical contexts that they (and we ourselves) can appear as scientific objects or natural kinds. By prioritizing this stance at the expense of others, objectivist accounts obscure the existential foundations on which such a stance rests. As a result, the objectivist insistence that the success of one's life be measured in terms of the individual's conformity to certain scientific laws of animal development is in danger of losing the link to the self for whom that development can *matter*.

Similarly, the 'subjective' component of our striving must be reconceptualized, since being a self is not about creating a private arena of experiences and pleasures, a private storehouse of good qualia that can be understood in isolation from the world. Rather, being a self is inescapably bound up with a sense of being individually at stake in whether I succeed or fail at trying to be who I am. But, crucially, such 'subjective' striving to be who one is can be understood only in conjunction with the 'objective' worldly roles and truths in terms of which we act out that striving and assess its success. Each of us answers the question 'Who am I?' by successfully acting into various possibilities of who one can be: philosopher, physician, psychic, etc. and in light of the constraints posed to us by the givens of nature. Meeting the requirements of these worldly constraints gives content to our self-assessments – criteria that are rooted in something more than private experiences understood as separable from the world. These different worldly possibilities I act into and take up as expressions of who I am are not just externally observable 'facts' about me, then – though they are surely that as well. They are the way I live out the project of who I will be. It is because we exist embedded in these networks of meaning and reference – the world understood not as a collection of objects but as the space in which human striving finds its shape and direction – that we can make sense of the practical project of living well that ethics is tasked with understanding.[41]

There is no self without the world that gives that self the objects and contexts of mattering that define its struggle to be, and there is no 'human nature' without the first-person domain of lived agency – both because humans are not humans without it and because the scientific endeavour wherein we see the world in terms of a domain of third-personal truths about natural kinds presupposes that agency. If this is right, the self can be neither an isolable arena of desires and preferences to be satisfied nor simply a scientific object whose functionality can be assessed without reference to the fact that we experience ourselves as tasked with the project of striving to be.[42] Rather, each of us is entrusted with an existence that is both constrained and enabled by the world. How well we negotiate this way of being in the world – both by changing the world and by changing ourselves – determines whether we are flourishing.

Practical Rationality

One way in which to conceptualize this middle terrain on which human life occurs – this status as neither subjective nor objective but simultaneously both – is in terms of practical rationality. On this view, human flourishing is equivalent to well-performed activity of the specifically human dimension of the soul – namely, rationality. Aristotle emphasizes that human beings perform this characteristic activity well when they choose things that are 'noble' or worth doing for their own sake – not simply when they are useful or pleasant.[43] Rationality is humanity's 'function' because it is our characteristic activity, informing all other aspects of our lives through the normative orientation that it provides. Thus any naturalistic emphasis on goals shared by all higher animals appears to be misleading, since it is the excellent use of our capacity to *reason* – properly understood – that is humanity's 'function' in Aristotle's

---

[41] See Heidegger 1985, §12.
[42] Thus for Aristotle, flourishing requires consciousness, will, and disposition. See Whiting 1988, 43.
[43] See, for example, *NE*, III.8.1117a4–6, *NE*, II.6. 1106b–1107a, and *NE*, VI.5.1140a25–28. See Luthra 2015 for discussion.

sense of the term (*NE*, I.7.1098a18–24). This is not to say that pursuits and capacities shared with other living things are irrelevant to human flourishing but rather that the presence of reason in the life of the human animal transforms them. As Korsgaard points out, each part supervenes on the one below and 'the addition of each new part of the soul changes the *sense* in which the thing is said to be alive or have a life, *both* by influencing the way the "lower" functions are carried out and by adding new kinds of activities' (2008, 142). This point forces us to question whether it is misleading to start with plants and other animals as some approaches to virtue ethics do, since the higher capacities cannot just be added on to an existing substratum like frosting on a cake.[44] Rather, the higher capacities transform the way the lower capacities are lived – for example, the human relationship to food and sex is vastly different from that of the other animals, even though there is obviously a sense in which we too are shaped by our instincts to pursue those ends. This represents a change in both *what* we do and *how* we do those things shared by plants and animals.[45] Despite the fact that the human soul shares the nutritive and appetitive dimensions present in plants and animals, then, the presence of reason transforms the manner in which these 'lower' dimensions manifest in human life. Our relationship to our bodies and their needs, our desires and passions, and our social identities are all shaped in light of human rationality. It is only on these grounds that one can characterize reason as *the* activity or structure that allows us to be what we are.

This obviously changes the naturalist picture substantially. No longer are we simply reading off characteristic activities from observation of the human animal and using the criteria we derive from that observation to assess the quality of individual lives. Rather, we have taken the view that

---

[44] See Foot 2001 and Hursthouse 1999, for example. This is not to suggest that they neglect the role of reason. See, for example, Foot 2001, 52–65 and Hursthouse 1999, 217–238. Hursthouse notes that once reason is involved, our interpretation of 'our characteristic way of going on' becomes 'avowedly normative' because it is 'to do what we can rightly see we have reason to do' (223). This is still to be understood as a kind of naturalism, however, since 'it is still the case that human beings are ethically good in so far as their ethically relevant aspects foster the four ends appropriate to a social animal, in the way characteristic of that species' (224).

[45] Thus the scope that reason is taken to have on this reading allows it to meet Hurka's criterion of an 'essential property' – which are properties necessary for a creature 'to count as human' and that 'play a central role in explaining its other properties ... [each] must explain at least a large portion of the kind's behaviour rather than just some arbitrarily restricted part' (1999, 48). However, Hurka suggests that the development of rationality does not require other-regarding virtuous action (1999, 50) and so rationality fails to serve the role that naturalist virtue ethicists hope it does – namely, as a trait that can guarantee the kind of moral awareness that we take to be necessary for flourishing. We will return to this point later.

practical reason's responsivity to the good is that aspect of human nature that should be used when assessing the extent to which human lives are fulfilling their 'function'. And since this activity is fundamentally evaluative, it cannot be understood as 'natural' in the simple way that the other goals of higher-order animals are. As a result, the shift of attention to reason allows us access to a normativity that seemed lacking in simple naturalism. Reason allows us to distinguish between the givens of nature that do motivate us and the reasons that ought to in a way that encompasses both the subjectivist and objectivist insights: reason itself can be understood as a natural capacity that it is our natural function to realize, even though the demands of rational integrity that claim us can manifest as such only from the stance of the agent condemned to action. Since the subject matter of ethics is not simple desires but *reasons* for why one ought to act or be in a certain way, it is hoped that this invocation of a natural rationality that nevertheless permits distance from the natural allows us to build a bridge from the natural to the normative in a way that does not isolate assessments of the agent's flourishing from objective conditions of human nature – as the subjectivist accounts appeared to do. In so doing, flourishing is conceptualized as a state of good fit between the agent and the world in which neither can be understood without the other.

In order for this approach to work, however, we will need to get clear on the nature of practical rationality. In particular, we need to resist the tendency to understand practical rationality solely as a kind of deliberative decision procedure – an explicit cognitive activity of judgment formation and application. In contrast – and in keeping with the discussion above about the way in which virtue can be understood as a kind of skill – I want to suggest that our characteristic way of being is best understood as a kind of pre-theoretical normative attunement to the world – an implicit understanding of one's possibilities in terms of conditions of success and failure, good and bad responses to the reasons that claim us. It is a background sense of oneself as being called to do only what one has reason to do. Though it is possible to engage in explicit deliberations, this only sometimes occurs in an average human life – it cannot be taken as the norm in our understanding of human agency. For the most part I strive to be kind to my loved ones, to exercise moderation, to be patient in the face of obstacles because I understand on an unthematized level that the world and my place in it are at stake in this striving. Only rarely do these reasons show up as objects of critical reflection.[46]

---

[46] We will return to these issues in greater detail in Chapter 6.

Thus when we look to the phenomena we see that each of us is engaged in a fluid responsivity to the way the world shows up as mattering; a fluid engagement in the world grounded in the agent's sense of being at stake in accomplishing that self-world fit. And this investment in who I am trying to be in the world is not an inner thought or representation but a way I *exist*, a way of grasping oneself by acting into possibilities that the world presents in light of an unthematized understanding of how they will answer the existential question: 'Who am I?' Answering this question well is not a matter of indifference and, crucially, is not something I can do in isolation from the world or those who share it with me. Our responsibility for and commitment to living well can be what they are only in the worldly context of meaning in which they find content and direction. When I experience a correspondence of self and world I recognize that I am doing a good job at answering this question; I experience flourishing when I understand myself to be responding well to the ways the world claims me.

Clearly there is much more that should be said about these difficult topics and we will revisit many of them in the coming chapters. But the point is that we should be wary of an overly deliberative and action-focused account of practical rationality, since the recognition of specific reasons for action is grounded in our overarching commitment to realizing certain ways of being in the world – ways of being that are not themselves deliverances of deliberation or gain their normativity therefrom. Thus, when we take 'rationality' as the bridge between the objectivist and subjectivist accounts of human flourishing we must conceptualize that practical rationality as a normatively governed attunement to the way the world shows up as mattering and the care that I have for responding well to the claims that arise from it. Practical rationality is the norm-governed striving that enables a successful self-world fit by responding well to the reasons that claim us from out of a deep commitment to the success of that endeavour.

Three Dimensions of Being in the World Well

We have seen, then, that we must question interpretations of flourishing that prioritize either a private self or a public world in favour of a condition that rejects the dichotomy. But this rejection should not allow us to overlook the fact that those views are pointing to something important. In the account that follows I will argue that human existence is characterized by a capacity to adopt multiple perspectives on this embeddedness of the self in the world – perspectives that provide different kinds or classes of reason. As we will discuss in greater detail in the following chapter, normative claims on our agency arise from three distinct normative domains, all of which provide different reasons for action and belief and none of which is fully reducible to the others. These domains of normative claim correspond to the different perspectives we can take on the world: first-person, second-person, and third-person. Each of these stances represents a different way of understanding how to act out the project of realizing self-world fit.

From the first-person perspective, the agent is claimed by the pull of her own particular desires, interests, and projects, including the fundamental project of being an agent at all. She sees the worldly possibilities of striving available to her primarily through the lens of her own potentialities being realized in the world. From the second-person perspective, the agent experiences herself as claimed by other persons: challenged to acknowledge reasons that do not derive simply from the satisfaction of her individual possibilities of worldly self-becoming. Rather, she recognizes that she has reason to enable the other person's possibilities – and that this relationship to the other person is itself constitutive of what it means for her to be in the world well. From the third-person perspective, the rational agent is claimed by her membership in the human community and its intersubjective projects aimed at establishing and understanding a shared world. She sees herself as one among many, and as a result certain kinds of reason move her; certain possibilities of self-world fit arise from out of that perspective. Practical rationality, I will argue, must be understood as essentially 'three-dimensional' in this sense – each of these normative perspectives is a way of understanding possibilities of being in the world well. Each perspective offers different possibilities of self-world unity in ways that deny the legitimacy of the subjective/objective dichotomy but nevertheless help explain why it has arisen: the first-person perspective's emphasis on the self as an individual and the third-person perspective's emphasis on the self as just another worldly object can be recognized as being at the root of the subjectivist and objectivist intuitions sketched out above. But those views tend to conceptualize these perspectives in ways that obscure the fact that these are orientations of meaning that arise at the interface of self and world – they cannot be reduced to one or the other component. Each perspective is both 'subjective' and 'objective' insofar as in all three cases the agent experiences herself as at stake in responding well to worldly criteria of success and failure. It is therefore essential that we keep sight of the fact that all three perspectives are ways of seeing and responding to what is the more fundamental project at stake in all of them: being in the world well such that the 'subjective' and the 'objective' are both recognized as necessary and mutually imbricated constitutive elements of a life excellently lived.

As we will see in coming chapters, this plurality of perspectives on how to live in the world well is experienced as a complex and ongoingly negotiated unity. The task of flourishing – living the kind of life characteristic of human excellence – is to accommodate the demands of all three perspectives in a way that meets their different requirements while negotiating any conflicts that arise among them.[47] My approach follows the existentialists, however, by insisting that such negotiation work and striving for unity can never overcome or settle the fundamental tension that results from this normative complexity.[48] We must resist the idea that all legitimate reasons for action can fit neatly in a simple hierarchy or single normative scale. Insisting on always prioritizing others over the self, for example, denies the legitimate role that pleasure and self-development play in each person's life, just as insisting that each person be treated as an equal and interchangeable rational unit can obscure the importance of the specificity of human relationships. The moral challenge we face is living well in the face of this tension. We cannot simply adopt a theoretical perspective from which this plurality appears to dissolve but rather must commit ourselves to both meeting the standards intrinsic to each normative perspective and doing so in a way that negotiates conflicts that will inevitably arise between them. Because the claims of the different normative domains must be played off against each other over time, an agent's success in doing so cannot be measured on the basis of individual acts but must look to her life as a whole. Only then can one assess whether the different kinds of claim are being given appropriate weight and proportion in someone's life.

---

[47] The issue of harmonizing these different areas of claim will be examined in Chapters 3 and 4. The idea of there being three different domains of ethical life can also be found in Hegel 1991 and, more recently, Slote 2001, where he argues that 'I think, in other words, that we should treat self-concern as a third kind or category of caring comparable to intimate caring and to humane or humanitarian caring, so that we can think of the moral individual as exemplifying a three-way balance among these kinds of caring' (77). Though there are obvious overlaps with Slote's account, I reject his agent-based approach in which the goodness of acts and lives is ultimately founded on the virtuous inner states of agents, since this strikes me as another version of a subjectivist non-cognitivism that decouples the agent from the world. For a critique in this vein, see Russell 2008: 'If anything is clear, it should be that whether one has reasons to be benevolent rather than cruel does not simply depend on whatever desires one may happen to have' (342).

[48] The existentialists were profoundly influenced by the Romantics in this regard. See Isaiah Berlin's *The Roots of Romanticism* (1999) for discussion of corresponding themes in Romanticism.

To be a self is to be in a relationship to the world that cannot be conceptualized from a single normative perspective: we are not isolated actors representing a world that is over and against us as an array of objects important only for triggering enjoyable experiences. Nor are we simply animals whose lived experience of self-understanding, striving, and joy can be understood as secondary or incidental to the project of living well. So too must we recognize that flourishing involves being bound not simply by our own preferences or by objective worldly facts but also by the individual others to whom we experience ourselves as answerable in love and responsibility. Rather than demonstrating the primacy of one such stance (as ethical theories regularly attempt to do), the task of flourishing – living the kind of life characteristic of human excellence – is to accommodate the demands of all three perspectives in a way that does not unduly prioritize one above the others but rather negotiates their sometimes conflicting demands. In doing so we respond well to the complex possibilities of self-world fit we are called to realize.

CHAPTER 2

Three Domains of Reason

Any account of flourishing must start with an accurate picture of the kind of being we are hoping will flourish. Human beings are defined by a striving to succeed at being who they are, and this success finds its object and its measure in the relationships that we have to the domain of significance we call the world. Ethics is tasked with the work of understanding the complex interplay of claims governing our striving to be in the world well. In what follows, I will examine the three classes of normative demand by which we find ourselves claimed.

First-Person Reasons

On my account, living an excellent life – flourishing – necessarily requires responding well to the demands that arise within the first-person normative domain. But what do we mean by such a 'first-person domain'? Are we speaking simply of the first-personal I of bare agency or experience or of the normatively governed self that experiences itself as concerned to do a good job at being who it is in its particularity? The answer is both, but only insofar as these aspects of self-givenness can manifest as practical imperatives. The mere fact of being conscious, for example, defines my existence but is not the source of any practical *oughts*.

In terms of the first kind of first-person claim, accounts of practical agency like Korsgaard's argue that there are certain constitutive norms governing us simply insofar as we are agents. To be an agent, she argues, is to be efficacious and autonomous – it is to perform actions that manifest in the world the way you want and such that they can be understood as genuinely coming from *you*, not simply from some force acting on you (2008, 45, 112; 2009, 82). Insofar as you are engaged in action you are bound by the constraint that your proposed action not violate the efficacy and autonomy constraints constitutive of the agency that makes such action possible. On Korsgaard's reading, the categorical and hypothetical imperatives are the practical principles specifying those constraints (2008, 23; 2009, 179).

Without a reasons-responsiveness that transcends changes in time and circumstance – in a word, without the constancy characteristic of commitment – efficacy and autonomy become impossible. Efficaciousness in the world demands constancy across changing circumstances – both internal and external (2008, 57). The spontaneous willing of an end definitive of agency is not mere wishing but rather committing oneself to realizing that end. As such, it demands an agency committed to the constancy that unites and gives meaning to particular actions. It demands, in other words, commitment to the unification of means with end that is specified by the hypothetical imperative.

The categorical imperative similarly functions as a constitutive norm of agency by testing proposed actions to see if they are universalizable. Only thus can you know if the reasons that you are acting on transcend the specificity of your own particular agency at this moment and in these circumstances such that they are consistent with the self-unification work over time necessary for agential integrity.

With this aspect of her account I am largely in agreement – all agents have reason to behave in ways that secure the minimal levels of coherence and integrity necessary to be agents at all. This is the foundational level of first-person reasons. However, we need not accept Korsgaard's claim that these minimal norms of agency can be the source of all normativity as such.[1] On my view this cannot account for the entire normative landscape – or even all of its first-personal claims. In terms of the latter, we must also recognize that each person operates with a more substantive experience of himself as having a unique set of dispositions, preferences, and capacities that he experiences himself as called on to respect.

This requirement has been encapsulated in the dictum: 'Become who you are' – the idea being that it is possible to *succeed* or *fail* at being oneself, that one can do a better or worse job at responding to claims of self-realization. But what can this mean? How do we make distinctions among first-person claims – claims from the self to itself – such that we have reason to choose some rather than others?

In the *Nicomachean Ethics*, Aristotle addresses this question by distinguishing between what might be called legitimate and illegitimate forms of self-love. He acknowledges that people tend to criticize those engaged in self-love, pointing out that on the common view, it is 'The bad person

---

[1] See Enoch 2006 for critique of this view. We will revisit this in Chapter 6.

[who] does everything for his own sake, the more so the more wicked he is' (1168a), and the good person, on the contrary, 'acts for the sake of what is noble, and the more so the better he is; and he acts for the sake of his friend, neglecting his own interest' (1168b).

In contrast to this view, Aristotle also argues that the stance of friendship – according to which one wishes goods for the other person for his own sake – is also the stance that one must take toward *oneself*: a person is 'most of all a friend to himself and so ought also to love himself most of all' (1168b), the reason being that all the features of friendship toward others extend from this relation (of a person to himself) (1168b). The correct kind of self-love creates a noble character from which healthy friendships can arise.

Aristotle argues that when used as a term of reproach, 'self-love' refers to the tendency to assign oneself the larger share of money, honours, and bodily pleasures – objects of competition among the masses. But *genuine* self-love involves assigning oneself not material goods but noble and virtuous tasks:

> But a person like this seems to be more of a self-lover. At any rate he assigns to himself what is noblest and best above all, and gratifies the most authoritative element within himself, obeying it in everything. (1168b)

> In all praiseworthy actions, then, the good person is seen to assign himself the larger share of what is noble. So, as we have said, we ought to be self-lovers. But in the way the masses are, we should not. (1169a–1169b)

Here we see that there is an important distinction being made between bad and good forms of self-interest: the former involving pursuits that do not realize one's best or truest self but rather indulge in immediate gratifications and shallow goods.

On some accounts, the best way to cash out this idea is in terms of universal categories of rationality or human nature. In other words, I do a good job at loving myself if I realize an innate rationality or nature shared by all human beings. Thus the flourishing agent meets certain universal criteria of flourishing and does so by specifying them within the particular constraints of her own life. This is no doubt true and speaks to the fact that each of the normative perspectives is both 'subjective' and 'objective'. But if we take seriously Aristotle's injunction that self-love is basically treating yourself as you would a friend, we see that this cannot be the whole story. After all, what I want for my friend is not simply that she realizes some generic human nature within her particular life – though I wish this as well – but that she does so while also bringing her idiosyncratic style of being to its best and fullest expression. And this, surely, is what we want for ourselves – not simply that we meet generic external standards of what we should be – but that we bring into being the best version of our own particularity while doing so. We wish to express our own unique gifts and projects in a way that both manifests general human excellence and expresses the particularity of who we are.[2]

As Marya Schechtman (2004) points out, however, we seem to have two competing intuitions about how to understand this kind of successful self-becoming. On one model of agency, being who you are means allowing the unique and natural self with which you are born to find complete expression. Such a view relies on a kind of Romanticism – epitomized in Herder's description of the self as a unique flower bud that blossoms into itself insofar as destructive external forces do not interfere with that process.[3] This view conceptualizes the self as having a unique set of dispositions and capacities that it experiences itself as called on to realize. Here the fundamental obstacles are unthinking conformity and the corruptions of luxury – namely, conditions that obscure or destroy one's unique gifts. On this model the standard by which one chooses among competing incentives is the self's inner sense of its own strength and nature – an inchoate sense of rightness that cannot be codified or fully communicated because it is so radically singular, though the worldly norms that govern its expression will nevertheless be public.[4] On this kind of substantive model of self-becoming, what matters is not simply the formal relationship that I bear to my own agency, but rather the manner in which the content of what I value and choose is expressive of the given particularity of my unique identity.

In contrast, we also see approaches in which the self is understood in much more proactive and creative terms – it is not a unique pre-given set of desires and capacities that we must reveal and protect but is rather the product of an ongoing project of self-making in which we assess our given desires and capacities, endorsing some and rejecting others. We have already seen a version of this approach in Korsgaard's work. We also see

---

[2] Historically, there have been many different ways to conceptualize our reasons for this kind of self-realization, e.g. 'God's plan'.

[3] 'May you fare well, innocent youth, on a chaste stem, from a noble seed, you a healthy, firmly shut bud, Not blooming and unfolded too early, so as soon to wither, not rocking luxuriously in the breath of mild zephyrs' (Herder 2002, 225). Absence of interference is not sufficient for Herder, however: a certain kind of culture is also necessary for self-realization.

[4] 'In his heart every man knows quite well that, being unique, he will be in the world only once and that no imaginable chance will for a second time gather together into a unity so strangely variegated an assortment as he is' (Nietzsche 1997, 127). See Conant 2010.

it in thinkers like Harry Frankfurt. Both argue that being a self requires us to achieve and maintain a kind of diachronic integrity by way of procedures of endorsement and deliberative vetting. In this way, both thinkers reject the glorification of the 'natural' that is operative in the Romantic self-expressive view and emphasize, instead, that each person's body is the site of multiple competing incentives, only some of which I should acknowledge as genuinely *me*, no matter how 'natural' or 'internal' those incentives may be. On this approach, it is the act of identification – of taking responsible ownership by endorsing some incentives rather than others – that is the ultimate marker of flourishing agency, not simply the act of protecting and promoting natural urges that are granted legitimacy simply on the basis of that naturalness.[5]

It seems clear that there is something right about both of these intuitions. The malleability of and conflict among preferences – along with the thought that something being 'natural' or 'given' is not necessarily an argument for promoting it – causes us to question the Romantic model. But the recognition that the particularity of who we are can be lost – distorted or obscured because of overly rigid demands for conformity and rational control – makes us hesitant to abandon it.[6] After all, a typical worry about Kant-inspired accounts of the Korsgaardian variety is that there is no *me* left if we reduce the self to mere diachronic rational integrity. Successful instances of becoming who you are will therefore require negotiating both of these first-person demands or constraints on the self and balancing them against each other throughout one's life.

These two models offer different ways for understanding the criteria according to which we should evaluate projects of self-realization. On the self-expression model, our interpretations of what we have been and our choice of what we will be are understood as being in the service of an innate and radically unique sense of rightness or fit with different possibilities that the world offers – a sense that will provide the ultimate criterion on the basis of which to choose among possibilities and protect against distorting influences. But on the self-control model, one's projects are chosen on the basis of a kind of ideal of who one might be; an ideal that is relatively unconstrained by the given conditions and is experienced as the object of yearning and ambition. As we have seen,

---

[5] Of course, Frankfurt acknowledges that there is a kind of care that we simply find ourselves in the grip of, and this establishes how things can matter for us (1998, 80–94, 86–87). See also Williams on identity-constituting ground projects (1981, 1–19, 40–53).

[6] See Friedman 1986.

such an ideal can be modeled in formal or substantive terms. In the former case, the ideal is bare agency-promoting efficacy and autonomy, grounded in universal features of practical rationality as such. In the latter case the ideal is embodied in particular exemplars with whom the agent identifies.[7] In both cases we see how the first-person task of self-becoming offers specific ways of understanding the relationship between self, other, and worldly categories.

It is important to be wary of characterizing the self-control model in overly libertarian terms, since even idealized visions of who one might be are not simply objects of arbitrary will but are rather constrained by certain givens – namely, the fact that we care about being agents and the fact that we find ourselves in the grip of a sense that we ought to be a certain way in the world – which governs and motivates the ideals and exemplars we choose to emulate. Similarly, we should not characterize the Romantic model in overly passive terms, since recognizing feelings of rightness and their potentially corrupting influences requires active interpretation work.

There are also important temporal aspects of these competing intuitions about selfhood. For example, the Romantic conception – whereby we are in some sense thrown into a particular configuration of selfhood – is more in the grip of the past: it emphasizes the purity and priority of the origin. The emphasis is on remembering and maintaining the self in a form uncorrupted by worldly temptations to conformity or dissolution. One also sees something of this kind of orientation in the backward-looking emphasis evident in much narrative theory, whereby selfhood is understood as being constituted by a unifying story that stitches together who one has been with who one now is. On such accounts, understanding who one is now – and who one might become – arises out of a narrative understanding of what has come before. Though such accounts seek to resist Romantic ideas about an essential self simply waiting to be revealed by the narrative – emphasizing, rather, the creative and interpretive work performed by the narration – there is nevertheless a tendency to view the key task as being the identification of one's past experiences with one's present self.[8]

---

[7] This will be a central issue in Chapter 5.
[8] For example, many of the thought experiments about personal identity examine lost or 'transplanted' memories to determine if and how the self can be understood to survive such disruptions to memory. Parfit 1984 uses such examples to conclude that identity is not as important as one might in fact think. Schechtman 1996 challenges Parfit's view and attempts to provide a narrative account of psychological continuity that resists this backward-looking tendency by insisting that by 'narrative' we in fact mean a 'way one addresses life' or a 'script' (111) that shapes the character of one's life as a whole, including the

In contrast to this Romantic fidelity to the past, the self-creation conception of self-becoming tends to emphasize the future, arguing that we constitute ourselves through our forward-looking commitments to our own unified agency and the projects that it enables – we prioritize the future in the form of an ideal of unity or self-realization that is brought about by our forward-looking deliberative planning. We see this kind of priority of the future in thinkers such as Michael Bratman, who argue that long-term planning gives a normative shape and direction to one's agency, decoupling the agent from immediate urges so that she can see her life as something to be organized in light of the self that she might become.[9] This allows us to distinguish simple continuous desires from plans that bear an essential referential connection between their 'earlier intention and later intentional execution' (Bratman 2007, 30).

In describing this planning agency, Bratman makes a distinction between self-governing policies, which coordinate and organize 'the agent's temporally extended life in ways that constitute and support Lockean continuities and connections' (Bratman 2007, 41), and ideals, which also organize and structure our lives over time but do so with less rigid constraints on consistency and coherence. We can perhaps read this in terms of the distinction made above between formal and substantive accounts of self-creation: the former specifying constraints imposed by the requirement that we accomplish a minimal level of integrity such that a unified agency is possible, and the latter specifying the creative self-shaping realized by adopting substantive life ideals. We might read this, in other words, as a distinction between a minimal threshold of agency and the direction of its development. In either case, however, the point is that our choice of specific acts and desires is always guided by a diachronic understanding of who we are trying to be, not simply what we are trying to do.[10]

The difficult work of responding well to first-person norms involves negotiating this tension between the active and passive, futural and

---

way that life unfolds into the future (105–114). I discuss this idea further in the next section. We see a similar emphasis on the essential role of backward-looking temporality in Nietzsche's second essay of the *Genealogy* (1989b), wherein being a sovereign individual – a genuine self – depends on the will having the ability to carry itself through the vicissitudes of time such that a past commitment is maintained into the present. Thus Nietzsche distinguishes between a 'protracted will' and 'short-willed' creatures when thinking about the possibility of self-becoming, and he does so in terms of memory (59–60).

[9] 'We do not simply act from moment to moment. Instead, we settle on complex – and, typically, partial and hierarchically structured – future-directed plans of action, and these play basic roles in support of the organization and coordination of our activities over time' (Bratman 2007, 26). See also Frankfurt 1998, 83; Velleman 2006, 271.

[10] See Rodgers and Warmke 2015 for a response to situationism in this vein.

historical dimensions of the self – challenging ourselves to realize our best possible self but within the boundaries established by the givens of our unique configuration of abilities, preferences, and visions of the possible. Our task is to express our freedom for self-creation in a way that does not do violence to what we have been given to be. In future chapters we will see that the mimesis relationship to the exemplar embodies this kind of negotiation of the active and passive. We model our active self-creation on exemplars for whom we feel a kind of natural love and admiration – an experience of unchosen responsivity that is echoed in the feeling of fit between self and world that we accomplish by emulating them. And this task is further constrained by the given requirement that we accomplish a minimal level of rational integrity such that our projects of self-becoming do not fragment into incoherence.

Style

The task of unifying these competing evaluative stances such that one can differentiate between better and worse forms of individual preference-satisfaction essentially requires one to adopt a governing ideal that both constrains one to an overarching unity of self-improvement and yet feels like a natural extension of who one innately is. One way to think about how these two standards of self-becoming – of self-creation and self-control – can be brought together is through Nietzsche's idea of giving *style* to one's character.

> One thing is needful – To 'give style' to one's character – a great and rare art! It is practised by those who survey all the strengths and weaknesses of their nature and then fit them into an artistic plan until ... even weaknesses delight the eye ... [W]hen the work is finished, it becomes evident how the constraint of a single taste governed and formed everything large and small ... It will be the strong and domineering natures that enjoy their finest gaiety in such constraint and perfection under a law of their own ... Conversely, it is the weak characters ... that hate the constraint of style: they feel that if this bitterly evil compulsion were to be imposed on them, they would be demeaned – they become slaves as soon as they serve; they hate to serve. (2001, 290)

Note that in this description Nietzsche emphasizes first the task of *surveying* what one has been given: 'all the strengths and weaknesses of their nature'. The implication here is that one is taking stock of the innate conditions – whether natural or inherited from one's culture – that will shape and constrain the task ahead.

Contrary to the Romantic picture of self-becoming, however, he insists that the form for which one strives is not yet fully present in one's existing form. Thus the process of self-becoming requires that one *transform* oneself, not simply that one avoid corrupting influences to allow one's true self to shine through:

> Every artist knows how far from any feeling of letting himself go his most 'natural' state is – the free ordering, placing, disposing, giving form in the moment of 'inspiration' – and how strictly and subtly he obeys thousand-fold laws precisely then, laws that precisely on account of their hardness and determination defy all formulation through concepts ... [G]iven that, something always develops, and has developed, for whose sake it is worth while to live on earth; for example, virtue, art, music, dance, reason, spirituality. (Nietzsche 1989a, §188)

We can see then that the two modes of constraint are operative in Nietzsche's account: the constraints of the given and the constraints of the chosen. The work of self-becoming, he argues, is the work of bringing these two modes of constraint into such a harmony that they are no longer experienced *as* constraining but rather as the necessary condition for the possibility of being who one is – the desired consequence being that one experiences one's life on earth as 'worthwhile.'

The notion of style is well suited to capture this kind of stance because it is a way of understanding limitations on one's choices not as shackles but as vehicles of self-differentiation and expression. Though *my* style of being rules out NASCAR racing and laissez-faire attitudes toward tidiness, closing down those possibilities is not experienced as a penalty but rather as a realization of who I feel myself to be.

The art historian Alexander Nagel describes style as 'the state in which one feels the least separation between one's character and one's body'. If we expand this beyond the notion of sartorial or physical style, we can understand style as a condition in which one experiences a feeling of fit – or 'least separation' between who one is and one's way of manifesting in the world. Note that this seems to involve seeing particular events and choices in terms of the overarching global sense of who one is; namely, each choice or urge – each particular worldly manifestation – is viewed not in isolation but as emblematic of one's identity; i.e. someone is the 'kind of person' who plays backgammon or is a vegan. A person's style is the way in which she understands a certain relationship between whole and part – identity and particular activity or object – and acts in light of that mereological insight.[11] It is an implicit interpretive frame according to which given preferences are winnowed and shaped to realize a unifying vision of one's true identity or best self.[12]

This is at the heart of what Nietzsche means by the requirement that one sees oneself at a distance in order to become who one is.[13] Seeing oneself at a *distance* can be understood as occupying a stance wherein one is unmoved by immediate urges as having a particular claim to endorsement. It is a tendency to focus on a certain configuration of one's life as a whole as opposed to a disparate collection of short-term projects or urges. This is captured by Nietzsche's insistence on the necessity of a kind of self-directed cruelty, whereby one's present urges are ignored or crushed in light of the ideal of future becoming. Thus in *On the Genealogy of Morals* he speaks of 'this secret self-ravishment, this artists' cruelty, this delight in imposing a form upon oneself as a hard, recalcitrant, suffering material and in burning a will, a critique, a contradiction, a contempt, a No into it' (1989b, §18). To take this kind of stance on oneself requires a fierce honesty about the degree to which one is failing to be the self that one might be: 'What is the greatest experience you can have? It is the hour of the great contempt. The hour in which your happiness, too arouses your disgust, and even your reason and your virtue' (Nietzsche 1995, §3, 13).

We see again the Romantic impulse here: the idea of a kind of innate selfhood that will be unleashed by the process of self-transformation. Thus Nietzsche suggests that the great person's 'hostility is at bottom directed against that which, though he finds it in himself, is not truly himself' (1997, 145). Further, knowing how to set up the ideal on the basis of which this cruel self-shaping is legitimate requires an intimate knowledge of who one already is. Nietzsche insists that you must look back on your life and ask:

> What have you truly loved up to now, what has drawn your soul aloft, what has mastered it and at the same time blessed it? Set up these revered objects before you and perhaps their nature and their sequence will give you a law, the fundamental law of your own true self. Compare these objects one with another, see how one completes, expands, surpasses, transfigures another, how they constituted a stepladder upon which you have clambered up to

---

[11] We will revisit this in Chapter 7.
[12] See also Nehemas 1985. Here we should note that such artistic norms and commitments to a style are always indebted to both shared aesthetic traditions and individual exemplars – a point that highlights the fact that even first-person striving to be oneself cannot be understood as a private or purely 'subjective' project but is a way of responding to the task of being in the world well.
[13] See Nietzsche 2001, §78, §80, and §82.

yourself as you are now; for your true nature lies, not concealed deep within you, but immeasurably high above you, or at least above that which you usually take yourself to be. (1997, 129)

The problem for most people, however, is a tendency to deny one kind of constraint by focusing entirely on the other. Thus the lazy and the cowardly insist on a fatalistic conception of identity, equating the givenness of their nature with an absolute powerlessness that licenses them to abdicate all responsibility for doing the hard work of building the stepladder and clambering up to themselves upon it. There are also grandiose and self-important souls, however, who insist that their freedom for self-creation is utterly unconstrained, that the menu of lives from which to choose is untrammeled by who they are or where they come from.

But what we have seen in this too-brief discussion of the nature of first-person reasons is that responding to them well requires one to negotiate between given and ideal modes of living one's unique style of being in the world, denying neither the limits imposed by the givens of one's nature nor the freedom to shape those givens in light of who one thinks one ought to be. Each of us feels the pressure of this requirement – a requirement that cannot be translated into third-personal or second-personal terms but rather is intrinsic to our sense that we are each entrusted with our own self-realization. Or better: that we each have our own style of being. To be a true friend to oneself is to nurture and appreciate that style, heeding its constraints not as external impositions but as authentic expressions of who one is.

Second-Person Claims

From the second-person perspective the agent is claimed by demands made on her by the specific others with whom she comes in contact. The genuinely flourishing agent occupies a world that is not treated as hers alone. She is claimed by the interests of others, but not merely as vehicles and obstacles to her own project of self-becoming. Rather, the second-person perspective involves seeing that the specific first-person desires and projects of the *other* person provide *me* with reasons for action – reasons unmediated by third-person categorizations or first-person pragmatic concerns. The complete absence of the ability to take this kind of second-personal stance, I take it, would manifest only in cases of sociopathy or perhaps severe blindness to other minds – cases in which the agent is able to recognize in a kind of third-personal way that there are 'others' but is unable to feel the other person's desires and projects as a reason for *him* to act. Human flourishing requires one to succeed within this perspective by responding appropriately to the second-person claims of others in their struggles to be. It requires, in other words, that one be at least minimally responsive to the needs of others for their own sake.

The notion of the 'second-person claim' is perhaps most closely associated with Stephen Darwall, who has argued for a distinct class of agent-relative reasons – what he calls second-person reasons – that arise from relationships of accountability between persons:

> A second-personal reason is one whose validity depends on presupposed authority and accountability relations between persons and, therefore, on the possibility of the reason's being addressed person-to-person ... As second-personal reasons always derive from agents' relations to one another, they are invariably fundamentally agent-relative. (2006, 8)

This agent-relativity does not permit us to conclude, however, that second-person claims can simply be reduced to *first*-person claims. Rather, they occupy a distinct normative terrain wherein their demandingness arises from the person-to-person relationship and our mutual standing within that relationship to hold each other accountable. Darwall emphasizes this reciprocality in what he calls Fichte's point:

> Any second-personal claim or 'summons' (*Aufforderung*) presupposes a common competence, authority, and, therefore, responsibility as free and rational, a mutual second-personality that addresser and addressee share and that is appropriately recognized reciprocally. (2006, 21)

Though I am in agreement with Darwall's specification of a distinct class of second-person reasons, in what follows I will argue that he fails to adequately distinguish them from third-personal agent-neutral reasons. To see why this is so, we must turn briefly to the work of Emmanuel Lévinas, whose account of the ethical encounter in many ways anticipated Darwall's idea of a 'second person reason' – though Lévinas's view also contains important differences, the key one for our purposes being the *asymmetry* of such encounters. Unlike Darwall, Lévinas argues that second-person reasons cannot be experienced as reciprocal except by leaving the second-person stance to view the relationship as if from the outside.

According to Lévinas, the historical tendency of both philosophy and political movements has been to 'totalize' – namely, to categorize and make predictable on the basis of generalizing systems with a common unit of comparison.[14] Lévinas rejects this tendency, arguing that we must acknowledge the kind of resistance or excessiveness that the other person poses to every conceptual framework that might be employed to define or contain her. The plurality of persons characterized by such incommensurability disrupts and precedes political and conceptual totalities. This can become evident to us in face-to-face relationships with others, in which we directly encounter a presence that testifies to a perspective on the world that can never be subsumed to one's own without remainder. Thus according to Lévinas, there are possibilities of encounter that interrupt and challenge the self and its tendency to domesticate all that initially appears 'other' to the safe confines of the knowable and the same. In such encounters one is subjected to a presence that resists one's powers of appropriation and categorization.

Importantly, this resistance to one's totalizing tendencies does not occur in the form of force against force but rather as a challenge to one's self-understanding as having a *right* to force. Lévinas calls this 'the resistance of what has no resistance – the ethical resistance' (2007, 199).[15] The fundamental feature of second-person claims, he argues, is that they are characterized for the recipient by an experience of being challenged, of being called into question. The other person shows up in the second-person encounter as a presence that contests and questions me – an experience that prompts me to recognize that my unthinking freedom must answer for itself. It is no longer experienced as legitimate by default. Ethics at its heart just *is* this ability to see that one's preferences are not automatically self-legitimating but must answer to and for the others who share the world. Absent the encounter with such a source of external normative claim, each of us would simply live free in the world, possessing and consuming it as a reflection of our own will. In the face-to-face encounter with the other person, on the contrary, we experience such self-servingness as potentially *unjust* – as *taking* from the other person something to which she too has a claim: 'Morality begins when freedom, instead of being justified by itself, feels itself to be arbitrary and violent' (Lévinas 2007, 84).[16]

It is of course a further question as to what exactly we are obligated to do or be in light of this experience of claim from the other person. But we must recognize first of all that the nature of this kind of claim experience

---

[14] See Mensch 2015.
[15] See Crowell 1998 and 2012; Smith 2012.
[16] Kompridis 2011 discusses this kind of experience using the notion of a *decentering* of the self: an unsettling whole-sensibility shake-up that cannot be proceduralized (214–215).

rules out speaking of it as *reciprocal*, at least from within the perspective where the claim shows up as such. To recognize self and other as equal – and thus our relationship as reciprocal – would require an external totalizing perspective from which we could engage in such comparison. But once we occupy such a perspective of comparison, Lévinas suggests, we have exited the second-personal face-to-face mode of relationship in which we feel answerable to a presence that resists our ability to contain it. We have entered, instead, a kind of neutral third-person stance where that specificity and resistance is covered over in the service of finding commonalities and equivalences. Once we exit the terrain of the second-person stance, then, the very phenomenon that we are hoping to capture – the resistance and challenge the other person poses to my tendency to subsume everything to my concepts and systems, along with the claim that I respond to the other as such a being – is lost:

> The reversibility of the relation where the terms are indifferently read from left to right and from right to left would couple them the *one* to the *other*; they would complete one another in a system visible from the outside. The intended transcendence would be thus reabsorbed into the unity of the system, destroying the radical alterity of the other. (Lévinas 2007, 35–36)

This is the problem with accounts that start by thinking of us all as being of the same *kind* – as rational animals or transcendental subjects or bearers of a mutual authority to make demands. To think of us as all the same in this way looks at the self/other relationship as if from the outside.[17]

Lévinas is not denying that we *can* do this – certainly this is both possible and necessary, as we will discuss in the upcoming section on third-person claims. But it is important to recognize that when we do so, we are translating a second-person demand into something else, since second-person authority does not show up in our experience as an agent-neutral activity or status that we are all equally capable of engaging in or displaying, but rather as a kind of *breach* or *interruption* in the self-interested focus on one's own preference-satisfaction.

With this brief sketch of Lévinas's view in hand, how should we interpret Darwall's understanding of second-person reasons? Though it seems clear that Darwall is pointing to the same kind of experience of immediate moral claim in the encounter with individual others – a claim whose authority makes a demand on one directly – he differs from Lévinas

---

[17] G. A. Cohen similarly argues that impersonal defenses of harmful actions that seem reasonable in the abstract suddenly become offensive when someone uses them to the face of the person being directly harmed by them (1991, 272–273).

in his use of justificatory language that seeks to ground the authority operating in such claims via third-personal categories:

> To enter intelligibly into the second-person stance and make claims on and demands of one another at all, I argue, you and I must presuppose that we share a common second-person authority, competence and responsibility simply as free and rational agents. (2006, 5)

But knowing that the other person belongs to a particular category – e.g. 'free and rational agent' – is not a necessary condition for *experiencing* her as a being who demands that I heed her presence. Rather, the experience of being claimed is itself constitutive of the recognition. It is only afterward, argues Lévinas, that we theorize about *why* our freedom is or ought to be limited by the other's presence. As soon as we do this, however, we have absented ourselves from the immediacy of the second-person claim itself:

> The radical separation between the same and the other means precisely that it is impossible to place oneself outside of the correlation between the same and the other so as to record the correspondence or the non-correspondence ... Otherwise the same and the other would be reunited under one gaze, and the absolute distance that separates them filled in. (2007, 36)

The problem with Darwall's account, in other words, is that it slides into looking at the second-personal self/other relationship from a third-person perspective – from a perspective that could see us as reciprocal, as equally balanced. But for Lévinas such a perspective is closed to us – at least from within the immediacy of the face-to-face encounter – which is the only perspective from which the authoritative demand of the other person can be genuinely revealed as such. Darwall himself seems to recognize this at points – wanting to exclude a general and external stance: 'What the second-person stance excludes is the third-person perspective, that is, regarding, for practical purposes, others (and oneself), not in relation to oneself, but as they are (or one is) "objectively" or "agent-neutrally"' (2006, 9). But he consistently undermines this recognition by speaking of both members of the ethical relationship as sharing common features that justify the authority of the claims they make: 'any second-personal address whatsoever presupposes a common second-personal competence, responsibility, and authority that addresser and addressee share as free and rational agents' (2006, 23). In doing so, Darwall characterizes the relationship in terms that ultimately distort the normative experience that he is attempting to describe, since he attributes to each participant a normative status that is at odds with the lived experience of being in such a relationship.

In contrast, Lévinas insists:

> This ... expression of the original accusative mode in which the presence of the Other to the I is attested, does not permit itself to be rationalized into a common concept of 'humanity', the ontological symmetry or *Gleichberechtigung* [equal rights] of free, autonomous subjects ... The Other does not derive her right to judge me by virtue of an equivalent right that I would have to judge her, since such equivalence would exchange for the primordial ethical phenomenon of obligation the interminable rhetorical and political one of negotiation. (2007, 27)

In the second-person encounter I am claimed by an incomparable presence that challenges my narcissistic tendency to view all things through the lens of my own projects and desires. But in the third-personal stance of politics, self and other are viewed as equal bearers of rights – seeing each other in light of a shared neutral term (e.g. citizen) that applies indifferently to all of us. The problem with Darwall's account, in other words, is confusing the ethical and the political by translating the immediate demandingness of the second-person encounter – which challenges me to recognize a normative source outside me – into third-person claims, whose demandingness arises from the experience of being one among many with the unique obligations that arise therefrom.[18]

This discussion of Darwall and Lévinas has not been intended to suggest that they are alone in their efforts to understand the nature of second-person claims or distinguish them from the third-person normative domain. One can also find important resources for doing so in feminist theorists such as Nel Noddings and Carol Gilligan, who resist the tendency to read all moral relationships in terms of a distanced and anonymous mode of engagement or, as they put it, a tendency to translate caring into justice.[19] What all of these thinkers are asking us to see is the impossibility of translating without remainder the immediate moral claim of the individual other person into first-person or third-person reasons. Acknowledging the distinctness of this class of normative claim means acknowledging that human flourishing requires responsivity to its

---

[18] This tendency is not unique to Darwall. For example, LeBar 2009 claims, 'When I engage in second-personal reasoning, I consider what I ought to do as one of a community of rational agents' (648).

[19] See Gilligan 1982 and Noddings 1984. See also Slote 1999, where he argues that the desire to integrate the second person with the third person violates the second person (26). Further discussion can be found in Blum 1988 and Crittenden 1999.

demands. Flourishing requires, in other words, acknowledging the other person's claims as having an innate normative authority and acting in light of this fact – a stance that will require us not only to accommodate our projects to those of others but also to recognize the communal character of those projects themselves insofar as others play a constitutive role in them.

Third-Person Constraints

So far we have considered the way that human beings experience themselves as being in the grip of claims that come both from themselves and from the individuals whom they encounter in the world. But as we will see in this section, it is important to recognize that we understand self and other not simply as unique and isolated individuals but also as members of communities in which we are merely one among many occupying a shared world. From this stance one looks beyond the specificity of one's projects and the demands of one's particular relationships to consider one's position in the human community and the world at large.[20]

This stance involves a shift in emphasis from that which differentiates self and other to that which is or ought to be shared among all of us. Since we share both a common status as rational human agents *and* we share the world in which that agency must be coordinated with others, the third-person perspective and the constraints it places on us can take a number of

[20] I wish to remain agnostic on the (enormous) question of whether the moral claim that animals make on us (if they do) falls into the second-person or the third-person domain, i.e. whether we feel an immediate claim to accommodate *this* animal's struggle to be, or if we recognize the need to share the world with animals in a more general way. I suspect it is probably both, but making that case would go far beyond the scope of the book. I am also bracketing the (similarly enormous) question of whether the environment itself can make a moral claim on us, and if so, whether such a claim falls into the first-person, second-person, or third-person domain – i.e. whether we are obligated to protect the environment so that we can accomplish individual long-term projects, so that future generations can, or so that we create and maintain a sustainable shared world. I suspect that the best way to accommodate the idea that the environment itself makes a claim on us in non-instrumental ways is via the third-person perspective. Alternatively, one might suggest that the environment makes a different kind of claim – e.g. an aesthetic one. It would require a significant expansion of this project to show how aesthetic claims can be understood to fit within the taxonomy of practical reason that I am articulating here. We should also note that phenomenology cannot give an account of animal/environment flourishing per se – i.e. in complete isolation from the lived experience of human agents, since doing so would rely on a speculative metaphysics closed to the phenomenologist. If we talk about animals or the environment from the phenomenological perspective, we must do so in terms of the ways in which their claims to value show up for *us* as such – we cannot, for example, simply make use of a natural law theoretical presupposition of the divine order and value of the universe understood in isolation from any human experience of its value as such.

different forms. What unites them, however, is a shared concern for and commitment to what might be called *objectivity*. To understand the claims arising from this normative terrain – and thus the way in which meeting them is constitutive of flourishing – we must therefore think through the nature of the demand for objectivity.

Generally speaking, the notion of 'objectivity' tends to refer both to a reality external to the mind and to a condition of being uninfluenced by personal feelings or bias. Naturally the debates on what exactly these conditions entail are numerous and cannot possibly be canvassed adequately here.[21] Instead what I hope to do in this section is show that both of these general understandings of the meaning of objectivity arise naturally from an agent's experience of herself as being one among a multiplicity of perspectives that must be coordinated and accommodated in her modeling of the world and her place within it.

Husserl and the Question of Physical Objectivity

The most straightforward way to find our way into this discussion is to examine how an objective understanding of the physical reality of the external world is possible. This is an issue that Edmund Husserl famously tackles in the *Cartesian Meditations* by showing the manner in which scientific objectivity arises from our recognition of other perceivers as capable of accessing different aspects of a shared physical environment.[22]

Husserl first discusses how a certain kind of quasi-objectivity can be accomplished from within the solipsistic confines of a single perceptual system insofar as something presents itself as having a kind of constancy and coherence of givenness for all five of the perceiver's senses. On the basis of this constancy and coherence the agent is led to believe that the object of her perceptual attention is in fact objectively there – i.e. that it stands over against her not as a hallucination but as a genuinely external reality. As Husserl points out, however, from such a condition of solitude one would never be able to tell if one's whole perceptual system were out of whack, i.e. that the agreement among the senses was not a sign of the reality of the object but rather of the pathology of the agent. The solipsistic

---

[21] Indeed, on one reading the question of objectivity is the question of epistemology itself, though that too is contested.
[22] See Husserl 1999. He also discusses how the ideal of objective truth arises from humanity's search for consensus in Husserl 1970.

agent would have nothing to verify her perceptions against and would therefore take her experiences to be accurate representations of reality even if they were in fact merely delusions. They would, after all, consistently confirm her expectations and appear to provide reliable information about navigating the environment.

As a result, Husserl concludes that the only way to achieve greater objectivity than this is if we escape the confines of our own perspective to compare it with those of others. To a certain degree this is simply what objective physical reality *means*: namely, that which is continuously and harmoniously present – or possibly present – to the perceptions of all knowers. Indeed, if it were not for the presence of these others, Husserl points out, we would have neither the motivation nor the ability to develop a more complex understanding of objectivity than the kind of quasi or 'private' objectivity we can achieve as solitary knowers, namely, reliable patterns of experience that are consistently confirmed by one's perceptions.

But the fact is that we do encounter such others and test our individual perceptions against theirs. We recognize that the things that other people perceive from 'over there' are also identified as being the same as the things I see from 'over here' (Husserl 1999, 148/119). This procedure of referencing the perceptions of other knowers is for the most part implicit and automatic – though, as we will see, it is formalized and made explicit in the sciences.

When we shift from our abstract examination of a 'solipsistic subject', then, we recognize that the experience of a plurality of perspectives other than one's own transforms the individual's private experiences from being equivalent to 'the world' to being recognized as simply one perspective among many on an objective world shared by all of us. And though our individual experiences are different – each of us having a different perspective on the physical objects present to us – they become unified in confirming the shared reality of the object whose perceptual profiles are given to each of us differently.[23]

The experience of this kind of 'thereness for everyone' would not be possible in the absence of a stance according to which other members of the community of experiencers show up as analogous to oneself. The agent must see himself as one among many, all of whom have the same basic status (Husserl 1999, 157–158/129). In other words, the very idea of an

---

[23] Zahavi 2001 examines the feasibility of this approach. Husserl expands on this point to encompass the shared, communal structure of the space of possibilities more generally.

'objective world' bears within it a necessary reference to the intersubjective coordination of a plurality of all perceivers.[24]

Out of this ongoing non-formalized experience of the world as an object of shared intersubjective agreement – in which I overcome the relativity and incompleteness of my own perspective through an implicit reference to the perspectives of others who are recognized as analogous knowers – a higher or more thorough level of objectivity can eventually arise, i.e. the objectivity accomplished by science. This is achieved, Husserl argues, by abstracting further from the agent-relativity of perception to find an identical content of qualities in *any possible* experience. The scientific project, in other words, is aimed at transforming shared perceptual possibilities into intellectual models that remove the relativity and incompleteness built into all perception – namely, its embeddedness in a particular limited perspective. The result is what Husserl calls the logico-mathematical 'physicalistic thing' of the sciences, which is not itself a perceptual object but rather a model for possible perceptions. In this scientific modeling all objects become characterized as forms or movements within a conceptual reconstruction of objective spatiotemporal reality. But doing so requires the community of knowers to step back from perception itself, which is inherently perspectival and relative – to develop a mathematical reconstruction or schematic of reality that can be known only conceptually. As he notes in *Ideas II*: 'Objective space is not sensuous'; it 'does not allow of being grasped by the vision of the eyes but only by the understanding'.[25]

Thus scientific understanding embodies a more robust instantiation of the third-person perspective insofar as it occupies a further remove from the lived experience of individual perception, enabling us to grasp objects in a way that is completely non-relative to any particular agent's embodied status. In doing so, it requires that the 'one among many' to which we are positing ourselves as belonging is conceptualized as bare perspectives stripped of any of the distinguishing features of human embodied perceiving. Such idealizing models of intersubjective perceptual experience are extremely useful since they help us predict possibilities of perception for any possible knower without being tied to any particular perceptual

---

[24] 'The Objective world as an *idea* – the ideal correlate of an intersubjective (intersubjectively communalized) experience, which ideally can be carried on as constantly harmonious – is essentially related to intersubjectivity (itself constituted as having the ideality of endless openness), whose component particular subjects are equipped with mutually corresponding and harmonious constitutive systems' (Husserl 1999, 137–138/107–108).

[25] Husserl 1989, 83/88.

system. In doing so, they set up a norm that governs our claims about what is physically real and thereby provide us with a tool for determining when a particular agent's perceptual system is pathological.[26]

From within the third-person perspective the recognition of oneself as one among many in a shared world brings with it a demand that one respect the plurality of perspectives and ultimately the scientific project to which it gives rise, since its purpose is the coordination of all relevant perceivers such that we are able to establish truths about the physical reality we all share. The fact that we share the world with a multitude of others imposes on us a need to find and create commonality among us.

Sensus Communis *and the Objectivity of the Cultural Sphere*

Having seen how this works in the sphere of physical reality, we can apply this interpretation of objectivity to other kinds of objects. Naturally the objects of a shared cultural space differ significantly from the objects of a shared physical space, but I will argue in this section that the third-person stance through which they appear as such displays the same underlying structure.[27] We can see this by considering Kant's notion of *sensus communis*, which he takes to be a necessary condition for the possibility of making aesthetic judgments about beautiful objects:

> By '*sensus **communis***' ... must be understood the idea of a **communal** sense, i.e., a faculty for judging that in its reflection takes account (*a priori*) of everyone else's way of representing in thought, in order **as it were** to hold its judgment up to human reason as a whole. (2000, 5:293, §40, emphasis in original)

It is this 'taking account of everyone's way of representing' that is of interest here. As we saw in Husserl's account of physical objectivity, the perceiving agent takes the other person's vantage point as offering perceptual information that confirms and expands on her own. She

---

[26] Husserl 1970 insists, however, that such formalizations will only ever be second-order insofar as they presuppose and proceed on the basis of existential sources of motivation and experience grounded in the shared life-world.

[27] The extent to which the natural and the social sciences are of a kind in terms of goals and methods conducive to objectivity is a debate that first found its modern expression in thinkers like Dilthey 2002 and Weber 1949. The issue turns to a large degree on the extent to which the social sciences are seen as capable of aperspectival knowledge. Though we cannot hope to resolve such a complex issue here, Husserl's model can be helpful by leaving room for abstraction from the point of view of the knower while also acknowledging that such abstraction work is always grounded in and ultimately answerable to the practical agents who are motivated to engage in such modeling activities. The best we can hope for is a self-aware dialectic between the two. See also Daston 1992.

conceptualizes the object both from her own perspective and as if she were in the perceptual shoes of others. In the same way, non-physical 'objects' – such as laws and social norms, aesthetic objects, and historical categories – are similarly shared by members of a community in ways that involve an implicit reference to other people as occupying vantage points that confirm and expand on one's own. As in the case of perceptual objects, these kinds of intersubjective cultural objects implicitly presuppose in the other agents experiential systems analogous to one's own. '*Sensus communis*' is the capacity for doing so – for taking others to be analogous in epistemically or axiologically relevant ways such that the object under consideration is viewed as being a certain way not simply for me, but for all of us. Thus when I proclaim 'This is beautiful,' I am asserting not only that the object triggers in me a certain kind of experience but implicitly presupposing that it also triggers a similar experience in everyone else insofar as they share the same faculties.

Like Husserl, Kant insists we do not have to explicitly and deliberately compare our experiences with those of this or that actual other person in order to do this, but rather that we are naturally capable of occupying a third-personal stance – a 'universal standpoint' characterized by an understanding of oneself and one's objects as occurring in a public world surrounded by agents like ourselves:

> Now this happens by one holding his judgment up not so much to the actual as to the merely possible judgments of others, and putting himself into the position of everyone else, merely by abstracting from the limitations that contingently attach to our own judging. (2000, 5:294)

As in Husserl, Kant also makes room for the possibility of making this tendency more formal, deliberate, and explicit (2000, 5:295). Note, however, that on Kant's account, we can attribute analogous faculties to all humans when we make an aesthetic judgment because he believes that aesthetic experiences make use of the same faculties necessary for cognizing as such. In other words, the faculties required for thought *simpliciter* are the same ones required for their aesthetic free-play. Thus insofar as other people are conscious at all, he argues, we can assume their capacity to judge the same things beautiful that we do: 'This pleasure must necessarily rest on the same conditions in everyone, since they are subjective conditions of the possibility of cognition in general' (2000, 5:292–293). Of course, just because we *can* share this experience does not mean we all already do. It means simply that we *ought* to based on the capacities that we have. So by saying one 'ought' to see something as beautiful, one is indicating that aesthetic pleasure is not simply automatic but rather is an 'ideal norm' of intersubjective coordination based on universally shared capacities that are recognized as such (2000, 5:294). This is the essence of Enlightenment egalitarianism and Romanticism: the idea that beauty is a training away from our biases insofar as it prompts us to conceive of ourselves as one among a plurality of beings who are all fundamentally the same.

Despite these similarities, important differences between intersubjective physical and cultural objects must be highlighted. The perceptual systems of vision, touch, etc. can be more easily recognized as shared by all others than can the capacities that allow us to love beauty, value justice, and experience various kinds of meaning. As a consequence, reaching intersubjective agreement about physical reality – and recognizing pathological instances as such – is much easier than reaching a similar agreement about cultural objects, since the latter require us to engage in an ongoing dialogue about which capacities for meaning, value, and aesthetic appreciation we all in fact share and which are merely contingent or local. The problem, in other words, is that in the case of cultural objects what we need to come to agreement about is not just which objects are beautiful, valuable, or good, but also what it is about us that is universally shared such that the beautiful, the valuable, and the good can be understood *as* objectively shareable by all human beings.

It is here that we can recognize Hegel's great insight. Namely, that a communal project of this kind cannot be understood simply in terms of the decision procedures of individual agents. Rather, the demands of the third-person perspective naturally give rise to the need for communal practices and institutions that conceptualize, compare, and coordinate this multiplicity of agents.[28] We see this, for example, in political concepts and institutions such as political equality, citizenship, and civil rights, which embody a certain shared understanding of what kinds of creatures we all are and therefore what kinds of shared cultural objects and practices ought to arise as a result of that understanding. We also see the influential role that the third-person perspective has played in moral theories that insist on universalizability and neutrality, requirements that both embody a conception of how to coordinate a multiplicity of agents and endorse a

---

[28] Hegel 1991. The requirement that one adopt this community-oriented stance indicates one way that virtue ethics follows Hegel in moving beyond Kantianism's traditional focus on the decision procedure of individual agents to focus on the individual's embeddedness in a community and its practices (despite Kant's inclusion of certain institutions of etiquette in 1996, 6:428–437). See Annas 2002.

particular understanding of what kind of agents we must all be in order to be capable of that coordination.

These are projects, in other words, aimed at finding basic capacities and preferences that are universally and identically shared by all agents – capacities and preferences that we can then take to reliably reveal universal objects of value to all non-pathological cases. And in many of these approaches we can recognize both an informal intersubjective objectivity – an implicit shared sense of what we are all doing and why – and efforts to formalize this informal understanding to reach greater objectivity in our shared pursuits. In this we can see the analogy with the physical sciences, which seek to formalize our shared sense of what is objectively there for all of us. Just as the models of physical reality allow us to explain and predict a shared world untainted by the idiosyncracies of particular perceivers, the moral, political, and social-scientific models we devise can also help us to explain and predict a human reality untainted by the idiosyncracies of particular agents. Responding well to the demands of the third-person perspective requires, then, that one is responsive to the models of human striving and excellence given to us via moral theory and the other *Geisteswissenschaften*. In our efforts to become our best individual selves and respond well to the claims of particular others, we must not pursue those tasks in isolation from the human project of understanding what kind of creatures we all are and what kind of world we all share. We must look to the multitude of others and the public norms governing shared arenas of meaning. In the same way, responding well to third-person demands also requires us to be responsive to the findings of the physical sciences so that we operate with an accurate picture of how the shared objective world can both enable and constrain our possibilities for action.

We have seen, then, that from the third-person normative stance the harmony and integration of all agents' projects into a shared world is itself experienced as a reason for action.[29] This stance provides reasons for establishing and maintaining shared practices and institutions dedicated to the comparative weighing and coordination of the claims of multiple agents such that this integration is possible. Finally, the third-person stance also involves recognizing that genuine flourishing involves public deliberation about what an intersubjectively shareable vision of excellence

---

[29] This can perhaps be called the 'kingdom of ends' requirement; i.e. the third formulation of the Categorical Imperative demands that one coordinate one's rational pursuits with the rational pursuits of all others (see Kant 1997, especially section II). Farnham 2006 argues that this demand is also characteristic of a Stoic account of flourishing (443).

involves. So adopting the third-person stance does not involve merely acting in accord with existing social identities or institutions, but deliberatively participating in their creation or transformation in light of ideals of human excellence. Thus the third-person stance must also encompass the intersubjective project of struggling to answer what a good human life is and how to shape the world in such a way that it becomes possible. This is not limited to the normative framework of one's particular community but includes the universalizing projects of science, philosophy, art, and religion – humanity's attempts to find shared answers to questions regarding how the world is, what we are, and what living excellently in light of these facts demands.[30] Flourishing requires one to succeed within this third-person perspective by shaping one's life in light of the standards, institutions, and projects endorsed by the human community and through which one's obligation to all others can be managed.

Balancing the Claims

The distinction between these three perspectives should not mislead us as to their degree of separability. Each is intimately bound up with the others – my first-person projects and desires are informed by the possibilities articulated by the public arena and my relationships with others. My duties to those others are given shape in terms of cultural norms and my own projects. And the public arena is in turn structured by the many individuals who are engaged in the project of self-becoming. This is necessarily so once we reject the subject/object dichotomy – recognizing all three perspectives as giving rise to different elements of being in the world well.

But neither should this deep imbrication of perspectives blind us to their plurality. The complexity of human life cannot be removed simply by interpreting it through the lens of a single perspective. Any account of flourishing must accommodate the plurality of reason types that claim agents and constrain what counts as a life well lived. What one should do in any given situation must be decided at the intersection of these kinds of competing normative claim. Any act can be understood only in terms of its location in such a complex normative field; even those acts that are

---

[30] In this sense the notion of flourishing is deeply responsive to empirical claims. As LeBar 2005 notes, assessing what human excellence involves requires us to consider both what we share with others of our species and what is unique to each individual animal (177). This is entirely in keeping with Aristotle's claim that despite shared criteria of flourishing, our well-being is 'relative to us' (*NE*, II.6.1106b1–7).

characterized as purely 'selfish' or 'altruistic' can be conceived as such only in light of an understanding that in these cases certain reasons are being responded to at the expense of others – reasons that are also in some sense recognized as making a claim to legitimacy. In contrast to deontology and utilitarianism, then, this approach better enables us to acknowledge the possibility of legitimate – and even irresolvable – conflict, since built into the very conception of practical reason is responsiveness to different modes of normative demand. The task of flourishing, however, requires that agents negotiate a kind of balance among these seemingly incommensurable classes of normative claim.

In the coming chapters we will consider what is required in order to balance these competing and incommensurable classes of value against each other in the way that I have suggested the flourishing agent is skilled at doing. At this point, however, it is enough to say that there is no hierarchy or single scale for measuring one class of claim against the other; these multiple sources of normative claim cannot be reduced to a single kind of claim without remainder.[31]

Notes on Method

Before turning to those more substantive considerations, however, we should make note of the formal constraints that this normative plurality places on us. The requirement that we acknowledge all three normative stances applies not only to our practical engagement with the world but also to the theoretical approaches we adopt in order to better understand how to do so. If the self is simultaneously claimed by first-, second-, and third-person norms as equally legitimate normative sources, any theorization of human life that unduly prioritizes one such stance will falsify the way of being in the world that we are attempting to understand. Thus taking seriously the practical meaning of ethics requires us to think about the existential origins of the different methodological stances that one might take when engaged in ethical theory. The tendency has been to prioritize the third-person perspective by interpreting the function of moral philosophy to be the development of models and decision criteria in which each person is conceptualized as one among many, all of whom share the same basic features and occupy the same moral status as all others. This obviously has the advantage of doing the coordination and

---

[31] See Nagel 1979, 128–141 where he discusses a similar view endorsing the irreducibly plural nature of value. Nussbaum 1986 demonstrates that this is Aristotle's view.

comparison work that will be necessary for building and maintaining a world shared by a plurality of agents. But we must be aware of the dangers of misrepresenting the nature of moral experience as it is lived, according to which each of us experiences a complex web of tensions among competing claims from different normative sources – not all of which can be conceptualized in terms of the universal interchangeability of persons characteristic of the third-personal stance. A good deal of moral life does *not* involve an experience of oneself as just one among many who need to coordinate this plurality of equals. And any theoretical approach that insists on understanding or justifying all normative demands from a perspective in which we are all conceptualized as such will necessarily cover over what is specific to the other ways that we experience ourselves as claimed, the other kinds of reasons that we recognize as legitimate.

We would do well, then, to bracket any presuppositions about what counts as 'the' perspective from which to engage in analyses of what human flourishing is and to be responsive, instead, to a plurality of methodological approaches, since not all approaches are aimed at uncovering the same dimensions of lived moral agency. We must therefore tie our analyses to the different ways we can experience that agency from within, attempting to bring to light the logic underlying them without forcing them to fit a pre-established mold that is alien to them. If we are to take seriously the primacy of the practical stance in ethics, we must take seriously each of the different perspectives from which it is lived. It is for this reason that phenomenology – with its emphasis on analyzing different kinds of lived experience – is particularly helpful here.

Philosophy is often tasked with communicating non-universalizable experiences and conditions via general concepts and categories. As a result, its method can be conducive to unduly prioritizing the third-person perspective insofar as it strives to provide universally accessible and applicable arguments and justifications. It is incumbent on us to be aware of this fact, however, and to recognize and resist the inevitable distortions that can result – as we saw, for example, in the tendency to mischaracterize second-person normative authority by interpreting it via third-person categories wherein self and other are conceptualized as interchangeable and fundamentally identical tokens of a type. The kind of obligating force that the latter stance can produce is significantly different from the kind of authority we experience in the face of the other person's suffering or immediate demand for recognition. Though it is indeed possible to try to translate or explain this kind of immediate second-person claim in third-person explanatory categories, doing so distorts the nature of the authority at work there: in the former it resides in the decentering experience of being called into question, while in the latter it resides in the experience of sameness and equality.

In keeping with this recognition of the need for a moral theory that accommodates the plurality of perspectives, we should note that some figures from the philosophical tradition – one thinks in particular of Kierkegaard and Nietzsche – have understood their writing to be in the service of bringing about cultural and individual transformation, not providing universally accessible justifications and categorizations, and have made rhetorical choices on that basis. For such thinkers, it is impossible to get people to understand their own normative position if they are only required to conceptualize themselves as one among an anonymous and interchangeable many. Their philosophical style and methodology takes different forms because it is aimed at awakening the audience to a particular kind of first- and second-personal normative self-awareness, not at amassing a body of true facts about the kinds of features we must all share universally. In philosophy, as in life, then, we ought to make use of the different tools of self-understanding that are available to us instead of assuming in advance that one must have priority. Only then can we do justice to the matters at hand.

CHAPTER 3

Justice, the Virtues, and Existential Problem-Solving

> Justice is a constant and abiding will that renders every person his desert.
> – Aquinas, *Summa Theologiae* 2a2ae.58.1

Virtue

So far I have not examined in much detail what exactly a 'virtue' is, other than to say that the virtues are excellent character traits comprised of a set of interrelated beliefs, affective orientations, perceptual dispositions, and behavioural tendencies, all of which conduce to and are constitutive of an excellent human life. In light of the discussions in the previous chapters, we can see that this involves successfully responding to and balancing the legitimate claims arising from the three different domains of normativity within which human beings operate, namely, the claims posed by self, other, and shared world – all of which are themselves constitutive of the kind of self-world fit definitive of flourishing. On this account the virtues can be understood as ordered stances through which we are responsive to this plurality of reasons. But if this is so, we are left with questions regarding the role that the specific virtues play in this account of flourishing. After all, it seems possible to describe them *all* simply as appropriate responsiveness to practical reasons. What, then, differentiates them? Why is there more than one? Is there a limit to their number?[1]

Answering these questions relies on our recognition of the fact that human beings face specific challenges to accomplishing this balanced responsiveness to normative claims, challenges that we all face as part of the human condition. The virtues are character tendencies that allow us to

---

[1] As Russell points out, many contemporary virtue ethicists seem willing to multiply virtues ad infinitum. But that poses problems not only in terms of worries about cultural relativism, but also for meeting the demand that the virtues be capable of integration in a single agent. For discussion of this 'Enumeration Problem', see 2009, 143–236. See also Upton 2013 and Annas 2011, 96–98.

respond well to existential difficulties that afflict all human beings in virtue of the kind of existence that we live. Such 'existential problems' encompass challenges that arise as a result of inalienable features of the human condition. They refer to structural aspects of human existence including but not limited to the fact of mortality and temporal finitude, the conditions of material scarcity in which we typically operate, the hierarchical structure of social life, innate limitations of strength and ability, and the temptations posed by desire for bodily pleasure and aversion to pain. The lives that we live lie balanced between an agency that demands action and multiple given limitations that shape the possibilities of action available to us. We find ourselves thrown into a way of being that we did not choose and cannot fully control, but in terms of which we must shape our striving to exist in the world well. Though each one of us will be more or less inclined to find these existential constraints challenging depending on our personality and context, they are nevertheless universal structural features of the human experience that interfere with the project of living well.[2] For example, Aristotle notes 'In everything, we should be on our guard especially against the pleasant – pleasure, that is – because we are not impartial judges of it' (*NE*, 1109b). In other words, we all share the need for problem-solving in this arena; we all need to develop character strategies that will allow us to face this recurring challenge in such a way that a good life is a genuine possibility – namely, through the development of the virtue of temperance.

The virtues are mechanisms for successfully negotiating these different problem areas; they are ways in which we respond well to normative claims in the face of human limitation, dependency, and weakness of various kinds. As a result, there will be a limited number of true or 'cardinal' virtues because there is a limited number of such existential problems – i.e. challenges we all face simply qua human. Other 'virtues' may arise that are derivative of – or context-specific applications of – these central virtues, but insofar as they are not aimed at living well in the face of *universal* human challenges to doing so, they are not virtues proper. So though the flourishing agent is tasked in general with responding well to the claims of the three normative domains, the specificity of the virtues lies in their ability to help us do so in the face of different existential challenges that arise as we strive to meet this task.[3] As we will see in Chapter 7, for

---

[2] See MacIntyre 1999 and Nussbaum 1993.
[3] Swanton 2003 seems to have something somewhat similar in mind with the idea of the 'field' of a virtue, namely, the body of concerns on which it characteristically operates, such as tempting bodily

example, patience is the virtue that addresses the particular problem posed by temporal scarcity. In Chapters 8 and 9 we will examine how modesty helps us address hierarchies of differential success, while courage is the optimal character strategy for facing up to threats to life and identity.

One might object to any suggestion that the language of 'problem-solving' is appropriate here. Do we really want to suggest that existential limitations on strength, resources, time, etc. are 'problems' that the virtues can help us to 'solve'? Yes and no. They are problems insofar as they make it more difficult for us to respond fully to the practical reasons that claim us, and this is not a matter of indifference. Rather, they are experienced *as* problems – ways we experience ourselves as failing to do what we ought to do. When I realize that I cannot fully help Syrian refugees *and* do my job *and* save the environment *and* care for my family *and* pursue my hobbies, then the limited fund of time, money, and energy strikes me as an obstacle to realizing the way I ought to be in the world.

There are better and worse ways to respond to these obstacles innate to the human condition. Not everyone develops the affective, cognitive, perceptual, and behavioural skills necessary to live well in problematic circumstances – especially the most deeply challenging circumstances that life can present. The virtues are modes of comportment in which the agent is attuned to these limitations and committed to addressing them in ways that are effective at realizing a condition of normative responsiveness despite the challenges they pose. In this sense we can understand the virtues as problem-solving stances – while recognizing that there can be no ultimate solutions to these existential problems: in limiting us, they define the parameters of the human. As such, any 'solutions' that arise from the problem-solving stance of virtue cannot involve removing such limitations, but rather will show us how to live well in the face of them. Approaches that pretend to an ultimate solution use an inappropriate standard of success and in doing so only succeed in concealing the nature of the problem. Thus any legitimate solutions to these existential problems can only count as such if they acknowledge their irrevocability. For example, one can think of friendship as a virtue that addresses the human challenges of isolation and loneliness. But friendship addresses this challenge in a way that incorporates and acknowledges the contingency and incompleteness of any solution to the problem of loneliness – as opposed to, say, a drug or an operation that would deaden the part of the brain that

---

pleasures. However, she does not interpret the virtues as ways of responding well to existential problems.

produces such experiences. Friendship solves the existential problem of loneliness without concealing or ignoring the fact that the core of solitude at the heart of being a self – and the experiences of isolation that this will inevitably produce – will never be fully overcome while remaining what we are.[4]

Thus the virtues should be understood not as resolutions of a problem such that it ceases to be a problem but as excellent modes of acknowledging and negotiating irrevocable but problematic constraints. Being able to distinguish between legitimate and illegitimate responses of this kind will be part of the practical wisdom constitutive of the virtue itself, namely, knowing how to embody the goal of adequate yet balanced normative responsiveness in a way that is appropriate to the particular situation in which that goal is being pursued.

However, one might further object to talk of existential 'problem-solving' as too instrumental, in the sense that it portrays the virtuous agent as adopting a kind of means-ends rationality at odds with how we understand the virtues as *constitutive* of flourishing, not as mere tools for realizing some other independent state. But this worry is misguided. Flourishing is responding well to all of the legitimate reasons that claim one, and the virtues are simply ways of ongoingly doing so in the face of specific kinds of obstacle that can arise in every human life. They are constitutive of that condition of excellence, not extrinsic tools that will be abandoned once the goal is reached. The fact that they are responses to irrevocable existential challenges means that abandoning them is abandoning flourishing. Thus virtue ethics is not teleological in a consequentialist way, not only because it promotes aretaic as opposed to hedonic outcomes but because in contrast to the consequentialist agent, the virtuous person is not trying to *maximize* anything or promote some independent good.[5] In other words, the virtues are not understood as promoting an independent outcome at all, but rather as embodying excellence in particular problematic situations. We can therefore characterize them as problem-solving stances without endorsing a perfectionist consequentialism, since the 'solutions' they provide are to be understood as skillful modes of embodying valuable ways of being – not tools aimed at maximizing independent states. These valuable ways of being are made more difficult because of

---

[4] For Aristotle's remarks on friendship and whether it is to count as a virtue, see especially *Nicomachean Ethics* 8.1   1155a3;   8.2   1155b27–1156a1;   8.5   1157b25–1158a1;   9.5 1166b30–1167a1. Kant discusses this in 1996, 6:469–473.
[5] See Angier 2015a; Annas 1995a; Luthra 2015; Rasmussen 1999; and Watson 2003.

certain existential challenges to their expression that will never be overcome but only more or less effectively negotiated.

Worries about Relativism

One might question the idea that there can be such universal challenges to flourishing intrinsic to the human condition itself. After all, isn't all human experience culturally mediated? Are there really universal existential problems to which the virtues can be understood as answers?[6]

We can begin to answer this worry by returning briefly to the naturalist approach to flourishing we considered in Chapter 1.[7] There we expressed similar worries about the overly objective and third-personal tenor of that account, suggesting instead that any account of flourishing must be based in an understanding of human personhood that accommodates both objectivist *and* subjectivist intuitions through the notion of living well in the world. As such, it must include the manner in which each one of us actively takes up and interprets the worldly conditions in which we enact that striving. So too will universal existential features of human life – such as mortality and embodiment – be taken up differently by different individuals and cultures *as* challenges to flourishing. But such mediation is insufficient to eradicate the universality of these dilemmas and the pervasiveness with which they shape the human condition. To be a creature that is not defined by embodiment, temporality, or finitude is to be something other than human. Indeed, the very fact that we are all called to negotiate the plurality of normative terrains in our struggles to live well in the world is *itself* a universal feature of human experience, as we will see in our discussion of justice. Though there will be personal and cultural variation in how to understand these criteria and how to meet them, human life is unrecognizable as such if it fails to be defined by this normative plurality, just as it is unrecognizable without embodiment or finite temporality.[8] The virtues are the ways we address obstacles that arise

---

[6] As Nussbaum puts this objection: 'the Aristotelian idea that there can be a single non-relative discourse about human experience such as mortality or desire is a naïve one. There is no such bedrock of shared experience, and thus no single sphere of choice within which the virtue is the disposition to choose well' (1993, 254).

[7] We will also return to the question of relativism in Chapter 6.

[8] As we will discuss later, part of responding well to the domain of third-personal claims involves structuring the social world in a way that mitigates these pitfalls and conduces to human flourishing by providing institutional buffers against these existential problems.

from these universal features of existence that complicate but also define our ability to be in the world well.

Though there is no view from nowhere from which to assess whether these problems are truly universal, such an external view is not necessary for our purposes. We are not in the business of converting aliens or psychopaths to morality. And insofar as we are able to discuss the shape and meaning of our lives with persons from other cultures, we will be able to ascertain whether the existential problems to which our virtues respond are indeed universal features of the human experience – and thus *true* virtues – or simply specific to our own limited milieu and thus culturally relative quasi-virtues.[9] Cultural variability can therefore encompass both diversity in modes of response to different existential problems (e.g. a range of behaviours and attitudes will count as courage or patience) *and* variation in what counts as a 'virtue' itself – though on my account it is only the character strategies aimed at solving *existential* problems (rather than culturally specific ones) that count as true virtues. On this conception, then, we all face limitations and challenges built into our way of existing. Flourishing requires that we respond well to the three classes of normative claim that apply to us despite those challenges. The virtues are the character traits that enable us to do so.

Justice: Global Character State or Specific Virtue?

In our account so far, goodness of character has been conceptualized as a general or global condition in which one gives due regard to the competing domains of value, while the specific virtues are instantiations of that good character in the face of particular problem types shared by all human beings. Thus there is an overarching condition of human excellence – responding well to the different normative demands that claim us – and particular virtues are instantiations of this unified condition insofar as the agent faces up to different existential problems. Such a view is in keeping with Socratic and Stoic ethical theory, according to which – as John Cooper puts it – there is 'only a single unified condition, virtue itself, of which the particular virtues that we normally distinguish from one another are (in one way or another) only aspects' (1998, 233).[10] We can see this kind of approach quite explicitly in the *Apology*, where Socrates is

---

[9] See Benhabib 2002, 1–23. However, this is not to suggest that the line between existential and cultural components in a given practice necessarily will be clear.
[10] See also Annas 1995a, 79–83.

portrayed as committed to understanding and attaining this single unified condition – whether this is called 'wisdom', 'truth', or simply 'virtue' (i.e., *arête*, being a good human being) (29e–30a). In the *Republic*, Plato names this single unified condition *justice*:

> [Justice's] sphere is a person's inner activity; it is really a matter of oneself and the parts of oneself... Once [the just person] has set his own house in order, which is what he really should be concerned with ... once he has bound all the factors together and made himself a perfect unity instead of a plurality, self-disciplined and internally attuned: then and only then does he act ... In the course of this activity, it is conduct which preserves and promotes this inner condition of his that he regards as just and describes as fine ...; however, it is any conduct which disperses this condition that he regards as unjust. (Plato 1993:443c–e)

Why does Plato name this condition *justice*? What is it about this virtue that makes it a good candidate for naming the global condition of human excellence as such?[11] Why does justice bear the equivocal sense of being both another name for good character in general *and* just one virtue among many?

In other words: What is justice? This is obviously an enormous question with a correspondingly impressive history. Of late – thanks in no small part to John Rawls – the question has become almost exclusively focused on the question of justice as it applies to societies and institutions.[12] The idea of 'personal' justice – i.e. justice as a virtue characterizing individuals – is typically understood derivatively: as a tendency to promote or maintain just institutions. Though there is clearly an element of truth to this – it would be bizarre for individually just agents to play no part in the justice of institutions[13] – my purpose here is to focus on justice understood as a personal virtue. What is it to be a just person? Questions regarding the relationship between individuals who possess that virtue and its various political manifestations will be placed to the side. Thus henceforth all references to 'justice' will be understood as an agent's way of being in the world, whether as a specific virtue or understood more generally as the single unified condition of virtue itself.

Return for a moment to Plato's *Republic*. As we have seen, on the Platonic account justice is another term for the inner harmony of the

---

[11] See *NE*, 1129b26 for comparable claims from Aristotle.
[12] For example, on page 1 of *A Theory of Justice*, Rawls claims, 'Justice is the first virtue of social institutions, as truth is of systems of thought' (1999).
[13] For discussion of the relationship of virtue to political institutions, see Annas 1995a: 292–312; LeBar 2014, 270–271; Schmidtz and Thrasher 2014; Slote 1993 and 1998; and Wiggins 2004.

soul from which all good acts derive. Each person is motivated to create and maintain the harmony among the soul's elements that makes her a successful agent. As LeBar puts it, it seems that 'the reason the just person does not perform any of the proscribed actions is that doing so would upset this internal unity and harmony' (2014, 266).

But the problem with the Platonic account in this regard is that it appears to characterize the desired harmony as an infra-psychic arrangement of the 'parts' that comprise a self. A bit more rationality here, a little bit less spirit and appetite there, and *voila* – you're a just person. In doing so it conceptualizes this state of harmony as being basically a private one, theoretically capable of existing in a kind of isolation from the world and the others who share it – a conception of flourishing we questioned in Chapter 1.[14] A further (related) problem remains, however: namely, the fact that this account seems to characterize the motivation for being virtuous as self-serving. How can we respond to this objection?

The Motivational Egoism of Eudaimonism

Critics have argued that since the agent's own flourishing is taken to be the reason for which she makes all choices, virtue ethical accounts are inconsistent with the kind of motivation necessary for genuinely other-directed concern. As Hurka puts it:

> [T]he concept of flourishing is used as the central concept in a normative theory that is formally egoistic, deriving all of a person's normative reasons for action from a fundamental reason he has to pursue his own flourishing, or his own good. The theory may acknowledge derivative reasons to act that are other-regarding, such as reasons to benefit others or to refrain from harming them. But it insists that if these are reasons, it is only because they can be connected to each person's fundamental interest in his own achievement of flourishing. (1999, 45)

In other words, we may *appear* to desire other things for their own sake, but ultimately these things are desirable only insofar as we take them to conduce to our own flourishing. Indeed, Hurka suggests that eudaimonistic theories prompt one to read the relationship between specific normative claims and flourishing as one of indirect desire, whereby my desire for ice cream or my interest in helping others is 'really' a desire for a fulfilled

---

[14] See Nussbaum 1986, 290–317 on why this is an appealing (but ultimately misguided) element of Plato's approach.

human nature (Hurka 1999, 47). The worry is that 'all of a person's normative reasons for acting derive from his own flourishing.'[15]

But such an interpretation mistakenly assumes that striving to flourish is reducible to a first-person project aimed at realizing the desired end state of flourishing, understood as a benefit accruing to me alone. But people are always in the grip of three different classes of normative reasons for belief and action, and the assumption that one type of claim has ultimate priority – and can be separated off from the other normative domains such that one could grant it that priority – is inaccurate. A first-person desire for my own self-realization is not the ultimate motivating principle that underlies all of my actions, since second- and third-person reasons are equally constitutive of my field of motivations – and, indeed, none of these normative orientations can be understood as fully separable from the others but rather as deeply imbricated elements of a flourishing life. Robustly understood, there can be no self-realization without personal and political relationships with others. Nor can those relationships flourish in the absence of each self's commitment to being the best version of itself.

Flourishing means being in the world in a particular way, namely, as responsive to complex possibilities of self-world fit. The different classes of normative claim are constitutive of this complex state of being in the world well.[16] To flourish is to do a good job at answering to these normative demands – but this is a far cry from the idea that everything is ultimately reducible to a selfish desire for more good stuff for me. Hurka simply assumes that the virtue ethical commitment to the priority of excellent lives over right actions and good states means that specific agents are at

---

[15] Hurka 1999, 53. The objection that eudaimonism generally requires the wrong reason for ethical action is further discussed in Hurka 2001, 248–249; Swanton 1997; and Watson 2003.

[16] Or, as 'formally egoistic' approaches to eudaimonism argue, 'a person's happiness may consist just in acting on whatever reasons apply to him, whether they are self-regarding or other-regarding' (Farnham 2006, 434). The formal versus substantive egoism distinction comes from Williams 1985, 49–52. See also Annas 1995a, ch. 1 and Lebar 2009. LeBar points out that it is the substantive conceptions of the good that provoke most of the offense in egoism, but Plato and other ancient eudaimonists roundly reject such a substantive conception (644, n. 5). Heidegger similarly calls it 'outrageous nonsense' to suggest that our striving for excellent being in the world implies individualistic egoism (1984, 186). Or, as Aristotle says: 'if someone always takes trouble that he of all people does what is just or temperate or whatever else is in accordance with the virtues, and in general always makes what is noble his own, no one will call him a self-lover or blame him' (*NE*, IX.8.1168b).

bottom only motivated by the desire for their own well-being, even when they *appear* to be motivated by the desire to benefit others.[17]

But Aristotle and those who follow his lead argue that ethics demands a conception of the good human life as oriented toward a plurality of intrinsic goods that are to be valued for their own sake. The good person does what is right not because she is attempting to accomplish something else through the right action but because the right action is choice-worthy for its own sake, and there are multiple ways that acts and ends can be choice-worthy.

Hurka adopts a recursive account according to which the virtuous agent's attitudes are intrinsically valuable, but their value is dependent on more basic intrinsic goods such as pleasure and knowledge (2001, 12–13). And, crucially, those basic goods are understood as in some sense *independent* from the lives in which they are instantiated. As a result, his account perpetuates a version of the subject/object divide insofar as the value of the (subjective) virtue attitudes is taken to be entirely derivative from independent (objective) goods that are understood as more explanatorily basic, and those goods need have no necessary connection to the lives of the agents who strive to realize them. But Hurka goes too far in his efforts to decouple the states that we have reason to promote and the agency of the people involved, since he assumes that we can speak of valuable states like knowledge and pleasure as if they can exist in isolation from the lives that manifest them. Thus we can be oriented toward promoting 'pleasure as such' as opposed to *my* pleasure or *your* pleasure or *her* pleasure. But this is a highly abstract way to think about how practical agents actually live their agency, namely, as oriented toward negotiating normative claims that originate in persons striving to be in the world, not toward objective states of the world disconnected from persons as the ones for whom the pleasure will be pleasurable and the

---

[17] This is similar to an objection to the suggestion that virtues can be understood as skills, namely, that virtues differ from skills in being self-effacing. I.e. we should not aim at becoming just or patient, but at doing virtuous actions for the sake of the good; by contrast, we may legitimately aim at becoming good tennis players. As such, there is a disanalogy between skill and virtue. But this misunderstands the nature of the trying at work. On my account one can indeed *try* to be wise, just, courageous, since what one is trying to be is adequately responsive to the complex moral terrain – one is not trying to acquire some status for oneself but to be good. Thus trying to be just is not a self-serving focus on having a certain status for the self but an attempt to respond to first, second, and third claims simultaneously. Indeed, we might suggest that someone who tries to be a good pianist solely in order to be seen as a good pianist and accrue the corresponding status – and not also out of aesthetic appreciation of the value of music – is similarly misguided and will never achieve complete mastery in that skill because of a failure of fit between intention and the state it is aimed at realizing.

knowledge will be informative. 'Pleasure' and 'knowledge' are abstract terms for what are complex modes of being – ways in which we are embedded in the world through the intentional acts that express our care for living well with others. Thus these 'values' are not best understood as objective states that are valuable in isolation from the people who can experience them as such. Rather, they are better understood as the way that we succeed at responding well to the world, ways of achieving the optimal fit of self and world that is what we mean by *eudaimonia*. As such, these ways of achieving optimal fit – values – cannot be characterized as either 'subjective' or 'objective'. Being in the world well is a condition in which 'subjective' and 'objective' elements exist in a unity that challenges our ability to make that distinction. To speak of goods as entirely separate from those who desire and enjoy goods *as* good thereby obscures the way that the self is caught up in trying to be itself by way of the world and with others. It assumes that values are a certain kind of objective world-object that can be neatly separated off from equally independent pro-attitudes – attitudes experienced by a subject whose relationship to those values is contingent and purely external. But pleasure and knowledge are not states but *activities* – e.g. knowledge is the activity of responding correctly to certain kinds of situations or claims. So to speak of 'knowledge' in isolation from agents is to hypostasize descriptions of actions and then define those actions in terms of those abstract definitions that no longer maintain a necessary connection to the life living them.

By theorizing these goods in some sense independently from the lives in which they are instantiated, Hurka reinforces the subject/object divide. We can also note a related overreliance on the third-person stance here, wherein one is encouraged to conceptualize the goods in isolation from the particular relationships with self and others characteristic of the other two normative domains. Indeed, one is encouraged to disengage even from the intersubjective claims of experiencing oneself as one among many. Thus as in the case of the Husserlian 'physicalistic object' – i.e. the theoretical construct designed to eradicate the specificity built into perception – Hurka is engaged in a similar third-personal modeling activity, decoupling value objects from the flourishing lives in which they have their first and most central meaning. Though we have seen that this is one legitimate perspective to adopt, it is not the only perspective necessary for thinking about what it means to live in the world well – and indeed, can distort that thinking into a subject/object dualism that misrepresents human agency if we do not remain clear on what such models are actually able to represent.

What we must recognize, then, is that the one for whom flourishing matters is the agent who is claimed simultaneously by all three normative terrains, and the concern to respond to those claims well – the stance of justice – cannot be reduced to a form of self-servingness without giving one normative terrain unwarranted priority over the others – thereby misrepresenting the nature of the flourishing for which the agent strives.

The flourishing agent avoids unjust actions not simply because they throw the parts of the soul out of whack but because they fail to respond adequately to the plurality of normative domains by which she is claimed. The object of the just person's striving is not simply a harmonious soul as such, but rather what such a harmonious soul represents – namely, a way of being in the world whereby the agent is successfully responding to the legitimate normative claims that are made on her, a successful response that involves both responding to each of them well and achieving a kind of equilibrium among them.

Doing Justice

As Aristotle characterizes it in Book V of the *Nichomachean Ethics*, personal justice is primarily about the distribution of goods and ills, privileges and obligations. This distribution is governed by the overarching concept of what is *owed*. This is most obvious in cases of contract, where the parameters of what are owed are made explicit. One can see, then, why justice is regularly understood to be particularly concerned with contracts, and in particular the social contract by which the state is established and maintained. But more generally understood, justice can be characterized simply as the ability to gauge what is owed to whom and the willingness to abide by this understanding of how competing claims are to be negotiated. It is, in other words, the capacity to know which of the different claims on the table ought to be granted priority in any particular situation.

On such an account one can see how justice can be taken as a global stand-in for human flourishing as such, since we have defined the latter as living a life in which one is giving each normative terrain its *due*. And if justice is to be understood as a virtue, and the virtues are the ways we successfully navigate existential problems posed to our struggle to be in the world well, we can recognize that the problem justice solves is how to correctly distribute care and attention to the three competing terrains of normative demand, despite the fact that the human capacity for such care, attention, and material support is limited. Each normative domain makes legitimate claims on us, and to say that a person is *just* is to speak to the fact that she knows how and when to balance her responsiveness to those legitimate claims, despite being in the grip of the existential challenge of being (1) pulled in different directions by those claims and (2) unable to commit fully to any one of them because of limited existential resources. Justice can be understood as a specific character virtue insofar as its terrain of operation – i.e. the specific existential problem that it solves – just is the fact that we need to negotiate these competing normative claims. But when considered more generally, we see that this is the overall task of flourishing as such and the just person can therefore also be identified with the flourishing one (though the former might fail to flourish as a result of bad moral luck).

With this in mind, we can distinguish between the general and the specific senses of justice by emphasizing that the former – namely, the fact that 'justice' can be a stand-in for character excellence as such – just *is* the correct distribution of care to the three competing terrains of normative demand, despite the fact that the human capacity for such care, attention, and material support is limited, and for this reason conditions of competition inevitably arise. Thus the good person can be characterized generally as understanding the manner in which she owes degrees of responsiveness to the different kinds of obligation that claim her, while the idea of 'local' or specific justice – namely, the idea of justice as one virtue among many – is the manifestation of this same orientation when it comes not to the distribution of all of one's resources in the face of all of one's obligations but to the correct distribution of particular limited resources or benefits (money, social recognition, etc.) in the face of specific conflicting claims to those resources.[18] A just person, globally understood, is someone who is skilled at balancing the domains of first-person, second-person, and third-person claims as such; justice is simply another way of designating a life that is appropriately responsive to all three normative domains in any circumstances that may arise. But understood as one virtue among many, justice refers to the ability to know and care about what specific thing is owed to whom and when. It is the latter sense that we typically associate with the concept of justice, but based on the structural analogies between them it becomes possible to understand why ancient thinkers could defend the claim that justice is another word for good character as such.

[18] Annas 1995a, 312 argues that the doctrine of the mean cannot apply to justice as it does to the other virtues. Though I wish to remain agnostic on the feasibility of the doctrine of the mean, it is not clear that Annas's objections hold if one conceives of justice as relating to care for normative responsiveness as such. See *NE*, Book V for Aristotle's discussion of justice and in what sense it is a mean.

General and Specific Claims

One might object, however, that there are in fact no monolithic domains of normative claim – there are only the specific claims arising at particular times – thus the general versus specific justice distinction makes no sense. Though this may be true when it comes to *act* assessment, when we consider a life or character orientation as a whole, the distinction has merit. Consider, for example, a person who is faced with the decision to either pursue her career more actively or spend more time with her children. On my framework, this person is facing competing claims from the first- and second-person normative domains. Because of the structure of the situation she faces, she will have to prioritize one or the other in the foreseeable future – she cannot do both. This fact in itself is not automatically a violation of the injunction to give each normative domain its due. Part of the work of normative negotiation is knowing when to prioritize one kind of normative claim over another in this or that circumstance, since few circumstances will allow for each domain to be treated equally. We see this in Sartre's famous example of the young man forced to choose between caring for his mother and going to fight in the French Resistance; he must prioritize either a second- or a third-person claim. In such circumstances agents are faced with act choices that necessitate a significant imbalance in their normative responsiveness to the different classes of claim. But the flourishing agent will be aware of this and attempt to compensate for it in future decisions – which is why one must look to one's life as a whole to assess how best to do so.

In contrast, Michael Slote suggests that those who are committed to both caring and justice (what I am calling second- and third-person claims) do not typically think about the integration of these two different kinds of demand. Rather, 'they go about their lives, sometimes dealing with issues of justice, sometimes being involved in caring relationships – alternatively, sometimes acting from humanitarian concerns and sometimes acting out of concern for the perceived needs of people they know. And there is no more integration than that' (1999, 27). In other words, people are only ever aware of specific moral obligations, not of the need to integrate different classes of moral obligation, and to claim otherwise, he suggests, is to falsify the moral phenomenology. But consider the fact that people can and do draw back from their specific choices to ask questions like 'Am I a selfish person?' or 'Do I care too much about my loved ones and not enough about strangers who are in dire need?' 'How should I arrange my life so that these different kinds of reasons are given their due?' Those questions are questions about the kind of weighting that one is giving to the different normative domains in one's life – they are not (merely) questions about specific moral choices. But also contrary to what Slote suggests, questions of this kind do not necessarily require (or result in) an explicit moral principle or theory – either when asking or answering them. Rather, each of us feels pulled in competing normative directions, and the flourishing agent makes efforts to respond well to this tension across her life as a whole – efforts that often occur on a pre-theoretical level of awareness.

As a result, the language of 'balancing' or 'harmonizing' the classes of normative claim must be understood as an ongoing project of trying not to neglect any one of these domains of obligation by playing off specific manifestations of the different claim types against each other. We might describe this as a project akin to keeping aloft three sinking helium balloons – a task that will require us to lift only one at any given time. Failure at this task cannot be assessed by that fact alone, however, but only insofar as one is allowed to hit the ground.[19] For the most part, then, prioritizing one normative domain over another in a specific circumstance is a necessary part of keeping all of the balloons aloft. But this does not undermine the necessity of being on guard against general tendencies to give undue priority to one normative terrain over the others in one's life. Agents must see each choice both as responding to a specific circumstance and as representative of their own dispositions toward the different kinds of normative claim. Each of us must ultimately assess acts in light of the life that we are trying to live as a whole. This general orientation to the question of who one will be is given direction both by certain deontic constraints on what is permissible (to be discussed in Chapter 4) and by one's relationships to moral exemplars (to be discussed in Chapter 5). These orientations to both deontic limit and exemplary ideal operate under the general normative rule of justice: to act such that none of the normative terrains is completely neglected but given their (minimal) due in the project of responding well to their claims.

Prioritizing can represent moral failure in one of two ways: specific or general. First, the agent may choose the wrong claim to prioritize in a particular situation. Obviously, specifying which choice that would be

---

[19] What counts as 'hitting the ground' in this analogy – i.e. *complete* failure to respect the claims of a particular domain as such – will be discussed in Chapter 4 in the section entitled 'Deontic Constraints'. What follows here, in contrast, is a discussion of specific versus general conceptualizations of disordered responsivity.

would require us to first flesh out the example in great detail, but we can imagine obvious cases of such poor judgment, e.g. when one chooses to betray a friend in exchange for a modest boost to one's career. Second, the agent's specific decision – even if it might be considered the right act in isolation – may represent a general character pattern according to which one normative domain is consistently prioritized in a way that cumulatively prevents the others from being given their due in one's life. For example, considered in isolation, an overly self-sacrificing person's act of kindness might look like the virtuous choice, but when seen against the background of her general life tendency toward self-abnegation we can recognize it as a kind of moral failure. Thus the legitimacy of the general/specific distinction is evident when we recognize that it seems possible to have a character in which the three normative domains are *consistently* inappropriately weighted against each other in a particular way – an inappropriate weighting that could not necessarily be recognized by looking solely at specific decisions but only by looking at the shape of an agent's life as a whole. Such a generally unjust orientation will typically produce specific acts of injustice, but since specific acts of injustice can also arise in agents *without* them being globally normatively askew in this way – e.g. if they are mistaken about the nature of the specific circumstances – the distinction between general and specific justice is a fruitful one.

Self-Directed Justice?

The suggestion that we can characterize the person who is too willing to prioritize others over self as *unjust* may strike some as false. After all, personal justice is often thematized in terms of a willingness to give limited goods and benefits to others at great cost to oneself. Thus the second-personally oriented agent in the above example might seem to be a model of justice, not a failure of it. After all, isn't justice in fact concerned only with the question of what is owed *other* people, not with the question of what is owed to any legitimate claimant, including myself? (see *NE*, 1130a 3–10). This is taken to be so because it is often believed, as Foot puts it, that 'justice seems rather to benefit others, and to work to the disadvantage of the just man himself' (2002, 125).[20]

As Foot points out, however, 'In the *Republic* it is assumed that if justice is not a good to the just man, moralists who recommend it as a virtue are perpetrating a fraud' (2002, 126). In response to any Thrasymachus-inspired

---

[20] LeBar 2014, 268–270 also takes this stance. See also Annas 1995a, 291, 298.

'supposition that injustice is more profitable than justice', she argues that though it may 'turn out incidentally to be profitable', this is true only if particular just acts are considered in isolation (Foot 2002, 129). When understood as a character disposition that will be manifested over time in many relationships, however, it quickly becomes clear how injustice could be unprofitable for the individual despite incidental benefits that might accrue in isolated encounters (Foot 2002, 129). With this I am in agreement. There are indeed many consequentialist reasons for believing that playing fair is a better strategy in life. But this point does not address Foot's key assumption that the essential feature of justice is a tendency to give only *other* people what is owed them. If that assumption is true, it is difficult to see how my claim about responding to all three normative domains applies; it would seem, rather, that justice is simply about making sure to respond to only one such domain in the face of competing illegitimate desires: namely, responding to the second-person claims made on us by others despite competing claims by self (and possibly community).

But this seems wrong. Consider how we might say to someone, 'You do yourself an injustice' if that person is treating herself too harshly, i.e. in a way that we feel violates what she is due. We might also suspect someone of being unfair to himself if, say, he always gives up to others what is rightfully owed to him. Further, we can criticize someone who helps the specific other person with no consideration for the implications that will have for the community's ability to continue to manage the project of establishing a shared world. In such cases we can see that justice appears to be about giving *all* participants what is owed to them, even when that requires mandating the self-directed distribution of benefits that we typically believe to be a human default mode rooted in self-love.

Indeed, the natural disposition to prioritize one's desires and the fact that it can undermine our ability to do what is required is itself a kind of existential problem for which the virtue of generosity is the solution. The generous person does not allow first-person claims to negate the other classes of claim, even when highly desired goods in conditions of scarcity are at issue. Thus generosity is often required to work in concert with justice in order to accomplish the stance in which each legitimate claim is given its due:

> But fairness in our judgments of others, and especially our competitors, in turn depends upon generosity. Thus, for example, to acknowledge the value of others' work, Zeta needs to see this value. And in obscure or complex situations, where the merit may be hard to see, she will be far more likely to see it if she is generous, i.e., disposed to give more than justice requires. For

> a generous person is far more likely to entertain the hypothesis that she might have overlooked some relevant fact and that a further examination is called for. Generosity disposes a person to beneficial giving, whether this take the form of a material gift, or of praise, or of (as in this case) the benefit of the doubt. (Badhwar 1996, 324)

So while it may be the case that our natural tendency is to look out for ourselves and take what is our due (or more), this does not undermine the claim that justice understood in the general sense involves giving each kind of normative claim its due. Rather, it supports our claim that the specific virtues – such as generosity – will be necessary to solve problems that challenge our ability to accomplish this correct normative responsiveness. Justice depends on the other virtues in order to be what it is in the face of the many existential problems arising in our struggle to respond well to the reasons that claim us.

Like the other virtues, then, justice is a state in which one is overcoming an existential challenge to the project of being in the world well. But justice stands apart in the fact that the existential challenge to which it offers a solution is the basic fact of there being a plurality of normative domains to which we feel called to answer. The just person is she who distributes her care appropriately among this plurality of goods.

CHAPTER 4

Unity, Comparison, Constraint

The Unity of the Virtues

The relationship of the virtues of generosity and justice briefly sketched in the preceding chapter requires us not only to question views that limit justice to other-directed stances but also forces us to think more deeply about how the virtues relate to each other in general. Doing so requires us to examine the so-called unity of the virtues doctrine.

The unity of the virtues is a theory that has received a good deal of attention in virtue ethics.[1] This doctrine is typically understood in terms of the idea that 'one cannot have one virtue without having all of the others as well. In other words, if there is any one virtue that a person lacks, then it follows that this person does not have any of the other virtues' (Sreenivasan 2009, 197). Thus the person who displays genuine courage must also have the character traits of honesty, temperance, patience, etc.[2]

What are we to make of this claim? At first blush, it looks absurd. Indeed, objections to the doctrine of the unity of the virtues typically take the form of a simple counterexample: for instance, the 'criminal who appears to have self-control and courage but yet lacks justice or compassion' or 'friends or acquaintances who are scrupulously honest, but not very self-controlled in this or that way' (Carr 2003, 223).[3] How are we to understand the idea that having one virtue requires an agent to have all the virtues, when the world seems filled with agents who instantiate the virtues

---

[1] Badwhar 1996; Carr 2003; Cooper 1998; Irwin 1988 and 1997; McDowell 1998; Sreenivasan 2009; Watson 1984; Wolf 2007.
[2] To distinguish this position from the understanding of the virtues as being manifestations of a single state of excellence (the view defended in Chapter 3) Irwin calls it the 'reciprocity of the virtues', though most recent accounts do not follow this practice, focusing their attention on the 'unity of the virtues' problem understood in this latter sense (Irwin 1997).
[3] Williams 1985 suggests that we would do better to understand the virtues as we do other psychological dispositions and thus assume that a person can 'do better in one area than another' (36). Flanagan 1991 also rejects the unity of the virtues thesis (271).

to varying and often disjointed degrees? Further, the unity of the virtues thesis appears to be particularly worrying when the virtues are conceptualized as modes of being that solve or alleviate existential problems. Why should solving the problem of scarcity have anything to do with solving problems surrounding fear and danger?

In order to motivate the claim that there is something right about the unity of the virtues thesis, we must recognize that it depends on the intuition that 'true virtue cannot be something that leads its possessor morally astray' (Sreenivasan 2009, 199). Being fully virtuous means that you not only have the right instincts to be responsive to the goods by which we are claimed – which people with what Aristotle calls 'natural virtue' already have (*NE*, 1144b) – but you know *how* and *when* to deploy those instincts so that you do not fall into moral error even when the situation is morally complex. Though natural virtue is positively oriented toward good states of being, it is prone to mistakes about how to realize or embody those good ways of being; only full virtue is able to realize those goods with consistency and in a way that does not cause inadvertent harm, as the strong man who is blind is wont to do (*NE*, 1144b8–12). The person who is naturally compassionate will rightly wish to help those in need but is liable to make mistakes in attempting to accomplish that wish. For example, he may believe that he is permitted to help the homeless by giving them that which is not his to give; for instance, money that has been donated for medical research purposes (Sreenivasan 2009, 198–199).

What is required for full virtue is the ability to negotiate morally complex situations such that one's natural virtue finds correct expression by adjusting it to accommodate the constraints placed on it by the other virtues in their problem-solving strategies. Thus we must note again that virtue cannot be understood simply in terms of characteristic forms of action; courage is not simply a tendency to face danger and justice is not simply a tendency to distribute things evenly. Such a view – which Gary Watson calls the 'straight view' of a virtue (1984, 58) – has the counter-intuitive implication that it is possible to have too much of a virtue, thereby making it possible for the *virtue itself* to lead one into moral error. In contrast, any *genuine* virtue, on my view, must be understood as involving characteristic tendencies of behaviour only to the degree that they succeed at being appropriately responsive to the normative claims that they are meant to be responding to in the face of existential challenges. Thus fully possessing the virtue of courage means that facing danger will in fact be the right thing to do in order to respond appropriately to the legitimate claims by which one is bound. It therefore makes no sense to talk of someone being 'too' courageous.[4]

The relationship of this point to the idea of the unity of the virtues becomes clear when we recognize that the claims of different virtues require integration in their task of responding well to the different normative terrains, as Sreenivasan's example demonstrates in its clash between claims of compassion (helping the homeless) and claims of justice or honesty (not appropriating funds belonging to others). Unless an agent knows how and when to exercise a virtue in such conditions of apparent conflict, she cannot be said to truly possess the virtue. In other words, she will be unable to actually *solve* the existential problem that is challenging her ability to live well in the face of the norms that claim her, since her blindness to the kinds of limits that other existential problems place on her agency undermines her problem-solving ability as a whole.[5]

The flourishing agent must be alive to the many ways in which her struggle to act on the reasons that claim her can be derailed by a variety of existential challenges and she must be committed to integrating her problem-solving approach in the face of this fact. The doctrine of the unity of the virtues speaks to the fact that the project of responding well to the different types of reasons that claim us takes place in the face of multiple existential challenges to that project, any of which can disrupt one's striving to live excellently. When taken together, they pose complicated and overlapping problems to the agent striving to flourish. Complete virtue therefore requires: (1) normative responsiveness, (2) a character capable of responding well to the existential challenges complicating that responsiveness, and (3) an overarching sense of how to negotiate overlapping or competing existential challenges such that they can be integrated into the agent's life as a whole.

Understood in this way, one can see the force of the unity of the virtues thesis. One cannot have a full virtue unless one in some sense has all of them, since otherwise one would not be able to correctly adapt that virtue to accommodate the claims of the other virtues and would thereby fail to answer the challenge the virtue is meant to solve; i.e. it would not really be that virtue. If I do not understand the many ways in which my tripartite normative responsivity will be undermined by different existential

---

[4] McDowell 1998 claims that the plausibility of the unity of the virtues lies in 'the attractive idea that a virtue issues in nothing but right conduct' (52).
[5] As Cooper 1998 puts it, 'any knowledge about, say, the values involved in courage ... must see the place of these values in a single overall scheme of moral or ethical goods and bads, including all those involved in all the other ethical virtues' (266). Annas 1995a and Irwin 1988 make a similar point.

problems, I will be unable to develop reliable and far-reaching strategies to solve those problems. Rather, the narrowness of my understanding of the project of living well will undermine my efforts. Counterexamples of the so-called courageous criminal kind therefore fail to track the distinction between proto-virtues and the true virtues, since a person in possession of true courage would recognize that it must always be limited by considerations of honesty and justice if it is to fully and appropriately manifest a responsiveness to all the normative claims at stake and thereby count as solving the existential problem posed by fear and danger.[6]

Of course, we should here acknowledge that the virtues must be understood as a kind of continuum with natural proto-virtue on one end and complete or perfect virtue on the other. The more complete the virtue, the greater will be its integration with other, correspondingly complete virtues. As such, those of us who are somewhere in the middle may indeed *appear* to possess more of one virtue than another – and popular modes of character assessment might therefore attribute virtue to us. But once we are faced with a situation in which our failings in one virtue are related to failings in another, it will be evident that we do not in fact fully possess that virtue. The process of moving from a quasi-virtue to a full virtue will therefore require commitment to improvement across the board.[7]

Practical Intelligence

Aristotle's conception of *phronēsis* or practical intelligence[8] becomes of particular importance here, since it refers to the ability to reason well about

---

[6] I owe the expression 'proto-virtue' to Sreenivasan 2009, 199. See also Cooper 1998, 244–245, where he shows that for Socrates each virtue must respect the considerations specific to other virtues.

[7] This speaks to another reason why people have objected to the comparison of virtues with skills. Namely, people hold it to be illegitimate to want or try to be merely mediocre at virtue, while it is not in the case of skills like tennis. As such, there is a disanalogy. There are some interesting questions here, not least whether it is really possible to *try* to be mediocre at tennis or if, rather, it is more likely that in trying to play tennis we are oriented toward an ideal that we value – excellent tennis-playing – and though we try to instantiate it in our actions, the fact that we are also committed to other goods that require our time and attention means that we cannot always fully do so and must therefore settle for mediocrity. Since on my account the virtues are skills that are more central to leading a good life than, say, tennis, it is indeed true that we ought to dedicate more time and attention to realizing them in our lives. But such a hierarchy does not mean that comparing them to skills is illegitimate, since such hierarchies exist even among non-moral skills, e.g. I will dedicate more time to gardening than to juggling since the former is more central to my understanding of who I am trying to be.

[8] I follow Annas in this translation of *phronēsis* instead of the more common 'practical wisdom' since it is more suitable for 'the suggestions of inventiveness and problem-solving' (Annas 1995a, 73). See *NE*, 1140a24–26.

how to set and accomplish good ends. Broadly speaking, it is the ability to determine in particular circumstances how exactly to recognize and realize virtuous ends by way of specific constitutive acts.[9] Or, as McDowell puts it, 'concretely situation-specific discernment' (2007, 340). This is why Aristotle insists that the *phronimos* sees what to do 'at the right times, with reference to the right objects, and to the right people' (*NE*, 2.6 1106b21–22). *Phronēsis* is the way in which we decide what action specific circumstances now demand if we are to embody virtuous striving. As Aristotle puts it, the person with *phronēsis* 'is the one who tends to aim, in accordance with his calculation, at the best of the goods for a human being that are achievable in action' (*NE*, 1141b 16–18).[10] As Russell points out, this 'aiming at the best' characteristic of *phronēsis* 'includes an array of more particular practical capacities' including deliberative excellence, discriminatory comprehension, sensitivity, and intelligent instrumental discernment (2009, 20–24). Like cleverness, *phronēsis* involves skillful instrumental reasoning – but in *phronēsis* this rational ability has been put to the task of recognizing and realizing only valuable goals, whereas cleverness is indifferent to the moral quality of the ends it promotes or the manner in which those ends are to fit within the structure of one's life as a whole (*NE*, 1144a–b).[11] As such it is even less reliable in promoting flourishing than natural or proto-virtue is (Sreenivasan 2009, 200).

Phronēsis represents a key aspect of the ability to respond to competing claims such that one manifests a correct and stable expression of one's disposition toward virtue. Without practical wisdom serving as the guide for the problem-solving tendencies characteristic of virtue, those tendencies would be mistaken about how to solve the problems they are tasked with solving, not least because they would not accommodate the claims of the other virtues but rather proceed in a piecemeal and disjointed way.

---

[9] 'It is a commonplace of Aristotelian exegesis that Aristotle never really paused to analyze the distinction between two quite distinct relations, (A) the relation x bears to *telos* y when x will bring about y, and (B) the relation x bears to y when the existence of x will itself help to constitute y. For self-sufficient reasons we are committed in any case to making this distinction very often on behalf of Aristotle when he writes down the words *heneka* or *charin* (for the sake of). See e.g., Book I 1097bII' (Wiggins 1975, 32).

[10] Or, as Chappell 2006 puts it, such a person aims at 'practical truth', which consists in finding 'rational combinations of desires and beliefs to yield reasons', thereby showing the moral virtues *how* to reach their ends (141, 156).

[11] See Aristotle, *NE*, 1144a–b. Bostock 2000 and Natali 2001 both suggest that this is *all* that *phronēsis* is, but following Russell 2009, I hold that this cannot be the whole story, since the *phronimos* must also be skilled at deliberating about what those good ends themselves are in an agent's life as a whole. We will discuss this further in Chapter 6.

They would therefore not be fully virtuous in the way that virtue ethics understands them.[12]

In this sense *phronēsis* and the general sense of justice are deeply akin – both refer to the general ability to live excellently in the world by balancing and integrating competing normative claims in the face of existential challenges. Like justice, *phronēsis* plays the role of a kind of meta-virtue grounding the successful expression of every other complete virtue. Both are necessary for seeing how specific acts and claims are to fit into the shape of a virtuous agent's life as a whole. Both are skills necessary for realizing the same condition of responding well to the reasons that claim us, and both do so by grasping how the elements that go into that responding should be mobilized to the task, thereby 'making an appropriate goal determinate in one's particular circumstances' (Russell 2009, 25). This explains why Socrates can name wisdom as the global condition of virtue as such, while Plato can call it justice.

What differentiates them is that the former emphasizes the more intellectual aspect of good character, while the latter emphasizes the appetitive. The emphasis in justice is more on the emotions, appetites, and behavioural tendencies necessary for correctly balancing competing obligations in the face of existential threats to that balancing. *Phronēsis*, on the other hand, is more focused on the *know-how* necessary to do so through deliberative reasoning that is beholden to the claims of all the virtues. The intellectual virtues relate to the terrain of correct beliefs about practical issues and how they arise through good deliberation about human possibilities.[13] Thus Aristotle points out that cleverness is to natural virtue what practical wisdom is to real virtue. The former – cleverness and natural virtue – are both innate capacities (intellectual and affective) that become wisdom and justice when operating well – namely, by being able to take a kind of holistic view in which specific acts and orientations are understood as constituents of the good life as a whole. From such a perspective, all of the complex factors that could prevent moral responsiveness in this particular situation are accommodated and integrated. The merely clever and the 'naturally' virtuous, on the other hand, have not yet learned to see how particular acts must be tempered and shaped by their place in the whole of an agent's life. Aristotle differs from Socrates by more strongly emphasizing that both intellectual and affective virtue – *phronēsis* and justice – are

---

[12] See also Kamtekhar 2004, which argues that the idea of character in virtue ethics must involve 'the kind of stability or consistency that only knowledge could provide' (487).
[13] See *NE*, 1141b8–15 and Chappell 2006, 136–157 for an excellent discussion of these issues.

necessary constituents of this overarching integrity (*NE*, 1144b16–23). For the Aristotelian, the distinction between the 'types' of virtue cannot blind us to the fact of the deep imbrication of the intellectual and appetitive virtues. These two facets of living well are inseparable, since knowing what to do when it comes to correctly ordering one's normative responsiveness and being able to enact those priority judgments in one's life are mutually supportive dimensions of agency (see *NE*, 1139b12 and 1144a2). As Annas puts it:

> making the right judgments and decisions in an ever more unified and coherent way both presupposes and encourages development of the appropriate feelings and emotions. This is the thought behind Aristotle's insistence that intelligence is not the same as the cleverness that indifferently achieves a variety of aims; intelligence implies virtue, for you are not reasoning *intelligently* unless in your reasoning you are constrained by and sensitive to considerations of virtue. (1995a, 77)

Nevertheless, the fact that *phronēsis* is an intellectual virtue, while justice is a character virtue, allows us to accommodate the sense that someone can see what he is supposed to do in different virtue terrains but still fail to do it because his emotions and appetites are disordered. He does not have the correctly habituated character dispositions that will allow him to do it. Alternatively, one may be oriented toward and desirous of good ends but be intellectually weak when it comes to knowing how to recognize or bring them about in one's life. One can see, then, why *phronēsis* and the character virtues must work together – the former represents the good reasoning aimed at deciphering and accomplishing the legitimate ends constitutive of human excellence, while the latter represent the patterns of feeling, seeing, and acting that allow us to recognize and desire those ends as good. Both *phronēsis* and the appetitive virtues are different kinds of problem-solving modes in the life of the agent who is striving to respond appropriately to a plurality of normative demands in challenging conditions.

As we will see in Chapters 5 and 6, developing these capacities requires the gradual training of certain affective and cognitive abilities of discernment and deliberation. It requires habituation into a kind of practical know-how that cannot be codified and communicated in simple rules or descriptors. This is true for moral judgment as for carpentry or pottery – the master carpenter knows how to shape the specific piece of wood by reading its particular grain and heft, and this is not knowledge that can be listed and passed on in propositional form. It is for this reason that Aristotle insists that practical intelligence – despite being an intellectual virtue — cannot be understood as deductive scientific understanding concerned with the application of universal rules. This is in contrast with ethical theorists who argue that we can come up with a system of practical rules that will prepare us before the fact for the demands of every new situation, and allow us to see every case as falling under the system's authority.[14]

This does not mean that we should be radical particularists, though. We can and should attempt to understand particulars in terms of patterns and rules that we can use as helpful guidance — just as we do in other skillful activity. But such rules will always be open to questioning and revision. It is for this reason that the task of flourishing is necessarily one that calls for modesty, perplexity, and reflective self-questioning as we attempt to give each normative domain its due. Anything less would illegitimately cover over the difficulty we face in negotiating the irrevocable tensions that arise between these incommensurable normative domains.

Comparing the Incommensurable

The question remains, however, how *phronēsis* and justice actually do this work of choosing. We have seen in Chapter 3 that we cannot solve the problem of how to negotiate competing claims from the different normative terrains by reducing them all to the demands of a single normative perspective. Nor can we understand such negotiation work as occurring from a fourth meta-perspective providing clear standards to adjudicate among them. The orientation of care — by which I strive to be good at being who I am in the world — is not itself a higher-order normative perspective external to those domains that provides clear criteria for weighing claims arising from the three domains against each other. We experience all three kinds of claim in terms of our care to be in the world well — all addressed to the same 'I' at stake in its choices — but this fact does not itself provide specific standards for dealing with this normative complexity.

If that is so, what can talk of 'balancing' the competing normative terrains really mean? After all, if the first-, second-, and third-person domains are in fact specifying incommensurable modes of normative claim, how can practical wisdom balance them against each other in a

---

[14] Nussbaum 1986, 298. See Williams 1976, 171 for discussion of R. M. Hare on this issue.

non-arbitrary way? Doesn't this presuppose some form of intradomain comparison, or at least substantive ordinal assigning of significance?[15]

To understand the possibility of non-arbitrary decision-making in such cases, we must get clear on how agents can make justified choices between claims arising from the different normative domains. I have referred to these domains as 'incommensurable' at various stages so far, but we must now spell out what that amounts to. In *Making Comparisons Count*, Ruth Chang argues that there has been an unhelpful tendency in the literature to equate incommensurability with incomparability. She suggests that 'incommensurable' should be understood to refer to 'items that cannot be precisely measured by a single scale of units of value' (2015, xvii) – but that incommensurability does not necessarily entail *incomparability*. Indeed, we should hope that it does not, since 'the comparability of alternatives is necessary for the possibility of justified choice among them' (2015, xviii). In other words, if non-arbitrary choice is to be possible between options embodying incommensurable values, they must be comparable – but not by way of precise measurements against a single scale of units of value.

We make normative comparisons between instances of claim *within* each of the normative perspectives all the time, despite the absence of such a precise scale – for example, I can compare and choose between second-person claims for attention arising from my two daughters at any given moment. My general obligation to respond to each of these particular children is equal, but the demand for responsiveness in any given circumstance is not: today Mary has been sick and is consequently particularly emotionally needy; Lucy has had a fun-filled day already, etc. Much of this comparison work is relatively straightforward, but not always. The work of negotiating demands arising even from within the second-person normative domain alone can be exceedingly difficult. For example, how does one balance some mundane need of one's child against the extreme need of an acquaintance? This kind of balancing work becomes only more difficult when we must decide between claims arising from the different normative domains. How do I choose between self and other, community and individual in any given situation? The answer to such questions cannot be a metric or algorithm of comparison that would permit unambiguous answers. Rather, practical wisdom involves responding to the specificity of the different demands arising within each particular situation and knowing what to do in the face of them. But if the claims arising from

---

[15] I am grateful to an anonymous reviewer for pushing me to think more deeply about this.

the different normative domains are incommensurable, how is such comparison work possible?

Chang suggests that the solution lies in providing a broader conception of comparability, rejecting the notion that comparisons are necessarily scalar and hence that comparison is necessarily calculative (2015, 76). For example, there might be ordinal comparisons that do not admit of any unit of measurement (2015, 110–111). She also argues that it is possible to recognize particular cases as nominal or notable instantiations of a value and make comparisons on that basis, without having to appeal to a common unit of value (2015, 72–73). Charles Taylor makes a similar point when he notes that within any domain of value

> there will be matters that are central, and others that are more peripheral, questions where what makes this domain important are centrally at stake and others where something relatively minor is in play. Under the rubric of justice fall such weighty issues as the preservation of basic human rights, or the avoidance of brutal exploitation, on one extreme, and on the other, whether you took your fair share of the housework last week. (1997, 176)

Such distinctions of central/notable and peripheral/nominal can help us in cases that require us to compare what we can call higher and lower goods: for example, we might agree that friendship is intrinsically or 'emphatically' better than money (Chang 2015, 113), but by making use of the nominal/notable distinction we can make sense of the fact that '*some* tokens of higher type goods are intrinsically worse than *some* tokens of lower type goods' (Chang 2015, 115). Thus a small act of friendship need not automatically trump a huge amount of money, even if we agree that friendship is a higher good than money. As a result, we cannot simply grant one domain of value 'systematic priority' over the other (Taylor 1997, 176). All we can do is look to the situation and attempt to recognize the relative weight or importance a particular choice has relative to the domain of good to which it belongs. Central to this will be questioning what role a choice might play in the value landscape of one's life as a whole, understanding that every relationship – to self, other, and community – will have both a history and a future essential to determining its importance.

Such judgments of notability or importance are themselves normatively fraught, however. What counts as a nominal or notable instance of some value can itself be shaped by the symbolic or exemplary meaning that can be attributed to it. People regularly view particular choices as being representative of a certain kind of stand they are taking on what is valuable to them, of symbolically embodying the particular kind of life that they wish to lead and as such being 'notable' instances of that valued way of being.[16] Thus there can be choices in which the symbolic import of that choice for one's identity as a whole will take on a certain kind of outsize or 'kairotic' meaning (Taylor 1997, 180) – a fact that becomes particularly important for our discussions of patience and courage in Chapters 7 and 9. As a result, certain choices might, from one perspective, seem irrational insofar as they appear to opt for a nominal manifestation of a value over a notable one. But the status of the choice as unjustifiable may change when viewed in its wider symbolic meaning, i.e. when we see it as a case in which the choice is taken to express or symbolize the role that one wishes that value to play in one's life as a whole.

The idea of such identity-constitutive choices is essential for understanding comparability and justified choice. We can see this by considering another element of Chang's account. Generally speaking, Chang argues that comparisons are always made in terms of what she calls a 'covering value' that applies to both items being compared. In cases where there is no such covering value we face a situation not of incomparability but rather of *non-comparability* – in which the formal conditions of comparison fail. This distinction is important, she argues, because 'practical reason never presents us with a choice situation in which comparison of the alternative could fail on formal grounds' (2015, 84). In other words, in conditions of non-comparability the items are so different that the agent is not presented with a choice between them – and thus the need to compare them does not arise. In such conditions the possibility of comparison cannot even be understood as such (2015, 85). But she argues that these cases are in fact rare. Rather, she suggests that typically what *looks* like a case in which a 'covering value' is lacking is in fact a case where the options fall under the auspices of some unnamed covering value and as such they can be compared – and the notable versus nominal distinction can help reveal that fact. For example, if some action is nominally prudential but notably moral, we have more reason to do the latter even if the values at stake are incommensurable. And since we can make such determinations of relative

---

[16] Joseph Raz argues in *The Morality of Freedom* that belief in incomparability is itself constitutive of some goods, like friendship. In other words, commitment to the belief that friendship and, say, money are incomparable is itself part of what it is to hold friendship in the appropriately high regard (1986, 348–349). As Chang points out, however, being unable to compare things is not the same as holding that one thing is 'vastly, significantly, off-the-charts better' – since making the latter judgment demands comparison (2014, 103–104).

importance, she argues, there must be 'some value, however indefinite, in terms of which the judgment proceeds' (2015, 89).

But here we should question Chang's invocation of the idea of a nameless covering value and suggest instead that in such cases what is being compared are different configurations of possible identities, different possible ways of understanding how one might answer the question 'Who am I trying to be in the world?' Deciding to become a certain kind of human being does not rely on some unnamed covering value, but rather appeals to a sense of how particular choices ought to play out in terms of their meaning for the unity of a life as a whole. As Taylor puts it, 'In the end, what we are called on to do is not just carry out isolated acts, each one being right, but to live a life, and that means to be and become a certain kind of human being' (1997, 179). Each choice is made in the context of our care to be in the world well, in the context of our striving to be a certain kind of human being. As we will see in Chapter 5, moral exemplars play an essential role here, since they expose us to different admired possibilities of self-becoming and in so doing provide guidance in choosing who we will try to be.

Chang herself recognizes this to some degree when she discusses the idea of 'parity'. The tendency has been to assume that comparisons can result in only one of three relationships: 'better than', 'worse than', and 'equally good' – a view she refers to as the 'trichotomy thesis'. In contrast, she argues that we regularly find ourselves in situations where we judge two options to be 'on a par' – for example, Beethoven and Cezanne – which she characterizes as a fourth sui generis value relation. In such situations neither option is better, but neither are they 'equally good' insofar as a small improvement in one of them would not automatically allow us to recognize it as the better choice (Chang 2015, 121). Parity relationships of this kind are particularly important for understanding how practical reason can allow for the possibility of identity-defining choice:

> [I]f one alternative were always better than the others, practical reason would lead us around by the nose, always telling us what we are required to do if we are to be rational. And if alternatives are equally good, practical reason tells us that it does not matter which alternative we choose, for the alternatives are, with respect to whatever matters to the choice, exactly the same. In this case, we have 'freedom' to choose either, but the freedom to flip a coin is not the fundamental freedom that expresses a person's distinctive rational agency. (Chang 2015, 171)

Parity relations therefore provide a space for autonomous, identity-defining choice. For the most part agents face decisions that should not be understood in terms of questions of obligation or rational necessity – since a huge range of options will be rationally and morally permissible – but rather as constituting their unique personal identities through those choices. By choosing among options that are all deemed rationally justifiable, the agent takes a stand on what matters to her specifically; she expresses who she understands herself to be and in so doing becomes a certain kind of person.

One consequence of this discussion is that we must recognize that there will be a range of lives that display the kind of perspectival success and harmony characteristic of flourishing. For example, one person may prioritize the first-person project of developing her gifts, placing the demands of other and community second and third on her list of priorities and thereby taking a stand on who she understands herself to be. If she does so without failing to meet basic minimal demands arising from the second- and third-person perspectives, she can accomplish a kind of flourishing. So too with the agent who places the universal demands of the human community or the particular demands of a loved one above her own projects. Of course, agents will not necessarily prioritize one normative domain over the others; most will work toward responding to the different domains in ways that are roughly equal and mutually supportive. The diversity of ways in which to do so in different lives will nevertheless be enormous. To talk about perspectival harmony, then, does not commit us to the view that such harmonization work will be the same in all cases. Each normative domain is essential to flourishing, but there will be a range of lives that can be recognized as embodying the required tripartite normative responsiveness. This variability in what counts as flourishing is in keeping with Aristotle's admonition not to seek greater specificity than the subject matter will allow; it makes room for our sense that there is diversity in what counts as a good human life.

As we will see in the next section, however, not everything goes. What is ruled out are lives in which commitment to one perspective comes at the cost of completely failing to respond to the claims operative in the others. In other words, what is ruled out are lives in which agents fall below a certain level of moral decency in one or more of the normative terrains. A flourishing life cannot lack any of these goods entirely, and as a result flourishing must be governed by certain deontic constraints.

Deontic Constraints

Based on the emphasis on complexity, tension, diversity, and particularity throughout our discussion so far, one might object that this approach has no room for absolute moral prohibitions governing what we are permitted to do. Worries about the seeming absence of deontic constraints in virtue ethical accounts of justice are raised by Gopal Sreenivasan, who argues that virtue ethics is not a complete or self-sufficient moral theory because it has no room for the kind of deontic moral constraint operative in the concept of rights.[17] He acknowledges that justice is the virtue that is characteristically understood as sensitive to rights[18] but rejects the claim that the idea of personal justice can succeed in accounting for what we mean by rights. And unless it can, he argues, there is no way that the complete set of virtues can insulate an agent against moral error, and thus the virtue ethical claim to being a complete moral theory fails.

But is this right? What kind of moral sensitivity *is* captured in the idea of 'rights' and does the conception of justice outlined above encompass that kind of rights-responsiveness? Answering this will require (at a minimum) that we have a working conception of rights. Obviously this is an enormous topic, but for our purposes we can make a distinction between specific culturally sanctioned rights (such as the right to a fair trial) and the more ethically basic idea of what Sreenivasan calls minimal moral decency – i.e. the idea of there being certain deontic constraints that specify a lowest common denominator of morally acceptable behaviour. Though culturally sanctioned rights are meant to track requirements of minimal moral decency, it is not relevant to our discussion to specify if and when they do. Rather, we will focus only on whether the virtue of justice can accommodate the idea of rights as a moral threshold below which one may not go.

---

[17] Sreenivasan 2009 raises an objection to the unity of the virtues thesis by arguing that this thesis depends on a commitment to the idea of the moral self-sufficiency of the virtues, an idea rooted in the belief that virtue ethics represents a complete moral theory. This idea also requires one to be committed to (1) the idea that there are no genuine moral dilemmas and (2) the empirical compatibility of the virtues (203–205). I will be bracketing those considerations here – along with the larger argument regarding whether it is possible to be free of moral error – though it seems that questions of 'moral error' may lead us back into an ethic focused on action assessment rather than life assessment.

[18] See Adams 2006; Foot 2002; McDowell 1998.

Aristotle's own account of the virtue of 'particular justice' makes little reference to anything like rights.[19] But if we recall the distinction between particular and general justice outlined above, it becomes easier to see how justice can be understood as intrinsically sensitive to rights in the relevant way. As Sreenivasan argues, 'a character trait does not merely record, but also explains its possessor's reliable behaviour', but any kind of post-hoc conception of justice qua rights sensitivity cannot do so because it does not have any independent content that could explain that behaviour (2009, 210–211).[20] In other words, we cannot just say, 'Oh yes, and justice involves rights sensitivity too' unless we are able to explain how that rights sensitivity is intrinsic to that trait as we have understood it.

But on my account of justice as a character orientation in which one is appropriately responsive to the three different normative domains, this objection does not apply, since my account already specifies that agents must be minimally responsive to those normative domains if they are to count as living well in the world. Thus to be minimally moved by the second-person claims of others is to feel oneself obligated not to engage in gross moral violations such as torture, rape, brainwashing, or murder. These prohibitions specify the lowest common denominator for moral decency in that normative domain. They are the forms that minimal normative sensitivity takes within the domain of second-person claims. Similarly, the minimal level of self-concern necessary to constitute an acceptable level of sensitivity to first-person normative claims involves understanding *oneself* as a being against whom such behaviours are also illegitimate. I recognize certain moral limits in how I ought to allow myself to be treated – and those are my rights. Further, constraints on agent integrity demand that a certain level of coherence be maintained if one is to meet the minimal requirements of the first-person normative domain. The rights specific to the shared world will be somewhat more complicated, since they will be shaped by the constraints that a community understands itself as having to place on itself in order to ensure the possibility of such a shared world. Here we can think of certain universal or human rights that are often taken to be minimal requirements of this kind – such as freedom of speech and assembly. Without these guaranteed minimums, there can be none of the work of public comparison,

---

[19] Miller 1997 makes a case for the idea that Aristotle did have a conception of rights. See also Annas 1995a.
[20] See also Flanagan 1991, 279.

deliberation, and world-building that we take to be essential to the expression of the third-person stance.

The idea of deontic constraints fits with the conception of the virtues as problem-solving orientations, since it allows us to see how the different normative terrains can be protected against being overridden by the others. This is important because we have seen that the idea of negotiating the different classes of claim results in the idea that there will be a range of lives that display the kind of perspectival success and harmony characteristic of flourishing. Thus, *pace* Sreenivasan, the task of justice – to respond successfully to the different normative claims binding us in a way that does not illegitimately neglect any of them despite limited resources – does indeed naturally include the idea of sensitivity to 'rights', insofar as this concept is taken to specify minimal levels of normative responsivity. It is typically the case that communities come together to codify in law these minimal levels of moral decency with absolute prohibitions on certain behaviours that are taken to violate that moral minimum. This is one reason that justice has come to be so closely associated with political institutions and the degree to which they succeed at embodying those moral minimums. But as I hope to have shown here, this is only one part of the story.

The Impossibility of Flourishing

One might object, at this point, that the world we live in makes it *impossible* to adequately reply to the different obligations that claim us. In other words, the worry is that we find ourselves in a condition of bad moral luck that prevents flourishing because we are in the grip of jointly unsatisfiable yet legitimate ethical demands. The demands of needy refugees, the dying planet, victims of police brutality, one's family, career, etc. cannot *all* be given their due in one's life, can they? Indeed, don't we sometimes find ourselves facing situations in which there are direct conflicts of rights of even the minimalist kind that I have specified here? Mustn't we agree with Adorno's claim that there is no right living in a wrong world – and we must be in the 'wrong world' because it prevents us from satisfying all the claims to which we find ourselves subject?[21] Don't we live in a world where just and flourishing lives are *impossible*?

---

[21] For example, Adorno claims that 'wrong life cannot be lived rightly' (1991, 39). For discussion, see Freyenhagen 2013. See also Tessman 2015.

There are two possible ways in which this objection can be understood. The first way is as a historically contingent fact regarding the possibilities staked out for us by the social and political structures in which we happen to live; in late capitalism, for example. On this reading, it is impossible for us to flourish *now*, but it is not impossible per se. On the other hand, one could read this failure as a kind of existential fact – that no matter what social order we establish it will be impossible to meet the legitimate obligations that claim us because human beings are such that the multiplicity and far-reachingness of the claims that bind us means that they *necessarily* exceed our abilities to meet them.

We shall start with the latter objection, which sets up flourishing as an ideal that cannot possibly be realized. In other words, it basically decouples the conception of human excellence from the human lives in which that conception is meant to be realized. On that understanding, it is impossible to flourish. But why should we accept a vision of human excellence that cannot possibly be realized by humans? How could such an ideal possibly motivate human beings to strive for it, and why would we take it to apply to us?[22]

Recall again the discussion of the virtues as 'problem-solving'. There I emphasized that any 'solution' that a virtue can provide for an existential problem cannot be one that denies or overcomes the truth and irrevocability of the problem but must rather provide strategies for coping with the problem while acknowledging and responding to it as what it is – namely, as a fundamental feature of being human. In the same way, any conception of the balancing work done by those who possess the virtue of justice – whose existential problem is giving each normative terrain its due despite insufficient existential resources in the face of competing claims – must be one that makes doing this sufficiently well a genuine human possibility. Not necessarily for all humans all the time, of course, but for some of us some of the time. Otherwise, we will have fallen into producing conceptions of flourishing that might apply to angels or aliens but bear no relevance to ordinary human lives. Conceiving of justice as a possible human virtue means that it cannot be taken to 'solve' the existential problem by eradicating the tension intrinsic to our condition of normative plurality or the finitude of our capacities to respond. Denying this tension by reducing one normative domain to another or by attempting to eradicate the legitimacy of one altogether is ruled out by the idea of justice as a human virtue. Justice does not permit strategies that destroy or

---

[22] See Russell 2009, 123–130. This is an issue to which we will return in Chapter 5.

occlude one's responsivity to the three normative terrains despite the limitations we necessarily face in enacting this responsivity.

If it is true that some degree of flourishing is existentially possible for many or most people to achieve, then, we must give an account of why it *feels* impossible. Why would one claim that we will *necessarily* fail to give normative claims their due? There are several possible reasons for this. The first such reason is that this impossibility is only apparent – an appearance of impossibility that is in fact rooted in the selfish desire to avoid doing what one knows one can and ought to do. For example, we can think of people who say it's 'impossible' when what they really mean is that they are unwilling to give up their time, money, or power to that cause. Of course, second- or third-person obligations cannot always trump first-person claims to pursue one's own interests, but the tendency to say that meeting those obligations is *impossible* is as often as not an attempt to justify an illegitimate prioritizing of the first-person domain over the other moral domains. In general, then, we must be careful not to excuse complacency by cloaking it with the mantle of existential necessity.

On the other hand, one might claim that it is impossible to respond adequately to competing normative demands because the standards one uses to assess this are so high that *anything* one does will necessarily be deemed insufficient. As we have seen, this is typically the result of an inappropriate conception of what human excellence can look like. The feeling that one is constantly failing to meet one's obligations – that meeting them is objectively *impossible* – can often be the sign of a kind of masochistic perfectionism.[23] If one's standards are calibrated to a superhuman model, one will fail to meet them. We see evidence of this in the so-called mommy wars where women (but also men) feel like parenting failures because their other obligations (typically at work, but also in terms of community obligations, personal development, etc.) make it impossible to parent at the level deemed culturally desirable (e.g. by attending all of the child's sporting events, staging elaborate parties, or constantly paying devoted attention to the child). But this kind of 'failure' is no failure, but rather the inevitable outcome of holding oneself to unrealistic standards, a condition in which one's cultural or individual interpretation of one's obligations is at odds with what the normative terrains in fact demand.

---

[23] It can also feel impossible if we are too focused on individual choices and not on the shape of our lives as a whole, as we will discuss in Chapter 7's examination of the virtue of patience.

This point returns us to the question of how to respond to the other way of reading the objection to talk of 'balancing', namely, by viewing it not as an *existential* impossibility but rather as a culturally contingent impossibility true of our current social order. How are we to think of lives in which the current social or political landscape makes it impossible to meet all of the claims that bind one? After all, though it is easy to *say* that certain standards are too high, this does not automatically change the fact that we feel bound by them. One continues to feel oneself to be failing to meet standards that one's culture promotes as necessary to meet.

Further – and much more worryingly than failed birthday parties – one can also be trapped in a system not through illegitimately high standards, but because conditions of oppression, systemic poverty, and power inequality make it impossible, say, to feed one's children. In such cases we certainly would not say that one's feeling that it is impossible to give legitimate claims their due is because the standards in place are too high, but rather that the political conditions are such that one is prevented from meeting even the most basic moral obligations one can have. What can we say of those cases? Do they reveal the impossibility of flourishing?

First, we must concede that it might simply be true that there are regimes in which flourishing is impossible. One can think of lives torn apart by brutal political occupations, for example. In such conditions one may indeed be prevented from respecting even the basic deontic limits. But the poor souls facing such moral dilemmas are unlikely to be flourishing. It is a central feature of many versions of virtue ethics that they insist on the essential role played by moral luck in the possibility of flourishing. Flourishing requires conditions in which my first-person projects can be balanced against yours along with others in a shared world, thereby allowing agents to respond to the reasons that claim them and minimize cases of conflict. But such conditions are never fully in our control. Even appropriate responsivity to and integration of the normative perspectives cannot *guarantee* flourishing – there will always be natural disasters, disease, and politically unjust regimes that cannot be fully managed. Even the perfectly virtuous life can involve suffering and loss, the world being as it is. Because of this, we have no reason to believe that all humans are capable of living excellent lives – and defining the concept in such a way as to ensure that they can falsifies the meaning of flourishing as a concept that applies to the world as it really is.

It is important to recall, however, that from within the lived experience of those who are striving to live well in the world, there is no perspective from which to view their own bad moral luck as definitively ruling out flourishing. Thus moral bad luck does not remove the possibility of or motivation to *strive* for flourishing. Nor can we predict or rule out of hand the many creative ways in which the virtues might engage with *eudaimonia*-thwarting conditions to overcome or mitigate them. In cases of oppression and extreme hardship, striving for flourishing will be directed toward reforming the structures and conditions that are foreclosing full flourishing as a genuine possibility. For the virtuous agent, the existence of such tragic circumstances will be experienced as a demand for more robust forms of political action aimed at creating a world in which such violations are no longer possible. In other words, in such political conditions the main way in which third-person obligations of shared world-building manifest is in terms of the struggle for political transformation.[24] But this is only a more specific application of a characteristic feature of the third-person perspective in general: namely, the way it calls on us to create a shared world that conduces to human flourishing by providing institutional buffers against the political, natural, and existential problems that afflict us.

Thus in both the 'unrealistic standards' and the 'systemic oppression' cases, the virtuous response is to fight to transform the conditions preventing people from living fully good human lives. Obviously what that transformation work demands will vary depending on the nature of the structures that need transforming. For example, in the former case we could publicly criticize or mobilize against a social framework in which people are routinely expected to work a sixty-hour week. Or we might fight for better childcare options (or resist the idea that good parenting requires elaborate birthday parties). In the latter type of case, it will demand more radical action – strikes, protests, or political revolutions.

---

[24] See Tessman 2005, where she explicitly addresses the problems that arise as a result of the supposition that virtue is necessary but not sufficient for flourishing. When conditions of moral luck are in place that prevent flourishing, she argues, certain traits must be understood as 'burdened virtues': namely, good traits that are nevertheless decoupled from flourishing. Such traits count as virtues 'either by being a trait that would be good under better conditions (trait v_2), or by being a trait whose goodness or nobility comes from its potential to help bring about a world in which flourishing will be more possible (trait v_3), or by being a trait that can improve a life even if that life cannot be truly good (trait v_4). In any of these cases, the trait can (though will not necessarily) fall into the category of a burdened virtue, a category that captures those traits that would be missed if one were to simply work backward from a conception of full flourishing to a discovery of what is conducive to or constitutive of that sort of flourishing' (167). I am deeply sympathetic to Tessman's account. Since I view the task of the virtues to be enabling an adequate responsivity to the three normative terrains in the face of challenges to that task, naturally my account allows for a good deal of flexibility in what such enabling will involve depending on how the challenges manifest in different conditions. More recently Tessman has argued for the existence of impossible moral requirements (2015).

Depending on the extent of the bad moral luck, some of the lives dedicated to this transformative work will count as flourishing while some of them will not. As with any continuum concept, the location of the boundary between flourishing and not flourishing will be difficult to set or recognize. But what matters is not so much specifying those categorizations as understanding where and how it might be possible to achieve lives of greater flourishing.

It is important to recognize, however, that no matter what transformations and improvements we accomplish, the tensions and the finitude characteristic of the human condition will never be fully eradicated. No transformation in physical or political conditions can remove from human life the fact that our energy, our time, and our capacity to love are limited. These existential limits cannot be transcended without leaving behind human life as we know it and, with it, any corresponding conception of what a flourishing human life should look like. But barring a prior commitment to the existence of a divine planner who will guarantee against such tragic dilemmas and struggles, we have no reason to believe that such dilemmas and struggles are impossible or that their existence undermines my account. On the contrary, my account has the advantage of making room for what appears to be a simple fact about human normative life, namely, that it is unavoidably complex and there are no guarantees. Any conception of flourishing must accommodate this fact; our ideals must be grounded in the human, even when we set our sights on its most lofty possibilities of expression.

CHAPTER 5

Called to Be Oneself
Role Models and the Project of Becoming Virtuous

> Kids don't remember what you teach them. They remember what you are.
> – Jim Henson, 2005

> The highest reward for a man's toil is not what he gets for it but what he becomes by it.
> – John Ruskin, 1819–1900

Typically the assumption in moral philosophy has been that its job is to provide some kind of decision procedure for making moral choices. When considered in this vein, some have argued that virtue ethics cannot be a genuine rival to deontology and utilitarianism because rather than being a systematic theory of right action providing specific guidance on how to behave – guidance that applies to everyone – it (unhelpfully) tells us that right action just is what a virtuous agent would do.[1] Aristotle claims that the criterion of morally worthy choice is the mean 'as a person with practical wisdom (*phronēsis*) would determine it' (*NE*, 1106b35).

This virtue ethical claim seems uncontroversial insofar as it is entirely in keeping with our everyday moral practice: usually when we do not know what to do we consult someone for help – someone we think would know. The problem is that this approach appears to be circular. How are we supposed to identify the virtuous person to consult if we are not already virtuous and consequently know what virtuous actions and people look like? Doesn't this presuppose that we have an independent list of necessary and sufficient criteria in terms of which such agents are recognized – a list that is in fact operating as the ultimate standard?

This chapter will argue that this objection is misguided, or at least not as damning as it might initially appear. Rather than basing our normative assessments on abstract lists or rules, I will argue that role models both

---

[1] See Crisp 2015 for a recent iteration of this objection.

serve to inaugurate the process of becoming virtuous and continuously guide even the most well-developed moral agent in times of moral conflict and confusion. Moral exemplars are at the very foundation of all our efforts to be in the world well, and it is only after they have already started us on the path of moral development that we can eventually turn back to assess their legitimacy for that role. As such, it is only late in the moral game, so to speak, that one can be in a position to explicitly assess and choose a moral exemplar. As we will see in the next chapter, those initial exemplars – though often quite flawed – nevertheless give us tools for moral judgment that we may ultimately turn against them, leaving them behind for role models further up the moral ladder.[2]

Central to my approach in this regard is the belief that questions of this kind are ultimately questions of moral *development*; that 'the nature of the virtues is not a separate issue from how we cultivate the virtues' (Russell 2014, 18). Such a developmental approach emphasizes the idea that living well is an ongoing achievement that we can get better at doing; it is 'not the sort of achievement that reaching the peak of a mountain is – once it is done, it is done forever – but the sort that involves keeping sharp, learning, and improving' (Russell 2014, 17). Virtue is a project characterized by striving and the ongoing capacity for gradual improvement. Thus understanding moral development involves an examination of both the way in which children are introduced to the project of flourishing and the way this striving manifests across different levels of development throughout our whole lives. When someone develops well, she is virtuous, and we look to her to give us a sense of how to direct our own striving. As we will see, emphasizing such a developmental account of virtue will help us alleviate some worries about the circularity objection.

In what follows I will argue that the structure of successful moral development involves elements that correspond to the three normative perspectives that I have specified in previous chapters. Different components of moral development are motivated and shaped by the claims intrinsic to the different normative domains. As a result, the process of learning to flourish itself embodies the tripartite structure that it is striving to more perfectly realize. These three elements can be specified as habituation, imitation, and critical comparison, which map on to the first-person,

---

[2] See Zagzebski 2006, 58–59. My approach here overlaps with Zagzebski's work on moral exemplars – especially in her recent book *Exemplarist Moral Theory* (2017) – but my own thinking on this issue developed independently of hers. A central difference is that Zagzebski attempts to build a comprehensive ethical theory out of admiration for exemplars, whereas I aim to fit the exemplar relationship within a broadly virtue ethical approach.

second-person, and third-person normative domains, respectively. As the domains themselves, these components of moral development should not be understood in isolation from each other, but rather as mutually supportive constitutive elements of the unified process of development.

The most important and basic concept for understanding moral development is that of *mimesis*, or imitation of an exemplar. It is the basis for the virtue ethical claim that the virtuous person is the ultimate criterion for assessing moral choice. This dimension of moral development corresponds primarily to the second-person perspective, since it is founded on love and admiration for specific others whom we take to be models of the way of being in the world that we wish to realize in our own lives. Discussion of this mimetic urge will lead us to another key element of moral development: habituation. Habituation corresponds primarily to the first-person normative domain since it is the process of forming a second nature within ourselves through practice. As such it involves the increasing realization of an idealized self that we take pleasure in becoming. Finally, we will see in Chapter 6 that moral development demands a social context in which our developing orientation toward flourishing is both enforced and strengthened, not only through participation in formal social institutions, but also in the critical comparison that allows us to test and fine-tune our sense of what is worthy of emulation and how to best pursue it. This element of moral development corresponds primarily to the third-person perspective, since it involves the comparative integration of a plurality of agents in a shared world.

As we have seen, *eudaimonia* is responding well to the three different classes of moral claim that grip us. The virtues are those stances that instantiate flourishing by coping with existential challenges to this task of norm responsivity. In what follows I will demonstrate that the process of moral development also embodies the structure of flourishing insofar as it involves responding to these three different terrains of normative demand.

Exemplars

The virtue ethical emphasis on the virtuous agent as the ultimate standard of moral assessment can sometimes distract from what I take to be a key insight at work in the idea of moral exemplars, namely, that we must begin with role models and the second-person perspective, since the task of human self-becoming is not a path on which we set out ourselves alone but is rather triggered by the loving relationship with the other person. Thus the question of circularity in a sense comes too late in the game, since it presupposes an agent who is developed enough to be able to deliberate about and choose a moral exemplar. Rather, I will argue that it is through one's attachment to specific loved others that we come to grasp and strive for a particular way of being in the world at all, and this attachment is not initially a matter of choice.

Before examining this point in detail, however, let us think a bit further about what it means for something to *be* an exemplar, and how that concept could relate to the structure of moral decision-making such that action guidance is possible. Generally speaking, the concept of an exemplar involves three aspects:

1. It is an example of something.
2. It is understood as something that ought to be copied or imitated.
3. It is understood as an ideal embodiment of the desired state or thing.

To understand how exemplarity can function in decision-making in the way that virtue ethics supposes, it will help to consider different ways of theorizing an agent's interpretation of the world via categories. Following John Jung Park's 2013 account, we can distinguish between the Classical Model, the Prototype Model, and the Exemplar Model.

According to the Classical Model, categories such as 'dog' or 'courage' refer to sets of necessary and sufficient conditions – or *definitions* – in terms of which we assess particular instances. We see this in Plato's theory of the Forms, for example, but the assumption that this is how moral concepts must be structured is a recurring theme in philosophy[3] and one that virtue ethics typically rejects, since it tends to view moral decision-making as the quasi-mechanical application of a set of codified rules for classifying action types. The real work on that account is in getting clear what the definitions are – and the rest simply follows. Thus Annas criticizes these as 'computer manual models' of moral decision-making, the idea being that it is possible to come up with a decision procedure for instantiating a virtue like 'justice' that could be stated in such complete and unambiguous terms that any non-virtuous person could understand and apply it correctly.[4] This classical model plays no role in the position I am defending here; I will put it to the side as another instance in which ethics is distorted by theoretical models at odds with its practical essence.

In contrast to this classical view of how concepts function, Park discusses what he calls the Prototype Model, wherein agents assess and categorize particulars on the basis of a 'list of statistically frequent features

---

[3] See Park 2013, 238–239 for other examples.
[4] Annas 2013, 680. See also Hursthouse 1999, 40.

that are a summary representation of the members of a category' (2013, 239). Importantly, this list does not specify necessary and sufficient conditions for membership in the category but is rather a family of concepts typically associated with that category. The greater the degree of similarity that an object displays to this 'family', the more that object is taken to be a good or typical example of it. This idea of degrees of membership is in contrast to the classical model, which 'predicts that there will be no typicality effects because so long as a potential member satisfies the necessary and sufficient conditions, each member should be regarded equally amongst its other members' (Park 2013, 246).

As we have seen, virtue ethics is in keeping with the prototype model insofar as that model resists the idea that ethical principles could be completely codifiable in action-guiding rules or principles that specify necessary and sufficient conditions for counting as an instance of a moral concept.[5] Further, it sometimes endorses the idea that we can specify a range of characteristic affects and behaviours as instances of the different virtues. We see this kind of approach in Hursthouse's idea of the 'v-rules', which she introduces to solve the circularity problem. The idea being that our concepts of the specific virtues carry with them action-guiding conceptual content in the form of a cluster of characteristic affects, beliefs, and behaviours associated with each virtue. By consulting the concept of each virtue and the v-rules embodied therein, she suggests, we will be able to determine when different actions more or less completely meet the prototype for that category. We can look to the v-rules implicit in our general understanding of what the different virtues demand of us and garner a sense of what we ought to do:

> Much valuable action guidance comes from avoiding courses of action that are irresponsible, feckless, lazy, inconsiderate, uncooperative, harsh, intolerant, indiscreet, incautious, unenterprising, pusillanimous, feeble, hypocritical, self-indulgent, materialistic, grasping, short-sighted, . . . and on and on. (Hursthouse 1999, 42)

Importantly for our circularity discussion, Hursthouse claims that we can specify these v-rules in abstraction from any particular people who embody them. We can know and try to emulate what good character traits are without having to look to a role model. Thus we often direct people to consult books on the virtues, we don't just tell them to 'imitate Mother Teresa'. Hursthouse suggests that it is only in cases of moral difficulty – for

---

[5] E.g. Hursthouse 1999, 25–42; Nussbaum 1986, 290–317.

example, when the demands of two virtues conflict – that we turn to moral role models for help in knowing what to do. As she puts it, role models provide 'fine-tuning' (1999, 81). And since we can specify the v-rules fairly robustly in isolation from such role models, they can serve as criteria for *recognizing* such role models, thereby solving the circularity problem.

Like other virtue ethicists, however, she claims that talking about a person's character still has primacy in the sense that good action is not just defined in terms of the action itself but also in terms of the person's beliefs, emotions, and general stance toward the world. As we have seen, we must emphasize the whole person – not just acts but also emotions and attitudes. This does not mean that we cannot specify certain moral rules (e.g. don't lie) since following those rules is part of what it is to be a person with the character trait of, say, honesty. But following moral rules is only part of that way of being:

> Virtue ethicists want to emphasize the fact that, if children are to be taught to be honest, they must be taught to love and prize the truth, and that *merely* teaching them not to lie will not achieve this end. But they need not deny that, to achieve this end, teaching them not to lie is useful, even indispensable. (Hursthouse 1999, 39)

So it is important to be clear that in specifying what we ought to do, the prototype model embodied in Hursthouse's v-rules is not focused strictly on right *action* but specifies *all* of the frequent features (including affective and motivational states) that we associate with possessing a virtue. Nevertheless, Hursthouse deviates from the typical neo-Aristotelian approach to right action by adopting this kind of prototype model of moral categorization rather than relying primarily on the idea of moral exemplars.

The prototype model has some strengths, but I will argue that it ultimately falsifies the phenomenology of moral experience and, in particular, moral development, and it does so by subsuming the second-personal dimension of moral development to the third-personal. Though the latter also has a role to play, it is only one aspect of the process of learning what virtue demands. To see why this is so, we will turn now to the final model of concept application: the exemplar model. This is a variation on the prototype model insofar as it too rejects the idea that a moral category specifies necessary and sufficient conditions and claims that the degree of an 'object's similarity to particular instances of a class determines membership' (Park 2013, 239). What distinguishes it from the prototype theory is that the latter characterizes the similarity assessment or categorization procedure in terms of comparison to a summary or list of typical features (e.g. v-rules), while exemplarity theory argues that similarity assessment occurs through comparison to a particular thing that has been taken as a normative instance or ideal instantiation of the category. Thus rather than thinking in terms of a specific abstract and disjunctive list as one does on the prototype model (e.g. barks, is furry, is four-legged, plays fetch), one thinks in terms of similarity to a concrete individual that is taken to stand in for the universal category when making the categorization (e.g. 'is more or less like Fido').[6]

In what follows, I will argue that the individual moral agent's decision procedure is originally to be understood in terms of this kind of exemplar model. Thus in moral development we are comparing ourselves with other *individual persons* and assessing our own successes in the struggle for excellence in terms of the model those individuals provide. We are not, for the most part, comparing ourselves to abstract lists. Our basic understanding of a good or flourishing life is founded on concrete examples that serve as touchstones embodying that meaning. Good acts are recognized and implemented by an agent by comparing herself against real or fictional exemplars; she interprets herself and her potential actions as more or less perfectly embodying that desired way of being in the world.[7] Though Hursthouse is right to isolate the v-rules as one important aspect of moral development and practice, I will argue that concrete exemplars play a more foundational role in practical rationality than lists of characteristic features that arise only on the basis of those exemplars.

Linda Zagzebski is a prominent defender of the idea that exemplarity must play a foundational role in ethical theory. She models her approach on Kripke's theory of rigid designation, wherein we are able to pick out members of a kind through ostension, even though we may be unable to explain what makes them members of that category. Thus we say, 'That is water' even if we may not understand the chemical composition that makes it what it is. In the same way, she argues, we can and do point to specific instances of moral goodness – 'that person there' – without necessarily being able to explain *why* that person counts as such an instance. This kind of basic grasping of individuals is, she argues, both in keeping with Aristotle's virtue ethics and a more promising way of

---

[6] This is not to suggest that the universal pre-exists the exemplar, as Park's account sometimes seems to imply. Rather, we gain access to the universal (insofar as we access it at all) via the exemplar.
[7] Chappell makes a similar distinction in discussing the role of ostension in certain kinds of practical knowledge (2012, 185).

grounding moral theories.[8] Zagzebski characterizes the way in which we choose or recognize exemplars as *admiration* – an emotion that (typically) triggers in us a desire to emulate (2013, 201).[9] Following Max Scheler's account, however, I suggest that in its most primal form, the relationship to the exemplar is better understood in terms of loving attachment.[10] Though love and admiration are of course similar in many ways, admiration suggests the attitude of an already developed agent capable of isolating the admirable qualities that make the exemplar admirable, while love is a more primal attachment that serves as a foundation for one's own self-understanding. Further, loving attachment leaves room for the kind of ambivalence that we might feel toward those we love[11] – an ambivalence that enables the kind of critical distance on which moral development will eventually depend. This difference is evident in Zagzebski's tendency to view exemplars primarily as morally exceptional persons that a community of relatively well-developed moral agents recognizes as such (e.g. Mother Teresa).[12] While this is an important way in which moral exemplarity functions in a culture, I believe that such conceptions begin too far up on the developmental ladder, since our original exemplars – the ones who first start us on the path toward flourishing – are fallible parents and caretakers, not moral saints.[13] These original exemplars are both unchosen and provide the first models of how to be in the world. These are the models that we initially strive to emulate, despite the fact that they often turn out to be unworthy of that role – as we discover in the course of our development. But at the very beginning, our loving attachment to our role models knows no such critical distance.

The Second-Person Claim: Mimetic Love

One of the key ways in which this kind of original attachment manifests is in terms of *mimesis*, or imitation, since the child strives to be like the loved one who models ways to be. On this Aristotle-inspired account, mimesis is

---

[8] See Zagzebski 2006; 2010; 2013; and 2017.
[9] See also Algoe and Haidt 2009; Velleman 2002; Vianello et al. 2010; and Zagzebski 2017.
[10] 'Every soul is conjoined with a personal exemplar by some kind of *love* ... there is always a passionate and affective relation' (Scheler 1987, 133).
[11] Ambivalence plays a central role in attachment theory (Bowlby 1988).
[12] For discussion of different kinds of exemplars, see Blum 1988 and Zagzebski 2017, 37–40.
[13] Olberding 2012 distinguishes between partial and total exemplars – the latter being the (much more rare) full-blown moral saints.

taken to be the absolute bedrock of a child's cognitive and moral development:

> For it is an instinct of human beings, from childhood, to engage in mimesis (indeed, this distinguishes them from other animals: man is the most mimetic of all, and it is through mimesis that he develops his earliest understanding); and equally natural that everyone enjoys mimetic objects. (*NE*, 1448b4–10)[14]

Contrary to many interpretations of this phenomenon, however, it is not primarily or initially specific *acts* that should be taken as the objects of this early loving mimesis. In keeping with my argument from Chapter 1 that the object of moral assessment is primarily *lives*, not isolated *acts*, Scheler emphasizes that the exemplar is initially and primarily grasped as a unity or whole. We love and wish to emulate the other person not as a set of atomic qualities or act tendencies, but in her mode of being in the world – her *gestalt*, her style:

> We entertain attachments and apathies we cannot explain to ourselves. Rather, we love or hate, first of all, whole and total persons on the basis of an *impression of their personal cast* [*Gestalt*]. Whenever we love or hate we also tend to consent or reject, to follow or to resist to follow. (1987, 147)

> We affirm in love, or negate in hatred, always the *complete whole of a person* before we affirm or negate individual actions and expressions of his moral tenor, before we recognize or reject values and propositions, before we obey or disobey orders from a person. There is no greater error as that in a psychology or sociology that says we love or hate persons only because they said or did this or that, or because they have certain traits of character or because of the looks of their noses or smiles. Our souls are not so didactic as our understanding which always lags behind our loves and hates. (1987, 147)[15]

Scheler characterizes the difference in terms of a distinction between a norm and a model or ideal. Whereas the former specifies the 'ought to be doneness' of specific acts, the latter specifies the 'ought to be-ness' of specific styles of being in the world.[16] Thus the prioritization of either

---

[14] Studies show that newborns learn through mimesis within weeks of birth (Meltzoff and Decety 2003; Meltzoff and Moore 1977; 1983; and 1989). For discussion, see Fossheim 2006, 109 and Garrels 2006.

[15] See also Jollimore's account of love as a kind of 'focused and devoted attention' that allows 'the full, unrestricted recognition of a human individual' (2011, 150).

[16] 'But the ideal ought which originates as a requirement in the intuited personal value of a person is not called norm, a name pertaining only to universally valued and universally ideal *propositions* of oughtness which have as content a valuable *action*. This ideal ought is called *a model*, or *an ideal*.

norm or model depends on whether an ethics attaches good and evil to acts or to persons. For both deontology and consequentialism, it is the former. Thus for Kant, a moral exemplar can only – or at least primarily[17] – be an anonymous instantiation of moral lawfulness, an instantiation that can serve as an example of the law's feasibility but is always to be understood as secondary to the law itself (Scheler 1973, 573).[18] But since the highest sense of human excellence is to be located in excellent lives, not in a supreme law or structured order, Scheler insists that we must consider the moral exemplar not simply 'as a mere subject (X) of possible acts of reason, i.e. "a rational person", but as an individual' (1973, 573). From a genetic and motivational viewpoint, model persons are '*more original* than norms' (Scheler 1973, 574) – a point in keeping with our discussion above about how prototype models of concepts depend on more basic exemplar models from which the list of common features is derived.[19]

This view is supported by arguments from Chapter 1 showing that the separation of act from the overarching intentionality of the agent's striving to be is deeply problematic. An act is meaningful only in terms of the context of intentional agency that establishes the standards in terms of which it succeeds or fails at being an act of a certain kind. This placement of an act against a background of the agent's striving to be is not merely an argument about conceptual priority in ethics, however, but a statement about what it is like to *be* an agent who sees others as agents. To see others as agents who can serve as patterns for one's own agency is to see them as caught up in the project of striving to be in the world, a project that gives direction and meaning to all of the specific activities in which they are engaged.

This orientation toward the exemplar's agency – as opposed to her specific actions – is evident in the fact that children adopt the goal or inferred intention that the other agent's behaviour is taken to embody. For example, Meltzoff and Decety found that toddlers complete the tasks that

---

A model is, like a norm, anchored in an evidential value of the person. But a model does not pertain to mere action, as is the case with a norm. It pertains first of all to a To-Be. One who has a model tends to *become* similar or equal to it, in that he experiences the ought-to-be on the basis of the value seen in the content of the model person. In addition, the *individual* value-essence of the person who serves as a model is not extinguished in the idea of the model, as is the case with a *norm*, which is universal by virtue of its content and validity' (Scheler 1973, 572).

[17] See O'Neill 1986 for discussion.
[18] Louden 1992 challenges this reading of Kant.
[19] '[T]here is a chain linking prototype theory to exemplar theory because if some moral concepts have prototype structure, then it is the case that at some earlier stage, moral concepts have exemplar structure. Thus, prototype theory, by way of concept acquisition, has built into the theory the existence of exemplar structure at some earlier time' (Park 2013, 245). We will discuss this further in Chapter 6.

they understand the experimenters as *attempting* to accomplish, rather than imitating the failed effort behaviours themselves: 'young toddlers can understand our goals even if we fail to fulfill them. They choose to imitate what we meant to do, rather than what we mistakenly do' (2003, 496). Such studies support reading mimesis as primarily an imitation of the overarching agency of the exemplar, and not just as emulation of particular isolable behaviours.[20] As Garrels puts it: 'Goals, intentions, and motives seem to organize the coordination of perception and action inherent in imitation at a much deeper level than surface behaviours' (2006, 66). Interestingly, this imitative adoption of the implied goal of the action does not occur when children observe incomplete or failed *machine* 'behaviour':

> Infants who viewed the uncompleted act by the mechanical device were no more likely to infer and complete the target goal than infants who were simply exposed to the toy without a demonstration. Apparently, infants do not attribute goals and intentions to inanimate objects. (Garrels 2006, 65)[21]

As we will see in Chapter 6, which discusses the role of the third-person perspective in moral development, prototype 'list of criteria' approaches to moral assessment are derivative of the exemplar model of categorization. At later stages of moral development children learn to separate out regularities of affect and act from the overarching gestalt of the beloved model such that abstract lists of assessment criteria can be developed. Once that has occurred, it is possible to use that list of assessment criteria to vet role models – as the circularity objection claims that we must do. But initially and primarily our moral development is characterized by a striving to be like beloved others who embody for us how to be in the world. The moral exemplar is the archetype of the life that we experience as ought-to-be-imitated, and specific actions or attitudes are emulated insofar as they are taken to be representative of the way of being of the loved other.[22] And, crucially for the circularity objection, the process of developing and applying that list of criteria will always be ultimately dependent on our understanding of the way the list captures the most fundamental object of moral assessment and imitation: human lives. Though we gradually learn

---

[20] Trevarthen et al. 1999 and Wohlschlager and Bekkering 2002. See also Garrels 2006 and Girard 2004.
[21] See also Hutto and Herschbach 2011; Kaye 1982, 121.
[22] Fossheim's account of mimesis sometimes seems to problematically emphasize image and representation – as he himself acknowledges (2006, 110). Ultimately what we are imitating, however, is ways of *being*, not representing, as his notion of 'practical mimesis' seems to recognize (111–112).

to distinguish specific acts or behaviours from the overarching world-orientation that we are initially drawn to imitate, interpreting when a specific act type should be emulated in a particular situation will always be shaped by the overarching question of what kind of person I am striving to be[23] and which beloved others help me envision an answer to that question. Because mimesis is primarily focused on an exemplary agent's overarching intentional stance in this way – not her discrete actions but her unique style of being in the world – mimetic development is profoundly second-personal in motive and realization; it focuses on the other person in her particularity, not simply on abstract act types.

Despite the tendency to assume that this orientation toward exemplars is something that we outgrow, even the most highly developed moral agents need the motivation and guidance of exemplars to show them what excellence can look like in changing circumstances – not only in the form of friendships, but also via fictional and historical figures.[24] Though one may overcome or outgrow specific role models, the need for role models exists as long as one has not yet achieved moral perfection. In other words: always.

The First-Person Claim: Habituation into Who You Can Be

Mimetic striving to emulate the beloved other is not the whole story, however. As Aristotle points out, the idea of *habituation* is also central to understanding moral development. Habituation is a process of practice and repetition whereby a learned response or activity takes on the qualities of ease and regularity that are typically reserved for natural or instinctual responses: 'as soon as a thing has become habitual, it is just as if it were natural; for habit is similar to nature; what happens often is akin to what happens always, natural events happening always, habitual events often.'[25] As such, habituation is sometimes referred to as acquiring a 'second nature' – namely, it refers to qualities or skills that have become so characteristic – so embedded in our character – as to approximate 'first nature' in their durability and predictability (*NE*, II.1 1103a14–21).

---

[23] Or *not* be. We should also note the role of a certain kind of anti-mimesis or revulsion that can occur in an encounter with agents who embody the kind of being in the world one wishes to avoid.
[24] MacIntyre 1984; Nussbaum 1999; and Zagzebski 2006 and 2017 emphasize the importance of narratives for this reason.
[25] Aristotle 1984a, I.11 1370a4–8.

For this reason, the development of the virtues is often compared to the development of practical skills, which are also built up primarily through imitation, habituation, and training rather than study of abstract principles.[26] Just as an agent can become a skilled builder only through building, she can become courageous only by performing courageous acts. Patterns of feeling and acting become customary by doing them often enough, and the same is true for excellences of character: we 'become good by doing good actions' (*NE*, 1105b10). This differs from things given to us by nature – like the capacity to see – which we do not have to acquire through practice (*NE*, II.1 1103a31). Both practical skills and virtues require practice and training and develop over time.

Russell points out that by characterizing moral development as a skill, Aristotle promotes what Russell calls a 'path-dependent approach', which interprets moral development against the background of a broader understanding of how people develop and improve generally (2014, 19). This approach is in contrast to the 'path-independent' approach to be found in thinkers like Kohlberg, who

> began with a purely philosophical picture of moral maturity – in particular, an explicitly neo-Kantian picture drawn from the work of philosophers like Hare, Frankena, and Rawls – and developed a theory of moral development as a progression through a series of developmental stages by which moral reasoning becomes increasingly explicit, and explicitly focused on purely formal and universal moral principles. (Russell 2014, 19–20)[27]

As Russell points out, the former approach has the advantage of placing moral development within the framework of ordinary human life, rather than granting it an exalted and foreign status that inhibits our ability to explain its structure or possibility.[28] Character development – as accomplished by mimesis, habituation, and critical comparison – is just another way in which we are able to get better through certain familiar patterns of practical striving, but in the case of the virtues, what we are getting better at is being able to embody and harmonize the three terrains of normative claim – the first-person, second-person, and third-person – in the face of fundamental challenges to that project.

What exactly is being habituated when we learn to be virtuous? Aristotle (and others) have argued that it is primarily the *emotions* that habituation is

---

[26] See Jacobson 2005 (especially 390–397) and Stichter 2007. See Chapter 1 for further discussion of the skill model of virtue.
[27] See also Haidt 2001.
[28] Crittenden 1999 demonstrates the trouble into which this kind of 'path independent' approach gets Kohlberg.

aimed at developing, not cognitive capacities, since the latter are more amenable to direct instruction, though they too are built up over time through experience. The affects and dispositions, on the other hand, are taken to be more resistant to the influence of reason and thus require forms of habituation and training that primarily harness pain, pleasure, and other irrational motivators such as music to the task: 'In educating the young we steer them by the rudders of pleasure and pain' (*NE*, 1172a21–22).[29] Insofar as the exemplar is virtuous, she will model an appropriate affective orientation toward good ends. Habituation is a form of supervised practice shaped by pre-rational desires and aversions that direct one toward those same good ends. Learning to love what the exemplar loves shapes the entire process of habituation; we learn to find pleasure in the objects that the loved other takes to be good.[30]

We have seen that mimesis involves taking up the objects pursued and valued by the exemplar. When coupled with patterns of habituation through repetition and reward, the pursuit of these ends becomes a normalized part of one's second nature:

> The underlying idea is that the child's sense of pleasure, which to begin with and for a long while is his only motive, should be hooked up with just and noble things so that his unreasoned evaluative responses may develop in connection with the right objects. (Burnyeat 1980, 80)[31]

This developmental model of virtue necessarily presupposes a distinction between the performance of quasi- or beginner virtue and virtue proper. The beginner performs acts that may appear virtuous from the outside but do not count as genuine virtue because she has not yet developed the characteristic ways of seeing and feeling intrinsic to genuine virtue. It is only by engaging in the former that one acquires the capacity for the latter. Thus if one is to genuinely learn virtue, it is not simply certain act types

---

[29] 'Aristotle owes to Plato, as he himself acknowledges at 2.3, the idea that these motivating evaluative responses are unreasoned – they develop before reason and are not at that stage grounded in a general view of the place of the virtues in the good life – and because they are unreasoned, other kinds of training must be devised to direct them on to the right kind of object: chiefly, guided practice and habituation' (Burnyeat 1980, 79). See also Coplan 2010 for a detailed rejection of the intellectualist picture.

[30] 'Enjoying and hating the right things seems to be most important for virtue of character. For pleasure and pain extend through the whole of our lives, and are of great importance for virtue and the happy life, since people decide to do what is pleasant, and avoid what is painful' (*NE*, 1172a23–26). Curzer 2001 gives Aristotle a quasi-Nietzschean reading according to which moral progress is primarily driven by the desire to avoid the pain of shame, regret, and punishment. This is an important point, but not one at odds with my account; loving imitation can involve motivation by fear and pain at the thought of being different from or rejected by the attachment figure.

[31] See also Curren 1999, 70.

that are to be normalized but rather ways of seeing, thinking, and feeling *in* those actions. To be virtuous requires desiring and pursuing the good in and through the action. One accomplishes this truly virtuous stance by performing the acts that one observes the exemplar performing, and in so doing gradually takes on the affective stances embodied in those acts. Repetition of behaviour helps to shape and normalize affective orientations because practice transforms the person who engages in it. The key point for our understanding of this first-personal dimension of moral development is that being habituated well means that a new set of behaviours and goals come to be experienced *as* pleasurable and natural.[32] As Burnyeat points out, many things offer little pleasure to those who do not know how to do them: e.g. chess, skiing, sewing, etc. – indeed, pretty much all skills meet this description. But through habituating practice, one both learns how to do it *and* that it is intrinsically rewarding.[33] In other words, one learns intrinsic motivation through habituation.

The Pavlov's Dog Objection

The irrationality and externality of this model of development has prompted some to argue that it is at odds with the self-direction and autonomy that we typically demand from genuine moral agents. How could this kind of habituation process ever produce agents who love and choose the good for its own sake, rather than simply out of an automatic association response? As Russell puts the worry: 'we might imagine that ethos is a kind of passive absorption of routine, and in fact the standard English rendering of ethos, "habit" or "habituation", can suggest exactly that in everyday usage' (2014, 24). The emotional habituation at the heart of moral education as Aristotle conceives it appears to be a kind of indoctrination; it establishes beliefs and behaviours that cannot be dislodged or transformed through critical analysis because the consequence of habituation is that 'one will tend to see what one has grown accustomed to as good' (Curren 1999, 74). And as Fossheim points out, Aristotle himself consistently treats pleasure and the noble as 'radically distinct forms of motivation, even when they are confused in some particular agent' – thus mere association via habituation seems unable to account for the transition from the one to the other (Fossheim 2006, 107). As such, habituation seems to involve a kind of coercive foreclosing of a child's options by

---

[32] See Burnyeat 1980, 74.
[33] See Burnyeat 1980, 77; Kamtekar 2004, 481.

'suppressing alternative conceptions of the good' in ways that make no use of rational persuasion (Curren 1999, 74). As a result, thinkers such as Lawrence Kohlberg famously reject the Aristotelian model of moral development as an irrational hodgepodge of habituated tendencies – a 'bag of virtues' (Kohlberg 1981, 31).[34]

A similar objection is evident in Kant, who critiques the teaching of morality through exemplification by pointing to the danger that the child will act in conformity with duty only out of habit, rather than acting for the sake of duty out of respect for the moral law.[35] In other words, the worry is that this kind of role modeling and habituation could never produce a morally autonomous agent. Though Kant agrees with Aristotle that judgment is a natural capacity that cannot be taught but only sharpened through practice – with examples serving as a kind of crutch for that practice[36] – ultimately judgment must learn to stand on its own.[37] If the 'crutch' of exemplars is too much present this will never happen. Rather, the power of judgment that is the basis of genuine morality will become stunted and weak.[38]

However, it is far from clear that this emphasis on developing autonomous judgment is incompatible with the endorsement of role models and habituation. As Julia Annas points out, the complexity of human life is such that rules – and exemplars – would have to be multiplied to infinity to actually capture all the different moral circumstances with which we might be faced. As a result, any appeal to imitation and habituation must be coupled with the development of the kind of practical judgment that we take to be a necessary feature of virtuous action since it allows us to respond well to the specificity of each situation.[39]

Our responsivity to the second-person call that the exemplar's presence makes on us draws us toward the condition of living well that we take her

---

[34] See also Maxwell and Reichenbach, who point out that 'the two strongly influential cultural currents of political liberalism and the modern ideal of authenticity picture, in different ways, the emotions as inviolably private and hence beyond the purview of legitimate educational intervention' (2005, 292).
[35] In *On Education*, Kant warns, 'All will be spoilt if moral training rests upon examples, threats, punishments, and so on. It would then be merely discipline. We must see that the child does right on account of his own maxims, and not merely from habit' (1900, para. 72). However, in 'The Doctrine of Virtue' he also explicitly endorses the use of examples and role models for developing good judgment and virtue (1996, 6:477–484). For helpful discussion, see Louden 1992.
[36] 'Examples are thus the go-cart of judgment; and those who are lacking in the natural talent [of judgment] can never dispense with them' (Kant 1965, A 134/B 173–174).
[37] Though Louden points out that Kant also seems to believe that no human being will ever be able to entirely dispense with the need for examples (1992, 309, 314).
[38] See Louden 1992, 306–318. Kant also worries that habituation can produce a fixation on a single conception of the good, the result being an inability to autonomously choose between different conceptions. See Siegel 2017.
[39] See also Hursthouse 1999, 54.

to embody. But this is not the whole picture. The relationship to the exemplar cannot be mere obedience or imitation on the basis of that second-personal call – at least if we are to account for the manner in which we enact that vision of living well within our own lives. The relationship to the exemplar is not simply a desire to please or obey but a dynamic interaction through which one is drawn or enticed forward toward growth. The exemplar does not merely create rote behaviour in those who follow her but evokes a transformation of self-understanding *through* this behaviour. Contrary to simplistic interpretations of early childhood mimicry as a mindless aping of observable action, then – interpretations that have played a long-standing and detrimental role in misrepresenting early childhood moral development – the imitation of exemplars must be recognized as an extremely complex and creative mode of social learning from very early on. For example, the extent of the child's mimicry depends on the chosen exemplar's willingness to develop a relationship with the infant, particularly by responding to mimicry in kind; studies show that 'young infants will smile and direct more visual attention to adults who are imitating them, while concentrating less on adults who simply respond' (Garrels 2006, 61). Further, older children will 'test' the adult's mutual mimesis by way of sudden changes to see if she is following in the game (Meltzoff and Decety 2003).

The increasing complexity of this mimetic relationship is evident in the fact that the learner must see *herself* as potentially being like the exemplar. She must understand herself as striving toward the realization of a future, better version of herself.[40] Such a self-understanding is a kind of tacit and pre-theoretical self-grasping of oneself in one's potentiality. This point gives us a more complicated interpretation of exemplarity: the exemplar who I follow is not simply the *other* person but also the self that I experience myself as capable of being when viewed through the lens of the model of life that she provides. I pursue the vision of this potential self that I experience when in her presence. Indeed, studies regularly show that the power of an exemplar depends on the extent to which a person can see

---

[40] This is an idea discussed extensively in Nietzsche's writing, especially in 'Schopenhauer as Educator' (1997). 'What one apparently needs is the capacity to say to oneself: "I am not myself." How can I not be myself? Nietzsche suggests that when you say these words ("This is not *my* self") to your "self", you acknowledge the existence of a self that is not who you presently are. Nietzsche courts this paradox of an absent self throughout his writing' (Conant 2010, 197). Velleman has suggested that admiration promotes emulation by wishful picturing of oneself in the image of the admired person (2002); one's hero is 'the image of the daydream self' (Warren 1972, 4). See also Zagzebski 2017, 136.

herself in that exemplar – shared race, gender, ability, interest, etc. increase the efficaciousness of the exemplar for promoting development.[41]

It is here that we can see how habituation manifests the first-person perspective. Habituation into patterns of feeling and doing demonstrates to me that I am *capable* of the traits that I take to be characteristic of the valued way of being. It is an initial making real of a possibility previously only yearned for. Habituation works to realize the new self that one envisions as a possibility because it gives content to that vision. The first-person experience of oneself going through the motions of doing what one said one would do, of acting patiently, generously, or courageously – *itself* comes to serve as a kind of norm against which I can compare my own future states. In other words, I come to experience myself as more and more closely approximating the self I am striving to become. Thus having experienced what it is like to act virtuously, I am better able to recognize and embody it on future occasions – occasions where the role model may be absent or not obviously relevant. In the experience of self-becoming via habituation, my second-person desire to be like the other is given shape by my first-person experiences of self-realization. This kind of transformation through habituation demands that one act 'as if' one were already other than what one originally understood oneself to be – an 'acting' revealing that one is indeed capable of this possibility. Going through the motions of virtue is to try on a model version of oneself, a version to which one becomes increasingly habituated and which provides the first-person pleasures of self-becoming.[42] Such pleasures are not external to the goodness of the orientation but intrinsic to it, since they are the first-person pleasures of realizing oneself as more closely approximating a flourishing human life. Through habituation we reach out toward our own potential self such that it is made a reality. In so doing, we become more independent in our capacity for moral evaluation.

To be in the presence of an exemplar is not merely to be shown a neutral possibility or even invited to realize it. Rather, the possibility of self-becoming

---

[41] See Algoe and Haidt 2009, 107; Lockwood and Kunda 1997; and Moberg 2000, 679. Lockwood and Kunda note that 'Models of attainable success can be inspiring and self-enhancing, whereas models of unattainable success can be threatening and deflating... in all our studies the superstars who provoked inspiration were members of participants' in-group' (1997, 93). Thus Sherman rejects Hursthouse's criticism of role modeling evident in her suggestion that the pregnant adolescent girl can gain nothing from thinking of Socrates as a role model: 'But her example makes my point. To an adolescent girl, Socrates is no concrete role model. He is an abstraction, little more fleshy than virtue with a capital "V"' (1999, 36). On the contrary, one must be able to see *oneself* in the exemplar if he is to serve as a genuine role model.

[42] See Fossheim 2006, 111–113.

presented by the exemplar is experienced as a kind of first-person *challenge* to which I am called to live up. The existential condition of agency is one in which I experience my identity as something that is at stake for me, and the presence of the exemplar makes real to me the danger that I might not accomplish the self that I understand myself as capable of becoming. According to Aristotle, emulation involves 'a kind of distress at the apparent presence among others like him by nature, of things honoured and possible for a person to acquire' (1984a, 161). But as Kristján Kristjánsson points out, this distress is unlike envy insofar as it prompts one to strive for goods without trying to prevent others from having them (2006, 42).[43] It is not pain at the thought of what others might have but rather pain at the thought of incomplete self-becoming. The summoning nature of the envisioned ideal self involves pain at the thought that I am not as I could be, the sense that I could lose something precious if I fail to rise to the occasion – namely, my better self.[44]

Teachers

A robust relationship with the exemplar is instrumental in this process of self-becoming, since he treats the learner *as if* she were capable of such behaviour.[45] A good exemplar also sees the child through the lens of her potential self, treating her as a would-be person by assuming the presence of certain cognitive and affective states and treating her in ways corresponding to those assumptions. These counterfactual presuppositions and imaginative anticipations help to bring those very conditions about:

> These early interactions may be considered pseudo-dialogues, initiated and sustained by the mother (or other caretaker) as he or she 'replies to' infant reactions, and in so doing, acts as if such reactions already have communicative meaning. ('You are bored, angry, hungry, enjoying yourself, aren't you?') (Spiecker 1999, 225)

---

[43] For further discussion, see Sanderse 2013, 36 and Zagzebski 2017, 52–59, where she discusses ways in which admiration might turn into envy and resentment – which she takes to be a significant danger threatening moral life.
[44] Burnyeat points out that shame can play a key role here, since its presence means the learner has begun to be motivated by goodness for its own sake, not merely instrumentally (1980, 79). Nietzsche also notes that the sign that you have attached your heart to an exemplar is that fact that you are ashamed of yourself, but in a motivating, not a paralyzing way (1997, 163).
[45] However, Bandura 1963 indicates that learning through modeling occurs even in the absence of reinforcement from teachers.

By treating the child *as* already having the capacities and orientations we wish to inculcate in her as a second nature, we prompt their development: 'it is precisely because parents play out this fiction that it eventually comes to be true.'[46]

For example, children are initially held to their commitments not because they have already developed a sense of responsible self-ownership but because we engage in practices that treat them as if they do – they are reproached, questioned, prompted; their lives are shaped by the expectations of others. In this way all of us learn to choose to do what reflects who we are striving to be, since that way of being is increasingly thrust on us from without. We emulate those around us not only in terms of the stance those others take on their own lives but also in terms of the stance they expect from us toward our own.[47] We see ourselves through the acts that they demand of us and the categories through which they interpret us.[48] As Fichte puts it in *The System of Ethics*:

> [T]he father and mother ... transfer to their child this concept of reason and freedom and ... treat the child in accordance with this presupposition, and in this case it could not fail to happen that traces of reason would, when summoned by this mutual interaction, manifest themselves in the child. (2005, 317)

Thus habituation means that the child is shown what it means to be a virtuous self by both acting and being treated as if she were one. This treating 'as if' can take a number of different forms. Maxwell and Reichenbach break up these practices into three general categories of 'pedagogical intervention':

1. Requests for reappraisals that shift emotional responses by offering a different interpretation of reality. For example, we might say: 'Don't be so upset. She didn't mean to step on your cap. It was an accident.'
2. Requests to 'adjust one's emotional expression in accord with normative expectations ... "Quit sulking!", "Calm down!", "Please, be nice!" and "Pull yourself together!" are all injunctions to make one feel what one does not at present feel.'

---

[46] Kaye 1982, 53. Sherman makes a similar point (1999, 45).
[47] See Pfeifer et al. 2008 and Coplan 2010, 145.
[48] Psychologists have found that children who are told that they *are* good at math perform better and try harder than students who are simply encouraged to *be* good at math (Miller et al. 1975). See also Kamtekar 2004, 490.

3. Requests 'to exercise the imagination, namely to engage in moral role-taking ... [e.g.] "How would you feel, if your brother did the same thing?"' (2005, 293–294)

These approaches facilitate development by encouraging the child to take on the perspective of the more virtuous agent, emulating the interpretations, emotions, and empathic imagination of the exemplar. These approaches thereby demonstrate to the child that there are alternative modes of response available and that they are expected to practice responding to the world in those ways.[49]

And, importantly for our response to worries about failures of autonomy, these practices are not modes of brainwashing or manipulation, but rather explicit solicitations of the developing agent's capacity for critical assessment and judgment.[50] In making such solicitations, the exemplar acts as if the child were capable of such judgment. Thus it is important to note here that the moral and intellectual virtues develop in tandem; the habituation of the emotions is coupled with exposure to broader activities of categorization that disengage from the particularity of the situation to see it as an instance of a particular kind. We say, 'That was cruel' or 'Why are you being so dishonest?'– we don't simply convey affective disapproval. Similarly, we highlight how specific actions do or do not conduce to overarching goals of flourishing: we point out that such and such instance is 'not a way to be a good person' or that some behaviour 'won't win you many friends'. In so doing we train the capacity for judgment and instrumental reasoning in conjunction with the emotions.[51] Through these kinds of feedback, teachers bring about a transformation in the way that the agent sees and feels about the world.[52] Rosalind Hursthouse points out the simultaneously cognitive and affective training at work when we say things such as 'You don't want that dirty nasty thing!' to children. Such responses teach the child 'not to want that sort of thing, and also ... that the nasty and dirty is such as to be undesirable and bad' (Hursthouse 1988, 213). The rational and the

---

[49] The fact that we are expected to train these emotions and affects demonstrates to us that we can take ownership of our emotional lives to a greater degree than is typically recognized (Sherman 1999, 35–36).
[50] Spiecker makes use of Ryle's distinction between habits and intelligent capabilities to capture this distinction. While the former are a kind of conditioning or indoctrination into routine, the latter involve intelligent sensitivity to variable circumstance (1999, 220–222). See also Maxwell and Reichenbach 2005, 295. We will return to this issue in Chapter 6.
[51] See Vasiliou 1996, 780 on this point.
[52] See Chappell 2006, 136–157 on the relationship between the desiderative and cognitive dimensions of virtue.

non-rational are deeply intertwined elements of our development, and training the latter need not inhibit the growth of the former.

The important function of this kind of environmental feedback extends beyond the explicit teaching provided by role models and caretakers. As Russell points out, the learning environment must be structured enough that regularities can be observed and practiced.[53] This speaks to the role of community and tradition in enabling effective moral education. But it also demonstrates the complexity of this kind of developmental account, since it is notoriously difficult to isolate and reinforce exactly what the role model is supposed to be modeling. Nevertheless we can and do teach our children to improve, despite the 'messiness' of the environment in which they are developing their capacities. It is important to recall that character excellence is not to be taken as some kind of supernatural ('path-independent') ability that is radically distinct from other kinds of skill acquisition. Rather, it is as mundane as childhood itself. Just as we would not say that a child who learns how to paint will only ever mindlessly ape those abilities observed in others, so too must we resist the suggestion that a child who learns how to be generous or brave will only ever be 'habituated' into those ways of being. This is not to suggest, however, that such development will not be complicated, piecemeal, and often ambiguous.

---

[53] Russell 2014, 37. See also Moberg 2000, who points out that the motivation of observers to acquire moral behaviour from role models is stronger if these models appear to be rewarded or more intrinsically satisfied as a result of their moral behaviour.

CHAPTER 6

Corrupting the Youth

In Chapter 5 we discussed how the structure of moral development is such that agents are guided by second-person love of the exemplar and by first-person transformations accomplished by habituation into a new self-understanding of the kind of person that they can be. We saw that exposure to the exemplar provides a tacit and pre-theoretical understanding of oneself in one's potentiality and as challenged to live up to the possibilities uncovered by that encounter. We saw that this involves developing critical assessment and application skills that allow agents to tailor the exemplar's lead to their specific circumstances. The result is that habituation into patterns of being that emulate the exemplar should be viewed not as mindless aping but rather as a creative taking up of the possibilities of identity that the agent recognizes as being at stake for her.

A major problem with this approach remains, however, namely, the fact that there seem to be no protections against having bad exemplars who model the wrong kinds of life.[1] This objection is particularly pressing because initially we do not really choose our role models – in a sense they choose us. Faulty role models shape our character before we are in a position to assess or resist the damage being done. Thus who and what we are exposed to as children appears definitive for how we conceive of human excellence and the way our emotions are ordered toward that end (Fossheim 2006, 116). Protecting children from poor role models is therefore of the utmost moral concern. As Aristotle puts it: 'we always like best whatever comes first. And therefore youth should be kept strangers to all that is bad, and especially to things which suggest vice or hate' (1984b, 1336b33–35).[2]

---

[1] See Presbie and Coiteux 1971, who found that 'culturally acceptable or unacceptable behaviours are both affected by vicarious reinforcement' (1038).
[2] See also *NE*, 1104b11.

Virtue ethics partly differs from other moral theories in its willingness to accept the implications of this point, namely, the idea that not everyone will flourish. If you have an exceptionally poor upbringing as a child, it is indeed difficult – if not impossible – to undo that damage. Moral development happens from the very beginning and those early foundations will determine the strength of the entire structure. Indeed, Aristotle famously starts the *Nichomachean Ethics* by specifying that the only students who might benefit from moral philosophy and argument are those who have been raised such that they (1) can recognize the noble when they see it and (2) are emotionally attuned to desire to be that way themselves: 'the soul of the student needs to have been prepared by habits for enjoying and hating nobly, like ground that is to nourish seed' (*NE*, 1179b23–31). Notice how different this is from moral theories aimed at providing a justification of morality that could convince even the moral skeptic or psychopath.[3] Aristotle did not think such attempts to be of much use: if you do not already love and yearn for the good – a loving that arises through gradual repeated exposure that transforms your sense of what is pleasant and good – then no amount of argument can change that (see *NE*, 3.5 1114a19–21). You cannot recognize examples of noble actions as such unless you have been trained to see them that way through practice and the gradual habituation of your emotions.[4]

The benefit of emphasizing this kind of habituated seeing is that it accounts for the kind of immediate and fluid responsiveness to moral affordances that we take to be characteristic of virtuous agents. According to this understanding of moral agency, virtuous agents simply see what is to be done without the need for explicit cognitive processing or analysis. John McDowell is perhaps the most famous recent proponent of characterizing virtue in these perceptual terms: as a habituated way of seeing defined above all by spontaneity and immediacy. He claims, for instance, that 'Occasion by occasion, one knows what to do, if one does, not by applying universal principles but by being a certain kind of person: one who sees situations in a certain distinctive way' (1998, 73). Or 'a kind person knows what it is like to be confronted with a requirement of kindness. The sensitivity is, we might say, a sort of perceptual capacity' (1998, 51).

---

[3] See Vasiliou 1996.
[4] Indeed, therapy is often conceptualized as a retraining of the emotions – a kind of second childhood, another chance at learning to love the noble. I am grateful to Alexandra Popescu for pointing this out to me.

More recently, thinkers such as Annas (2011), Döring (2007), Goldie (2007), and Hursthouse (1999) have also endorsed a kind of perceptual model of moral sensitivity that allows agents to simply 'see' normative reasons, evaluative properties, and/or deontic facts in a phenomenologically immediate way. Such an approach can already be found among phenomenologists like Heidegger and Lévinas, and if we look to Aristotle himself, we find claims about *phronēsis* that support this perceptual model: it is characterized as being concerned with particulars (*NE*, 1141b14) and as the 'eye of the soul' (*NE*, 1144a30). The phronimos is someone who is able to 'see correctly because experience has given them the eye' (*NE*, 1143b14). There is a good deal of debate about the extent to which this should be taken as perception in the literal sense. Döring (2007), for example, endorses a distinct kind of affective perception that bears many similarities to Heidegger's account of circumspective concern.[5]

On this perceptual model the presence of explicit deliberation is sometimes taken to be a sign of failure or underdevelopment. The expert chess-player does not need to consider the vast majority of possible moves but simply sees what is to be done – and that undeliberated immediacy is a sign of her mastery. In the same way, morally excellent people do not even consider whether to torture the innocent or break a promise; the fact that someone experiences those as live options means that he is a moral beginner or a poorly raised moral agent. He has not yet achieved the fluid mastery that manifests as a kind of immediate responsivity to the situation – with no hesitation or explicit choice-making necessary. The virtuous agent does not weigh options and then rule them out; rather, the most salient action possibility is immediately evident and present to the virtuous agent as 'the thing to do'.[6]

The phenomenology of such everyday moral experience – the immediacy of our evaluative seeing – seems to make this perceptual model 'almost inescapable in ethics' (Jacobson 2005, 389). A problem arises, however,

---

[5] The expanded sense of 'perception' often goes hand in hand with the skill model of virtue: 'On this Aristotelian view, the virtuous person has a special kind of skill that provides sensitivity to reasons. This skill model of virtue appeals to many proponents of virtue ethics, because it promises to domesticate the perceptual metaphor and to vindicate the claim that the virtuous person sees situations in a distinctive way: as comprising reasons to act. When someone possesses a practical ability – that is, a skill or form of know how – however mundane, we quite naturally say that he sees what to do (in the context of the relevant activity)' (Jacobson 2005, 389).

[6] McDowell characterizes this in terms of the notion of 'silencing': 'the relevant notion of salience cannot be understood except in terms of seeing something as a reason for acting that silences all others' (1998, 70). For this reason he also argues – *pace* Foot – that the claims of virtue are present as categorical, not hypothetical, imperatives (77). See also Dreyfus and Dreyfus 1991 and Goldie 2007.

when we recall the bad role models objection and we note that Aristotle's purported view that virtuous behaviour can be performed in this kind of immediate and spontaneous way seems to be inconsistent with his other claims about virtue needing to issue from rational (not just habituated) choice, which he characterizes as determined by deliberation (Finnigan 2015, 1).[7] Thus in response to worries about fluid action accounts that model practical rationality on perception, we find accounts that reject this view in favour of equating practical rationality with critical distance and deliberation.[8] Rather than being a sign of failure, critical deliberation is taken to be what distinguishes reasons from mere animal incentives. Korsgaard and other Kant-inspired views embody this approach.

According to Korsgaard, rational self-consciousness and the reflective distance that it produces put us in a position of having to assess incentives and act only on those that we decide to endorse: 'Once we are aware that we are inclined to act in a certain way on the ground of a certain incentive, we find ourselves faced with a decision, namely, whether we should do that' (2009, 115). As we saw in Chapter 2, she argues that an incentive counts as a reason for action insofar as it meets the conditions of the possibility of agency itself. Agency demands efficaciousness and autonomy – performing effective actions that come from you, not simply from some force acting on you (2008, 45, 112; 2009, 82). Insofar as you are engaged in action – which we are all 'condemned' to (2009, 1) – then you are bound by the norms of efficacy and autonomy constitutive of that agency, namely, the categorical and hypothetical imperatives (2008, 23). Human beings are rational insofar as they deliberate about what incentives are worth endorsing according to those legitimating principles of reason. Such critical deliberation serves as the decision procedure that distinguishes legitimate from illegitimate incentives.

The appeal of such a view is that it seems to provide some critical purchase on the immediate seeing and valuing that characterizes our everyday practical agency. As such, it appears to provide a solution to the worry about poor role models. But the problem for Korsgaard's approach and others like it is that they isolate the deliberative elements from the incentives to such a degree that it becomes difficult to account for

---

[7] Russell raises a similar objection: 'Unfortunately, Aristotle himself does not have a clear view about automaticity. On the one hand, he says that things we do "immediately" (*exaiphnês*) are not done from choice (*prohairesis*) since choice involves deliberation, and deliberation takes time. But on the other, he also says that a courageous person can decide "immediately" in virtue of his or her hexis, without prior preparation' (2014, 36).

[8] See Wrathall 2015, 194–197.

the fluid, norm-responsive action that must enact the deliverances of that deliberative endorsement without distorting the phenomenology of agency. Korsgaard herself is sensitive to the worry that she has isolated deliberation from action too much, suggesting that the idea of reflective endorsement need not involve an explicit act of reflection:

> Liberation from the government of instinct means that it is up to us to decide what justifies what, what counts as a reason for what, what is worth doing for the sake of what. We don't need to think of this, and in fact we shouldn't think of it, as a decision made prior to action: as often as not, it is a decision embodied in the action. (2009, 127)

But other aspects of her account militate against this solution; she is unable to explain how such an 'embodiment' fits with the rest of her account, since she characterizes agency in terms of a sharp divide between irrational instincts and the rational practices of reflective distancing and testing for universalizability that transform those instincts into reasons. But there is a vast normative middle ground between irrational instinct and rational deliberation. Affective tendencies and patterns of motivation and action are often pre-reflective identifications with and embodiments of reasons. They can be understood neither as irrational incentives that must all be made rational via reflective deliberation nor as the results of that deliberation. But by emphasizing reason's testing and legitimating function – its critical distance from incentive – the pre-theoretical norm-responsiveness constitutive of fluid action is lost (Crowell 2013 and 2017). The greater the initial polarization, the more difficult it is to understand how reason can speak for a whole that includes both of these disparate elements. The problem, in other words, is starting with an additive ontology of the self in which some parts are not normatively governed but must be made so via another part of the self.[9] In contrast, we must instead begin with an account of the self as being in the grip of the world and caring about responding well to its claims. In other words, we must begin with an account of the self as being normatively governed all the way down such that fluid action is itself characterized by a normative responsibility and responsivity that does not arise via deliberation but rather accounts for its possibility. But we must also be able to explain the possibility of interruption to such fluid action – interruption that can prompt agents to question how to go on with the interrupted practices and

---

[9] See Crowell 2013 and 2017; Enoch 2006. Döring 2007 discusses related Kantian difficulties in accounting for the motivational efficacy of normative practical reasons.

whether, indeed, they ought to. As we will see in what follows, such breakdowns can have varying degrees of scope and, consequently, different tools for deciding what to do in the face of them. In what follows I will outline several ways in which critical assessment stances can arise out of such interruptions to fluid action.

In order to do so, however, we must first think a bit further about the claim that *phronēsis* can be understood as a kind of perception. In doing so we must be careful not to illegitimately import an artificially simplistic perceptual epistemology into our conception of fluid practical agency.[10]

Rational Fluid Action

Thinkers who focus on the phenomenology of action insist that practical agency is best understood not in terms of discrete actions that are each deliberated in advance of execution but rather as a fluid interface with the world informed by normative responsivity.[11] We see a version of this, for example, in Finnigan's Bratman-inspired emphasis on the way in which plans and self-governing policies provide a teleological ordering that filters or frames what counts as a relevant option and thereby shapes fluid responsive action – without this having to be present to the agent's explicit awareness as such (2015, 16–21; see also Russell 2014, 33–35). For Finnigan, the explicitly deliberative choice of a plan is a necessary cognitive event in the agent's causal history – thereby accommodating the deliberative element. But once chosen, the normative structure provided by the plan means that the actions that result are not merely mechanical but rather informed by that teleological structure. One can make a similar case for how Korsgaard's account of practical identities function (1996).[12] Similarly, Velleman argues that practical reason is best understood as functioning in a kind of supervisory role that makes sense of what the agent is doing as he goes along – implementing the plan or realizing the practical identity, we might say – only intervening to provide explicit deliberation and course-correction in rare cases.[13] On his account,

[10] See Döring 2007; Finnigan 2015, 28–29; Goldie 2007, 348 n. 3; McDowell 1998, 72–73 for discussion on the extent to which characterizing virtue as a perceptual capacity should be taken literally.
[11] The following sections are particularly indebted to Matthew Burch and Steven Crowell.
[12] However, as we will see, we must be wary of endorsing interpretations of practical identity that require the agent to be aware of them as such. Rather, it is best to think of these as normatively governed abilities to be (*Seinkönnen*) only some of which are or could be explicitly present to the agent as such. See Crowell 2013 and 2017.
[13] See Velleman 2015. For Heideggerian accounts, see Crowell 2013 and Haugeland 1998 and 2013.

ongoingly norm-responsive fluid action is best understood as a kind of constant normative poise: a readiness to step in with deliberative assessment whenever cases of breakdown or anomaly reveal it to be necessary.[14]

But how are we to understand the 'readiness to step in' of Velleman's model and the ongoing shaping and framing that is operative in the agent's enactment of a plan or practical identity? Is it possible to understand this as fully compatible with the perceptual model, or does it commit us to the view that all action is at bottom deliberative or quasi-deliberative insofar as it betrays a kind of distance from the immediacy of the given circumstances?

Here we must note in particular that ordinary perception is itself not structured as a simple and immediate recording of unquestioned givens. Rather, even simple perceptual acts are governed by a series of expectations regarding how experience will continue to unfold in a meaningful way; perceptions operate within a normative field of fulfilled or thwarted intentions. To perceive the tree is to have my expectations continuously confirmed in the series of profiles that are presented to me. This means that the perceptual act implicitly refers to the ideal unity or meaning of the series of profiles given in perception. It refers to the object as that which will continue to present perceptual profiles in a harmonious and rule-governed way.[15] When this operation is proceeding smoothly, those expectations – or their justification – need not be explicitly referenced or thematized. I simply see the tree as a tree. But when there is an anomaly in the experience, the perceiver attempts to either establish the falsity of the anomalous perception or reconceive the nature of the object she is perceiving. The strangely behaving tree now becomes recognized as a movie prop, say – and a new horizon of perceptual intentions arises that is governed by a new norm in light of which the particular perceptions are meaningful. Perception is not simply the passive reception of sense data but a normatively governed activity in which the perceiver implicitly

---

[14] A version of this kind of approach can be found in what is known as dual process theory. See Kahneman 2011. See also Annas 2011, 37 on how anomalies in experience can produce confusion that prompts deliberation.

[15] See Husserl 1989. As Crowell puts this Husserlian insight: 'To "intend something objective" for instance, is not merely to enjoy some content (e.g. sense data) but to grasp "the intended as such" in light of what it is supposed to be, what it is or means to be such a thing. Only on such a normative basis can I be conscious of something *as* something, such that subsequent experiences can either "legitimate or correct" it. To "intend something objective" – to perceive that tree there – is not merely to be causally related to it; it is to take my experience to be corrigible in a certain way, namely, in light of the norms of treehood' (2013, 153). See also Noë 2006 on the view of perception as activity.

understands there to be possibilities of success or failure to which she must be responsive – an implicit understanding that only becomes explicit in conditions of interruption or failure.

In the same way, the practical agency operative in fluid action – affective, valuational, skillful perception of the practical context of action – is similarly normatively governed. We saw in the preceding chapter that the possibility of self-becoming presented by the exemplar is experienced as an ideal that I am called to approximate through my actions. As in ordinary perception, this requires an ongoing responsivity to the changing circumstances in light of the norm. The moral agent exercises creativity and skill in determining how best to instantiate the valued way of being in the particular situation. Such creative responsivity to the specificity of one's circumstances – a responsivity governed by the norm of who I am trying to be and in light of which things show up as appropriate or inappropriate – provides normative guidance without necessarily requiring explicit deliberation or even occurrent thoughts about who one is trying to be. But this lack of deliberation and explicit awareness is not the same as merely acting out of instinct, since it involves the intelligent responsiveness of the person trying to realize a meaningful possibility in the face of changing circumstance. Overcoming obstacles to one's striving to be therefore does not necessarily require explicit events of deliberation but is typically accomplished in a relatively unthinking way through the creative and intelligent responsiveness characteristic of the skillful practice itself. If the fly-swatter is missing, I use a magazine instead. If I cannot see what something is, I get closer before deciding.[16]

Interrupted Action

There are cases in which conflicts, uncertainties, and anomalies interrupt creative norm-governed responsivity and require us to step back and think more explicitly about what to do to continue pursuing the end to which we are committed. In such cases the agent does not know how to simply overcome the anomaly or conflict and continue gearing into the activities and commitments by which the world is ordinarily polarized into compelling action affordances. If my pen runs out, I might wet the tip, scribble on the page, or shake it. If it still refuses to work, I look for another one. But when such initial creative and skillful procedures of

---

[16] Annas 2011's discussion of the distinction between intelligent skill and mindless routine is helpful here.

clarification and resolution fail, the result is the need to think about what to do, and this can give rise to explicit practices of analysis, reason-weighing, and justification wherein we try to get clear on what exactly we are trying to accomplish in the practice and how to overcome obstacles to it. The fact that the normative perceptions operative in fluid action are phenomenologically non-inferential, then, does not mean they are incompatible with epistemic inference and rational justifications that may arise after the fact.[17]

Such deliberations are typically limited to a particular practical problem and decision context: can I remember the rest of the idea, or must I write it down immediately? As such, they pose minimal disruptions to one's praxis because they are not fundamental breaks with the overall project – e.g. working on a paper – but refinements and specifications of it. As Annas points out, the key feature here is that there is no disruption of intent (2011, 77). In other words, the commitment to the project is itself not open to question in such local deliberations but rather establishes the normative framework in terms of which any solution to the problem can show up as such. Though circumstances are such that it is not clear how best to do so, the agent continues to try to realize the project to which she is committed, and the norms internal to that project will determine the appropriateness of any proposed solution.

As a result of its localized character, this model cannot cope with the key objection raised in this chapter, however, since it cannot account for critical assessment of the general normative framework to which one is committed. It only speaks to how one can responsibly and creatively apply those standards to the complications specific to one's situation. But if one's normative orientation to the world is developed prior to and as a condition of recognizing morally relevant factors, how is it possible to achieve the critical distance necessary for assessing those practices themselves? Are we doomed simply to emulate our teachers, or is there a critical check on the agential trajectory into which we have been inculcated? Unless we can achieve some kind of critical distance from the exemplars who model the practical identities and life plans that shape our seeing of the world, there is no hope for an account of moral development that is not fully hostage to the moral quality of one's original exemplars. How, then, can we account for a more global critical distance in which I do not simply assess how best to enact a particular identity possibility in this particular situation, but rather assess that identity possibility itself?

---

[17] See Annas 2011, 27–29; Brandom 2002, 97; Crowell 2017; Doring 2007; Goldie 2007, 348–349.

The fundamentally public nature of human life and the normative terrain to which it introduces us – the claims of the shared world and the third-person perspective from which they manifest – are essential here. So far for the sake of simplicity we have discussed the role model relationship as if there were only one in each person's life. But every agent will have multiple role models, many of which will be experienced as in tension with each other. The conflicts that can arise between one's exemplars complicate those relationships substantially, calling for critical comparative assessment of the role models themselves. The plurality of role models means that a creative tension can arise among them such that the agent is increasingly required to isolate particular identity possibilities (carpenter, Catholic, cousin) as what ought to be imitated or avoided – as opposed to whole lives or general ways of being. The consequence is that the global loving emulation characteristic of the second-person orientation to the exemplar is increasingly broken into distinct practical identity-specific domains in terms of which role models can be compared in a more focused way.[18] Admirable activities and roles are isolated from the sense of the exemplar as a unified whole. For example, one might feel moved to emulate multiple people whose lives are characterized by very different career orientations: one person displays a commitment to social justice activism, another to a life of quiet scholarship, a third to full-time parenting. The practical impossibility of trying to emulate all of one's exemplars in a single career path forces the agent to consider which identities and practices to take up in her own life. It will force her, in other words, to take a more piecemeal approach to her exemplars, viewing them from a more critical stance as she chooses which elements to emulate. In circumstances where appealing styles of being come into conflict, then, the agent is forced to compare the different role models she feels called to imitate and decide if and when to follow those exemplars into particular practical identities or abilities to be in the world.[19]

These experiences of comparative tension often arise as a result of changing age or circumstance: one finds new loves, new objects of admiration, new ways of seeing the world – often without (fully) losing the old ones. The teen years, for example, are particularly characterized by experiences of conflict between the role models of childhood and those of the

---

[18] In one study researchers found a major difference between kindergarteners and sixth graders when it came to the power that the role model had in eliciting certain behaviours, with the older children relying more on internalized rules regarding normalized patterns of socially accepted behaviours, rather than on direct emulation of the role models (Lipscomb et al. 1982).
[19] See also Chapter 4's discussion of comparison.

changing peer group.[20] But due to the third-person perspective and the way that it enables us to see ourselves as one among many, this kind of comparative tension can arise at any time.[21]

Recall that the prototype and exemplar models are not mutually exclusive but rather that the former arises out of and depends on the latter. A grasp of general character or identity types is derived from exposure to multiple candidates for emulation, enabling the developing agent to see a specific action or identity possibility as an instantiation of excellent living in different circumstances. The experience of comparison and contrast between multiple admired agents increasingly allows one to see the trait or project and not just the agent as noble or 'to be imitated' (see *NE*, 2.9 1109b23; 4.5 1126b2–4). One isolates specific possibilities of being from the lives of the role models who first revealed those possibilities to one as desirable. I no longer simply wish to be like Jim, but to be a great conversationalist like Jim.

Further, viewing these exemplars as occupants of a shared public domain means seeing them in terms of all the others who also occupy similar publicly recognizable practical roles and identities – roles and identities whose governing norms can consequently be delineated in general and average ways. Heidegger calls this public normativity '*das Man*' – how 'one' does things. We come to see that our exemplars model different publicly specified abilities to be (*Seinkönnen*) as core elements of the lives that we take to be admirable – abilities governed by the conventions and public standards that define what counts as an instance of such an ability-to-be.

Because these public norms are underdetermined and must be taken up and applied in intelligent and context-responsive ways, we emulate our role models in terms of how they occupy particular public roles. We take guidance from their interpretations of public norms to help us develop our own. We understand others, then, in terms of both general public norms and their idiosyncratic ways of taking up and implementing them in their lives. We respond to the style in which they live the role, the manner in which they interpret its meaning. Here we see the virtues appearing as core constitutive elements of the style with which an exemplar occupies a particular role or identity. We admire someone because he is a patient teacher or a courageous emergency room nurse.

---

[20] See Beauvoir 1976 for a discussion of how recognition of the contingency of role models and norms marks the transition out of childhood. See also Sanderse 2013.
[21] See Arendt 1998 for discussion of the role of such plurality in human life.

Here again there can be cases of conflict as a result of the plurality of one's role models; our exemplars can model conflicting ways of embodying the norms that govern the roles and identities we are trying to occupy. We might simultaneously admire competing models of femininity, say, or admire the manner in which different people manifest the virtue of forgiveness in their lives. Though the role or practical identity is the same as far as conventions go, the interpretation of what these conventions mean and how they should be lived will be specific to different role models. The consequence, again, will be a creative tension that complicates our ability to occupy that identity and prompts the corresponding need to determine not only which practical identities to pursue, but how best to pursue them.

It is important to recognize that this kind of critical and creative comparison activity does not necessarily involve the conscious weighing and selecting of goals or styles of being – explicitly cognitive activities of reflective deliberation and discursive reason-giving – though it regularly prompts them. Faced with a practical dilemma that demands a choice between options that are at odds with various (aspects) of one's exemplars, the agent often engages in the deliberative analysis of reasons to prefer one option to the other – making lists of pros and cons, consulting others, etc. For example, perhaps one views having children as central to one's model of a happy family and desires to emulate women who are mothers – while also being drawn to environmentalists who embody their commitments by refusing to have children on an overcrowded planet. The person in that position must choose between conflicting models of the good life – comparison work that can in some cases rise from the pre-theoretical weighing of different identity possibilities to the explicitly cognitive activity of discursive thinking and reflection on reasons for and against.

There is clearly a good deal more to be said about how the stance of comparison moves from implicit weighing to deliberative reflection and reason-giving, but those discussions must be bracketed here. For our purposes I want to simply suggest that interruptions to fluid action often arise from conflicting models of the good life and solicit the kind of comparative stance that is the basis of deliberation. Indeed, comparison is the original meaning of 'deliberate' – a word that comes from the Latin *libra*, or scales. Creative tension among competing role models can in some circumstances give rise to explicit deliberations, then, but it is not always the case that it does. Rather, such tension often simply manifests as an experience of being out of sync with the world, of not knowing how to fit into the world with the spontaneity and ease one had before. New saliences make themselves known that are at odds with competing perceptions of what one should do and be. The agent must try to make sense of these conflicting visions of the world and her place in it. Whether such efforts take the form of explicit deliberations or not, the agent is called on to compare the manner in which those different possibilities of being speak to her understanding of who she is trying to be. Of course, often these experiences of conflict are never fully resolved but rather persist in an agent's life as a source of recurring normative ambiguity, inconsistency, and confusion. Many lives are marked by a lack of coherence generated by such conflicting commitments to competing exemplars of the good.

We have seen, then, that loving emulation of the exemplar as a whole is complicated by a plurality of exemplars and leads to comparisons that break up the emulation relationship into distinct traits, projects, and practical identities of various kinds. Once chosen, these different abilities-to-be can themselves be subjected to further (deliberative) comparison work as a result of competing exemplary instantiations of the norms internal to them. As a result of the normative tensions that can arise out of the plurality of one's exemplars, one can achieve some measure of critical distance from a particular role model and consequently work to decide which elements of that role model one wishes to emulate. In the final section of this chapter we will consider why such decisions should not be deemed arbitrary.

These critical comparison abilities are strengthened by the practices of reason-giving into which we are habituated as part of our intellectual development and which are constitutive of the public domain.[22] Because we can get better at this (deliberative) comparison work throughout our lives we can observe an enormous difference between stages of moral development: at the beginning one is committed to loving imitation of the whole person as a kind of unanalyzable unit, and hence the danger of going astray is very real. The capacity to isolate what is admirable and what is not depends on that loving relationship being interrupted or challenged by conflicts between competing exemplars and the creative comparison work that arises to resolve those conflicts. Despite the possibility of improvement and refinement in the execution of this critical comparative stance, the capacity itself is built into the third-person perspective: it is intrinsic to our ability to decouple from the immediacy of first- and second-person demands and consider their public context – to view each

---

[22] As Curren notes, 'if children are initiated into habitual practices of giving and taking reasons, including moral reasons, they will become both morally serious and committed critical thinkers, motivated by conceptions of themselves as both moral and devoted to the truth' (1999, 80).

of us as one among many. From such a perspective we are called not simply to imitate a particular loved one but to see those loved ones as modeling a range of different possibilities of being within a larger context of public possibilities – and to assess some as being better embodiments of those possibilities than others.

Though we might begin with an unarticulated yearning to be as the exemplar is, then, we can get better at isolating the abilities to be that more or less instantiate the inchoate vision of the good life that we are striving to accomplish. This capacity to grasp qualities and practical identities at some level of isolation from specific persons – and to compare and assess persons as potential role models in light of them – enables the agent to challenge or overcome earlier role models, establishing for herself in the process a more and more personalized vision of who she ought to be. The consequence is that we can achieve a kind of critical purchase on our role model relationships. We are not simply in loving thrall to our exemplars; through exposure to a plurality of competing models of the good life we are forced to engage in creative comparison work that involves endorsing some elements of some of our various role models and rejecting others.

This narrowing or qualification of the role played by specific exemplars is never sufficient to eradicate them from the moral landscape entirely, since no agent is ever in a position to have already experienced every possible complex situation. She must therefore look to the world for guidance on how best to answer the challenges that arise.[23] Our development toward excellence is never complete insofar as the task of living well in changing circumstances is never complete. When things become difficult we continue to question what kind of person we wish to be – looking to others to help us answer this. This is particularly the case insofar as we continue to need guidance throughout our lives not simply in terms of being the best friend, farmer, or film-enthusiast we might be – that is, meeting role-specific norms – but also in achieving the kind of tripartite normative balance across our lives that we saw was constitutive of flourishing. Each of us looks to role models both in terms of their exemplification of the particular abilities to be that we deem constitutive of the good life – especially insofar as these manifest the virtues – and in terms of the extent to which their lives as a whole display the normative balance that characterizes being in the world well. It is true that this will typically take the

---

[23] Garrels shows how Plato's dismissal of mimetic learning as a juvenile process that we eventually outgrow altogether had a huge influence on Western thought that is only now being overcome through the influence of empirical research that demonstrates otherwise (2006, 53).

form of emulating particular virtuous traits within the context of a specific ability to be – the patience of a teacher, say. But despite our increasing tendency to look to role models only for their excellent interpretations of this or that specific domain, we continue to need exemplars who model excellence in terms of the shape of lives as a whole – how to fit all of one's competing identities and obligations together into a normatively responsible unity.

Of course, one might object that at a certain point in moral development it becomes impossible to find relevant exemplars. But this helps explain the importance of the narrative arts in the developed agent's life, which portray possibilities of human excellence to which the average person might not otherwise be exposed.[24] It also explains why friendship with people of good character is so important for Aristotle: true friends are role models for adults, since they are excellent people living similar lives with whom we can identify.[25] By providing us with different perspectives on what good living looks like, friends can challenge the styles of being into which we have been habituated and help us become better versions of ourselves.

Invoking one's friends and favourite fictional characters as moral exemplars might seem problematic considering the moral reprobates that many of us count as friends. But for most people the process of moral development is not a smooth upward trajectory characterized by incrementally improving role models. On the contrary, role modeling is a complicated and messy mode of moral development, since agents typically look to a range of role models who sometimes embody vast disparities of excellence – both within and between the three normative domains. For example, one might look to one's friend Nancy, one's sister Heather, and to Jesus, Elizabeth Bennet, Hannah Arendt, and Gord Downie for conceptions of human excellence. The tensions among these competing exemplars must be negotiated and adapted to the specific conditions of one's own life through an ongoing process of (sometimes explicitly deliberative) comparison, as well as through trial and error and creative adaptations of all kinds. And this is not a process with a completion point or a single model of success, but a complicated experimental and creative

---

[24] See MacIntyre 1984 and Zagzebski 2006 on the importance of narrative in this regard. Narratives present the developed agent with increasingly complex problem cases that he himself has never directly encountered. As such, it prompts both exposure to highly context-specific role models and imaginative projection into morally challenging situations that may arise in the future.
[25] See Sherman 1999, 42, 46.

negotiation among competing self-conceptions – a negotiation that lasts for an agent's entire life.

This point allows us to respond to the question of whether role models should be ideal or realistic – paragons of virtue, or 'good enough,' average souls. On my account, the answer is both. Our visions of human excellence can and should be plural. Though paragons of virtue such as Mother Teresa remind us of what humanity is capable of, finding models in the ordinary folk who share our lives can often be both more motivating and more helpful, since they give us guidance even in circumstances in which a perfectly virtuous agent would never find herself.[26]

However, if we only look to those in our immediate environment for guidance, the creative tensions that can arise in the face of conflicting role models will be minimal – thereby limiting the degree to which our self-conception might be called into question. This worry is exacerbated when we realize that laws and other public institutions convey a community's general sense of what counts as a minimally decent life. Through these institutions the community binds itself to a certain shared vision of the basic requirements of flourishing, thereby providing a further constraint on who one will be able to experience as a role model. This fact returns us to the problem with which we opened the chapter: How it is possible to achieve critical purchase on the normative framework into which one has been habituated? We have seen how it is possible to achieve some critical distance from *particular* role models – through creative comparative tensions – but what if *all* our role models are corrupt? Addressing this worry requires us to consider the deepest and most comprehensive form of interruption to one's fluid engagement with the world – and the normative resources we have to deal with it.

Global Self-Questioning

So far we have seen that agents may be interrupted in the exercise of a particular skill or the expression of a particular practical identity, and when

---

[26] See Zagzebski 2013, 203: 'the important point here is that moral improvement may come in stages, and direct imitation of the exemplar may come only after a person has reached a certain level of moral development. Before that, the person does better at imitating persons who are better than he is, but not so much better that he cannot see clearly the path to becoming like the exemplar.' In *Human, All Too Human*, Nietzsche warns against choosing exemplars that are too far above us, since this can function as a strategy of evasion: 'our vanity, our self-love, promotes the cult of genius: for only if we think of him as being very remote from us, as a *miraculum*, does he not aggrieve us' (1996, §162, 86).

that happens negotiations and deliberations internal to that role allow us to determine how best to proceed in realizing that pursued skill or identity – without calling that pursuit itself into question. We also saw that fluid agency can be disrupted by conflicts that arise between role models, causing us to question which projects and pursuits are worthy of commitment, not simply how best to pursue them. But this intersubjective comparison solution to the worry about bad role models only seems to push the problem back to the level of communities, which may only provide sets of competing role models that are all flawed in the same ways.[27] Thus achieving fluid action by way of a critically deliberated unity between one's practices, practical identities, and role models might still be insufficient for addressing the worry of corrupted agency. The problem, then, is accounting for the critical purchase necessary to challenge conformity to cultural norms that are at odds with genuine human flourishing. Just because one has chosen among multiple bad role models – and displayed the critical distance from them necessary to do so – is no guarantee that one thereby escapes the corruption of bad role models. On the contrary, it may simply entrench it.

One solution to such relativist worries is to simply note that we are not typically limited to role models from our own political communities. Rather, we are regularly exposed to exemplars from other communities – both real and fictional – and this can again introduce creative tensions that call elements of our cultural framework into question. In other words, there can be a cultural analog to the experience of being exposed to a plurality of competing exemplars. Cultures do not occur in monolithic isolation – especially in the age of the internet.[28] Exposure to a plurality of cultures can trigger the need for critical comparison work and deliberation about the models of moral seeing to which one's culture is committed; other potential ways of organizing a culture can throw the normative obviousness of one's own culture into question.

But more importantly, we need to recognize that despite the publicity of the norms that govern the different styles of being to which we commit ourselves, each person's individual sense of being responsible for and at issue in these commitments means that they do not function as laws of nature that simply cause her to be this or that way. Rather, when we

---

[27] See Zagzebski 2006, 60–61. Jacobson 2005 raises the objection in terms of honour cultures, which characterize as virtuous what many outside those cultures believe is morally objectionable behaviour (394–395).

[28] See Benhabib 2002, ch. 2. As Aristotle noted: 'in our travels we can see how every human being is akin ... to a human being' (NE, 1155a20–22).

engage in a phenomenology of agency we recognize that from the perspective of the agent, there is always a kind of distance between her and the public norm to which she responds since its bindingness is contingent on her commitment to it. The fluid agency of everyday coping with the world – whereby things show up as appropriate or inappropriate – is itself grounded in the agent's commitment to the projects and roles in terms of which those affordances are meaningful: 'things can show up as serviceable or suitable (as opposed to simply being serviceable or suitable) only because I am trying to be something, only because some "possibility for being" (*Seinkönnen*; ability-to-be) is at issue for me' (Crowell 2017, 247).

This experience of oneself as at stake in what one does – as a care-driven trying to be in the world well by way of these public norms – means that one must always take a stance on how best to interpret those norms in the specificity of one's own life and in terms of what one understands to be at stake in them. We have already seen that this is necessary insofar as the guidance provided by public norms and one's role models can never be entirely definitive of what to do in any given circumstance. Practical intelligence is required to continually interpret and apply that guidance to one's life – a process that is not simply a mindless algorithm but a creative and experimental interpretation of what genuinely matters in those models of excellence:

> If such [public] norms were constitutive of [say] fatherhood, then in failing to live up to them, I could not be described as being a father badly, but only as not being a father at all. Phenomenologically, the norms that measure what [the agent] is trying to be are themselves at issue in that trying... My comportment, and not some accompanying mental process or intention, discloses what I take a 'good' father to be, and such comportment can bend the rules, even quite radically. To be a father is to exemplify an interpretation of what it means to be a father. As Heidegger began to say around 1928, in acting for the sake of being a father I stand as an exemplar (Vorbild) of what a father should be. Here, [one's] being seems to possess the modal character that Kant called 'exemplary necessity'. (Crowell 2017, 249)

Fluid norm-responsive action instantiates an agent's understanding of what is at stake in these norms; the way one creatively adapts one's norm-responsive action to the specific circumstances is a kind of testimony to how these ways of being ought to be understood. The relationship of the individual agent at stake in his endorsement of a particular identity to the norms governing it is necessarily one of creative uptake, whether this is explicitly recognized or not. Kierkegaard, Heidegger, and other existentialists have emphasized the many ways in which people are prone to avoid recognizing this fact, since doing so means refusing to accept their individual responsibility for determining who they will be. But these thinkers also emphasize that awareness of the freedom and responsibility underwriting our commitment to and creative appropriation of these public norms can be forced on us more directly in various kinds of breakdown experiences. We already saw localized forms of disruption and breakdown in which one's 'mindless' norm-responsive coping is challenged by anomalies or obstructions of various kinds, in response to which one must figure out how to get on with the project at hand. We also saw that more wide-reaching breakdowns can arise from conflict among role models – conflict that paralyzes fluid action and calls the agent to consider – either implicitly or explicitly – what exactly she values in the different possibilities of being embodied by those exemplars and hence how best to be who she is trying to be.

But we might also think of more radical forms of disruption to fluid action, in which all of the different possibilities of being among which to choose are called into question. Heidegger speaks of this kind of experience in terms of the concepts of existential anxiety and 'death' – in which the contingency and incompleteness of these ways of doing things are revealed as such. We will discuss the idea of existential death in greater detail in Chapter 9, when we consider the virtue of courage. For now it is sufficient to simply suggest that there are possible experiences in which the indeterminacy of our conventional ways of going about things is brought home to us and we come face to face with our individual responsibility for determining how to be in the world.

When faced with the awareness of this contingency and responsibility for interpreting what is at stake in the different practical identities our role models and cultures provide, we are not without critical normative resources in determining how to respond.[29] In other words, it is possible to achieve a kind of critical self-reflection about the fact of one's normative misalignment, even when the culture into which one has been habituated is itself corrupt. This is not to suggest that such radical questioning and transformation will be easy or frequent – but only that it is possible. To see this, we must return to the fundamentals of my account. Namely, to the claim that there are three normatively basic stances that provide us with reasons to be in certain ways rather than others. Though we learn from our neighbours and our culture how to interpret and apply the claims inherent

---

[29] Heidegger has been accused of this. For discussion of this 'decisionism' critique, see Burch 2010.

in those normative domains by way of public roles and identity possibilities, the stances themselves are foundational to being human and it is not possible to be habituated out of them altogether – no matter how bad one's role models. At least, not without having experienced a life of horrific abuse on a scale that would put one beyond the pale of moral discourse or development. Even if someone is entirely lacking in the virtues – the character capacities that allow one to respond well to the claims of the normative perspectives – that person would not thereby lack the perspectives themselves. She would still feel claimed by self, others, and the human community; she simply would not have the affective, cognitive, and behavioural skills necessary to respond well to those claims.

Certain existential conditions of norm-responsiveness make us the kind of beings that we are, conditions that are missed if we start with an anormative account of human nature and attempt to build them in after the fact. To be human is to see the world in terms of three classes of normative claim, and this circumscribes what can count as a good human life. Because of the normatively basic status of these stances, there is a feeling of fit that comes with successful expressions of the three perspectives; they can provide feedback on what ought to count as individual or cultural representations of human excellence.[30] Indeed, this is a fact that we have seen operative throughout the various manifestations of agency and its breakdowns: in cases of fluid action one is guided in one's creative uptake of public models by an individual sense of what is best about them. Similarly, when faced with competition among role models the individual is guided by her sense – however inchoate – of which elements of each role model represent lives worthy of emulation. In such cases this inchoate sense of what is best is ultimately rooted, I contend, in the three normative perspectives that govern our sense of how to be in the world well. So too in the case of more global or radical breakdowns in one's sense of certainty about what is best to do or be: in such cases one is called on to evaluate the different possibilities of being for one's life as a whole in light of a deep sense of being answerable to self, other, and the human community. There is a kind of minimalist normative responsiveness constitutive of human agency as such. We experience ourselves as claimed by the conditions that allow us to be selves in the world at all, and we deliberate alone and with others about what those conditions imply about how we should be. In doing so we appeal to the implicit sense of self-world fit that has been shaping our creative application of particular conventional

[30] See Friedman 1986, 30–31.

norms and our critical responsivity to competing role models throughout.[31]

It is clear that cultures can indeed train us into distorted ways of expressing these three normative perspectives – for example, the way that racism violates the second-person stance through first-person fear and selfishness coupled with a third-person narrative of the legitimacy of those orientations. But the fundamental status of the normative perspectives themselves means that it is possible to appeal to such agents on charges of inconsistency, pointing out that their endorsement of certain destructive interpretations of the perspectives is at odds with the basic nature of their normative claims. We can criticize such agents as failing to respect in their specific practices the general normative orientations that they themselves acknowledge on some level. And though such criticisms are generally insufficient for undoing the destructive forms of seeing into which those agents have been habituated, they can nevertheless prompt some people to recognize why they might have reason to pursue new forms of habituation, new avenues to the good – and to deliberate about how best to do so. Further, if I am right about the irreducibility of the normative perspectives, a person habituated into a fully vicious culture would be deeply unhappy; he would in no way be leading a flourishing life since he would feel claimed by the normative obligations built into the perspectives but would not have the tools necessary to respond to them well. In such a situation of

---

[31] We might view Korsgaard's deliberative account in light of normative perspectives constitutive of agency that are not themselves available to deliberative assessment but rather a condition of its possibility. The efficacy and autonomy conditions on agency that she specifies – coupled with the universalizability constraint on the publicity of reasons – can perhaps be understood to designate the constitutive roles that the norms of self-becoming, other-recognition, and shared world-building play in the possibility of being a self in the world – though my account understands these constitutive normative stances somewhat differently and Korsgaard herself tends to collapse what I am calling the second- and third-person perspectives into a single normative condition on agency. In Crowell's Heideggerian approach, we also see him arguing that one's foundational commitment to a certain interpretation of how best to be in the world involves 'a claim to validity that is addressed to others to whom I am, therefore, answerable' (2017, 250) – and that such answerability demands procedures of justification and reason-giving. But as Crowell points out, these procedures are not able to simply demonstrate their truth at this fundamental level since there are no higher shared norms to which agents can appeal in determining how we ought to be. Rather, all we ultimately have in conditions of radical breakdown are (1) certain formal norms governing the space of reason-giving into which third-order deliberations place us and (2) Kantian-style universalizability requirements according to which there is an unlimited horizon of others to whom we are answerable (2013, ch. 10 and 2017, 251). Unlike Korsgaard, however, Crowell makes more room for second-person recognition, according to which each of us is called to 'let the *other's reasons matter*' (2017, 253). McMullin 2013 makes an extended argument for the necessity of this kind of second-person recognition in Heidegger's philosophy. See Vasiliou 1996, 781–782. Drummond 2002 and 2016 provide Husserlian resources for thinking on these issues.

radical existential homelessness – in which one cannot achieve a sense of self-world fit because one's entire normative framework is deranged – the only recourse is to question the entire shape of one's life and world to discover the transformations necessary to make feeling at home in the world possible.[32]

This discussion should remind us of debates regarding whether *phronēsis* can be understood not only as a capacity to choose the appropriate means for realizing a particular end but also as a capacity for deliberating about good ends themselves. Some argue that it cannot, suggesting that since Aristotle claims that *phronēsis* is concerned only with 'particulars', it can only be focused on making decisions about particular actions and therefore cannot be involved in choosing which ends to adopt (Sherman 1989, 87). But as we have seen, there are different kinds of disruption to fluid action and the scope of questionability to which that disruption gives rise. When we question how best to realize a specific end, that end must be fixed in order for the relevant decision-making to function. But when those ends have themselves been called into question, different forms of critical questioning and deliberation can arise in which we compare competing interpretations of what human excellence should be like, at both the individual and the cultural level.[33] The possibility of those deeper forms of critical self-questioning is underwritten by every agent's sense that she is always at stake in her choices in a way that can never be completely elided by the normativity of the role models and the culture that have shaped her way of seeing the world. Rather, that sense of being at stake is always answerable to the three normative perspectives that are constitutive of the possibility of being in the world as we know it.

Concluding Thoughts

For many of us, most of the time, we typically know what to do in order to live well: strive for good work, good friendships, and good citizenship in the human community. The lives into which we have been habituated provide us with a set of worldly norms in terms of which to assess our success in doing so and – if we're lucky – we have been habituated into seeing and desiring the world in terms of the possibilities of excellence they afford. In such cases we respond to these norms in a fluid and

---

[32] Tessman 2005 provides an important discussion of the extent to which we are able to achieve virtue in conditions where flourishing is impossible or radically compromised.

[33] See Burch 2010, 214–215 and Russell 2009, 10.

undeliberated way, taking up the possible ways of being they provide and tailoring them to our lives and circumstances. But the fluidity of this practice should not be taken to exclude an abiding background sensitivity to the fact that who I will be is always at stake in my actions and that the world shows me more than one way to answer that question – a plurality of good actions, good projects, and good lives that can in some cases prompt me to radically rethink the kind of person I have become or wish to be. Even when things are proceeding smoothly, however, the agent implicitly acknowledges the possibility of getting things wrong, of questioning the norm, of pursuing different ways to be. This awareness need not show up in terms of an experienced inability to decide between compelling alternative possibilities but is typically operative in the agent's sense that she is at stake in her choices – that they have weight – and that she cares about living up to the way that they matter in her life. This orientation toward success and failure is constantly present as such on a pre-theoretical level – as is evident in the fact that the agent experiences ambiguous or mutually incompatible experiences as unacceptable, as problems that need a resolution.[34] Even when I am 'in the moment' – engaged in the moral perception of *phronēsis*, which simply 'sees' what is to be done – I am implicitly aware of myself as faced with the possibility of things being other than they currently appear to be. This awareness of being in the grip of possibility – which is at the heart of the human experience – only sometimes rises to the level of explicit consciousness or deliberative weighing but rather typically appears to me primarily as a sense of caring about what I do and striving to do it well. Because of the complexity and indeterminacy of the normative terrain in which that striving takes place, there is always the possibility of conflicts and breakdowns that provoke the need to think more explicitly about what one is trying to do and who one is trying to be. When we do so in radical fashion, we come face to face both with the conditions governing what it is to be a person in the world and with the other people with whom we must interpret how those conditions ought to shape our lives.

[34] See Haugeland 2013.

CHAPTER 7

Patience

> Patience, n. A minor form of despair, disguised as a virtue.
> – Ambrose Bierce, 1906

Like the other virtues, patience is directed toward overcoming a particular challenge to human excellence that is built into the human condition. In the case of patience, the immutable existential problem that it addresses is temporal finitude. Patience, I will argue, is our best hope for living a flourishing life in the face of a temporal limitedness that we can never escape.

There are two aspects to the manifestation of this temporal finitude in human life. The first is what I will call the dispersion problem: namely, we are dispersed across time and as a result we cannot be who we wish to be immediately or definitively. Indeed, the more identity-defining the pursuit is, the less capable it is of being quickly or completely realized at a particular point in time. This fact can prompt attitudes of impatience in which the overarching sense is that *things are taking too long*. On the other hand, temporal finitude also afflicts human life in terms of what I will call the scarcity problem: namely, every option we choose uses up the limited quantity of time allocated to us, so we must ration this limited resource. In this sense, impatience can manifest as the sense that *time is running out*. Clearly these are related: we typically feel that time is running out because things are taking too long. In what follows we will discuss these different aspects of the problem of temporal finitude and how patience helps us to live well in spite of this existential condition.

Enabling Agency

An example will help us better understand patience. My daughter is learning to read. The shapes on the page that leap immediately into significance for me are for her shifting, uncertain – offering up their meaning only through strenuous effort. She is exhausted by the work of it and as she tires, the pauses grow longer; she increasingly relies on guesswork despite a dogged refusal to surrender the task entirely. Patience demands that I resist my urge to intervene, to give her the word that comes so easily for me. It also demands gentleness, ruling out the urge to rush her along, to punish her for her inability – an urge that typically arises from my frustrated desire to do other things. Its overall pattern is one of self-restraint aimed at enabling the other person to accomplish what she is struggling to accomplish. It is an ability to sustain a calm commitment to the task at hand in a demanding situation that is at odds with one's immediate inclinations and desires.[1] It involves stepping back to allow the other person time to be what she is trying to be, despite the fact that this will prevent one from allocating that time to pursuing other possibilities.

A key aspect of patience is that I do not intervene in this striving and make it my own – even if the other person herself wishes that I would. Rather, I offer her my attentive but restrained presence as a kind of witness to her struggle.[2] Such attentive restraint involves a certain shared orientation toward realizing some possibility, then, but essential to this is the fact that it is the *other* person who realizes the goal, not simply *that* it is achieved. Though I want the book to be read, I want it to be read *by my daughter*. I fundamentally alter or qualify this desire such that it is genuinely satisfied only if the *other* person is the one who has brought it about.

This unique mode of attentive and supportive restraint is characteristic of patience and differentiates it from simple endurance. The latter also involves self-restraint but is accomplished primarily through a type of disengagement. When I endure someone I do not share the drama and meaning of his struggle – rather, I disengage so as not to interfere with it. Though the difference may be virtually indistinguishable from outside the relationship in question – in both cases there is a lack of intervention – the recipient of patience will not find it so. One can sense whether the other person is silently sharing an orientation to the task and a recognition of its purpose and difficulties, or if he is merely enduring the events, unmoved

---

[1] As Matthew Pianalto puts it, patience is the ability to bear adversity and thus not simply a form of waiting; rather, it involves notions of endurance, forbearance, and perseverance (2016b, 146). See also Pianalto 2016a. I am indebted to Matthew for sharing the book with me in an early form.

[2] Heidegger's contrast between 'leaping in' and 'leaping ahead' is relevant here: the former 'take[s] away "care" from the Other' – 'care' being understood here as each individual's striving to succeed at being who he is – while the latter 'helps the Other to become transparent to himself *in* his care and to become *free for* it' (1985, 158, 159).

by the intention being expressed in them or the agency that is being accomplished through that expression. Patience involves a deeper form of second-person recognition and accommodation of the other person's struggle to act in the world. Thus in patience we see a stance toward the other person that takes the expression of that other person's agency as more important than the particular goal itself – despite the struggle this will involve on her part and the restraint it will involve on mine.

Time Is Running Out

Patience bears an essential connection to temporality; it is the way we successfully cope with the existential fact that our lives play out in conditions of temporal scarcity.[3] The mantra of the impatient person is 'Hurry up! We are running out of time!' while the patient person, in contrast, says, 'Take your time'.[4] Impatient people experience time as a scarce commodity that must be rationed. Time shows up as such insofar as one is focused on alternative possibilities that are being foreclosed because time is being used as it is. Focusing on unrealized possibilities causes the possibility that *is* being realized to appear as an annoying drain on the limited time that is available. This experience of temporal scarcity is a function of the agent's focus on the other activities that are being ruled out by making use of time that way. In the case of my daughter's reading practice, the reading is experienced as a slow and burdensome drain on my patience insofar as I am thinking of the need to get the supper started or wanting to read my own novel instead.[5]

Note that the impatient person need not reject the value of the particular project being pursued per se; belief in its illegitimacy is not essential for

---

[3] The belief that patience bears an essential relationship to time is the norm, at least in the West: Kupfer 2007 describes patience as 'anger in the modality of time' (279). See also MacIntyre 1984, 202, and Rudd 2008, 491. Hurka 2001 is an exception here, since he references both the temporal interpretation of patience as waiting and a more atemporal understanding of patience as calm endurance of hardship (110). We will consider challenges to the temporal reading in later sections of this chapter.

[4] The idea of 'giving the other her time' is reminiscent of Heidegger's definition of justice in his reflections on the Anaximander fragment. On Heidegger's translation, the fragment reads: 'Whence things have their coming into being there they must also perish according to necessity; for they must pay a penalty and be judged for their injustice, according to the ordinance of time' (2002, 242). He takes this to indicate a deep relationship between temporality and justice, arguing that the root of all injustice is the attempt to maintain oneself in a type of constant presence, the grasping refusal to acknowledge that time is shared with others.

[5] As we will see, impatience can also arise because one is making use of an unrealistic standard when assessing how long things ought to take.

experiencing impatience. Rather, one must simply believe that the project is taking too long insofar as its use of scarce temporal resources rules out pursuing other valued projects. I can simultaneously recognize the value of my daughter learning to read and be annoyed at how long the practice involved in doing so takes. The extent of one's desire for realizing another possibility or one's anxiety about the consequences of neglecting those other possibilities can be a good predictor of impatience.

Of course, there will be cases where calm, restrained waiting aimed at enabling the other person to pursue his tasks may not in fact be virtuous but rather a kind of complacent obliviousness to what is at stake in how we allocate the limited time we have. We see the structure of the Aristotelian mean at work in this virtue: to be patient one must understand when self-restraint aimed at facilitating certain projects or preferences is demanded and when it is not. In patience the mean lies closer to self-restraint than self-assertion, since there is a human tendency to believe that one's own possibilities – and thus the time to be allocated to realizing them – are more important than those of others, especially in conditions of scarcity of the kind to which our temporal finitude condemns us. The patient person says, 'Take your time' – the words implicitly indicating recognition that time is not mine alone, that we must share our striving in a world where there is never enough time.[6]

Impatience, on the contrary, often arises out of an arrogant belief in the privileged status of the self. The impatient person judges people in terms of their ability to get out of the way to better enable him to pursue his own ends. He grants his preferences a default legitimacy and insists that time be allocated to him by interrupting and taking over or lashing out in impatient displays of anger and contempt.[7] Such a person believes that his projects and preferences always ought to take precedence over others, prompting an imbalance in the understanding of how to share the limited time that the world affords us for our striving.[8] Because the existential condition in which we live is one of temporal scarcity, this scarcity can exacerbate human tendencies to unduly prioritize first-person claims. In patience, one adopts a specifically other-directed stance that tempers the expression of these immediate first-person desires. Patience helps us to

---

[6] Lévinas characterizes patience as a condition in which 'the egoism of the will stands on the verge of an existence that no longer accents itself' (2007, 239).
[7] For discussion of the role anger plays in patience, see Pianalto 2014, 95 and Pianalto 2016a, especially ch. 5.
[8] Kupfer 2007, 275–276.

achieve normative balance then, despite the pressure that temporal finitude places on our ability to respond well to claims on our time.

Patience is not only an other-directed stance, however. Self-directed patience is clearly necessary if we are to accomplish challenging tasks requiring perseverance over time. Both kinds of patience involve overcoming one's immediate desire to end whatever suffering is associated with spending limited temporal resources on self-restrained persistence in the service of an activity whose rewards in the short term are limited. In the case of other-directed patience, this involves prioritizing the other person's possibilities over the immediate relief from frustration that impatiently seizing that time for oneself would provide. *Self*-directed patience similarly involves overcoming one's immediate desire to end the suffering associated with calm perseverance. But in this case, it involves prioritizing the successful expression of one's *own* agency, committing to the judgment that pursuing long-term goals is a better use of one's time than indulging in the immediate relief of giving up. It sacrifices immediate gratification in favour of nurturing one's longer-term identity-constitutive projects.[9]

In such self-directed patience we can see particularly clearly how the temporally extended nature of agency – the dispersal problem – shows up as an existential problem that threatens flourishing. Our projects can only rarely be immediately or definitively realized but must be sustained over time – typically in the face of countervailing desires to seek more immediate rewards instead. Patience helps us to solve this problem by taking a long view of human agency, accepting that we are dispersed across time in an ongoing and open-ended striving to be who we are. It requires committing the time to following through on unappealing tasks that are constitutive of the identity that is at stake in those tasks – or enabling the other person to follow through by unbegrudgingly giving her the time to do so.

Tolerant Patience for Strangers

So far the discussion of patience has been focused on those we know. But we must consider whether one can also display patience toward strangers. Am I always merely tolerating them insofar as I am not personally invested in their projects of self-becoming? When waiting in line at the bank it seems unlikely that the other person's developing competence with ATMs

---

[9] Psychological studies indicate that we are disposed to prefer immediate gratification over long-term reward, a tendency known as temporal discounting.

is the object of my patient orientation. Though such cases will often involve simple endurance, the attentive restraint that can be demonstrated in such isolated encounters with strangers can also be instances of patience insofar as one is concerned for the other person's *successful* completion of her goal or realization of her preference. In mere endurance the success of the other person's activities is a matter of indifference – I am simply waiting for their completion, regardless of their outcome. In patience, on the contrary, I encourage the other person to take the time necessary for its successful completion. As in the case of loving patience for a cherished child, then, patience for a stranger involves an endorsement of the value of realizing the goal or satisfying the preference – not simply as such, but insofar as it is enacted *by* the particular person toward whom patience is being displayed. Both involve a willingness to grant the other person's striving time to fulfill its end by restraining one's urge to use that limited time for one's own pursuits.

The key distinction to be found in the case of the stranger, however, lies in the nature of the endorsement of the other's agency that is operative. In the case of my daughter, loving respect for the child's developing personhood is itself what motivates me. My support is rooted in respect for the role that the successful pursuit of a goal or fulfillment of a preference is playing in this *particular* person's life. Such patience is grounded in personal knowledge of and concern for a specific person, a desire that this person as an individual will thrive. While such an orientation to the striving of the agent in her particularity is clearest in love for close friends and family, it can encompass a variety of relationships in which our care for the other person is rooted in second-person recognition of that person as an individual.

There can be a range of ways in which this kind of love for the individual can intersect with support for her projects. On the one hand, I might want the loved one to have the opportunity to express her agency in general and might be indifferent to the goal itself – or unable to recognize why it could be central to the identity of the beloved. Alternatively, one can recognize and value not only *that* this goal is central to the loved one's overarching project of self-becoming, but also *why* it would be so. In such a case, you value her ends for independent reasons, not simply because they are important to her as a beloved friend. We might call these instrumental versus intrinsically valued projects, respectively. Loving patience, when coupled with intrinsically valued projects, is the least difficult form of patience to practice. If you both love the person and value the activity she is striving to perform or enjoy, it becomes easier to step back and allow that person the time to pursue it. In some instances, this kind of stance might also overlap with the virtue of generosity. If the valued goal is shared by both people – and this valuing occurs in conditions of scarcity – the virtuous agent may be required to share not only the temporal arena in which to strive for those valued ends, but also the valued ends themselves.

But what of the stranger, for whom I feel no such love? In tolerant patience for strangers, one exercises self-restraint such that the other person's agency is enabled out of respect for what that non-interference represents. In other words, one takes as one's object not the well-being or projects of this person qua individual; rather, one refrains from interfering because one values the project of ensuring that the agency of all members of the community is accommodated. The objective of tolerant patience, in other words, is not nurturing any particular person's agency, but doing what is necessary to provide the shared public arena required for human agency in general to flourish.[10] Since a certain degree of autonomous choice and preference satisfaction is deemed essential for such flourishing – and these pursuits take time – each of us has reason not to interfere but rather to give each person time to pursue her projects. Insofar as I act patiently toward stranger X, I do so because I see in her a representative member of the community to which I belong and in which we all pursue our time-consuming striving.

Characteristic of this stance, then, is an interpretation of all other agents in terms of their status *as* members of the community. One sees others not simply in terms of the radical particularity of persons acknowledged in the second-person stance, but rather through a third-person perspective whereby others show up in terms of their 'humanity', 'citizenship', or 'rational personhood' – general categories applied to all, indicating a response to them as participants in a community of peers.[11] The accommodation of the other person's projects displayed in this third-personal

---

[10] Cohen 2004 explains tolerance: 'We must *value* our noninterference for it to count ... the noninterference must be properly principled' (73, emphasis added). According to Cohen, one can adopt a principled stance of non-interference either out of respect for the other person or because one values toleration itself (81) – a distinction that in some sense tracks my loving patience/tolerant patience distinction. A similar point is evident in Raphael 1988, 139.

[11] This point reveals the basis of a criticism leveled against Kantian ethics, namely, the worry that I am not really respecting *this person*, but rather a kind of anonymous bearer of the status 'rational'. Those who object to the anonymity of this stance are essentially objecting to the claim that this kind of third-personal orientation is not only necessary but *sufficient* for ethical life. On this point I am of course in complete agreement, since I distinguish the second- from the third-person modes of normative claim and view responding to both as constitutive of moral life and irreducible to each other.

mode of tolerant patience is an acknowledgment of membership in and facilitation of the intersubjective community as such.

Here again we can see the distinction between intrinsically and instrumentally valued projects. In the former case, it is easier for me to be patient with a stranger who is slow at sorting his recycling or helping his child, since those are projects I independently view as valuable. Indeed, in such cases we can often develop overlapping orientations of second-person (loving) patience and third-person (tolerant) patience, since the other person's commitment to things I value may prompt me to see him not merely as an anonymous member of the community but as a unique individual struggling to be himself. Tolerant patience for strangers becomes much more difficult, however, if the other person is engaged in a project that I deem unintelligible, unworthy of pursuit, or inconsistent with human dignity.[12] Indeed, in some such cases patience is not necessarily the appropriate stance to adopt. Rather, one ought to strive to help the other person see the error of his ways. This is exceptionally difficult moral terrain, however, since in most cases we are called on to adopt a stance of tolerant patience whereby we give the other person the time necessary to pursue a project or preference whose value we do not necessarily share. We grant the other person time to pursue his chosen ends despite our disapproval – a stance grounded in our commitment to the value of a community of autonomous agents able to express their agency as they see fit. Tolerant patience involves respect for the other agent's ability to decide for himself the relationship between the particular project and the task of self-becoming. Recognizing when to tolerate and when to resist a project or preference that one deems unworthy of choice will demand the utmost in practical wisdom.

Thus patience has first-person, second-person, and third-person dimensions to its expression. Despite the centrality of second-person heedfulness to the meaning of patience, then, it is important to note that this other-directedness is not without limit. Responding to the other person's struggle cannot come at undue cost to oneself: one must 'take time' for oneself. The agent who entirely eradicates her own desires and projects in the interest of the other person is not displaying patience or the perspectival harmony characteristic of a flourishing self, but rather self-abnegation.[13] As Nicholas Bommarito puts it: 'patience as weak servility is no

---

[12] See Williams 1996.
[13] This raises interesting questions about the role that acknowledgment and gratitude can play in alleviating normative imbalance. Must the recipient of patience be aware – or be made aware – that

patience at all' (2014, 277).[14] In the same way, the agent who always places the desires and projects of this or that individual person ahead of the community also fails to display the appropriately integrated stance. The demands that arise from the third-person perspective must also serve as a constraint on those of the first- and second-person. One's initial self-restraint can at a certain point shift from virtuous patience to a kind of obstructionism. If I insist on an individual's right to dither endlessly at the ATM despite the line of other claimants forming behind us – I can also fail to display the perspectival harmony required for flourishing.

The Temporal Orientation of Patience

In all three cases, then, we have seen that patience requires what can be called the 'long view' – i.e. seeing a particular project or preference in light of what it means for realizing human agency and the community structures that enable its fullest expression. Patience involves understanding the worth of the current use of time in light of its value to the person or the shared world more generally. The particular project or preference is seen not in isolation but rather as an expression of who that person is trying to be in and through the specific acts.

As it is typically understood, this stance has a fundamentally futural valence. In other words, patience is taken to be intrinsically related to temporality because of its emphasis on enabling future consequences – allocating one's time in the present on the basis of one's understanding of how that will affect the future. Thus common conceptions of patience typically view it as a character trait that helps agents reach whatever teleologically ordered ends they happen to have chosen, good or bad.[15]

---

the time he is taking is therefore not available to me for *my* projects? How can this be highlighted without it being an expression of resentment that undermines the experience of patience for the recipient? There are often institutional/cultural modes of recognition in place – e.g. Mother's Day, Nurse's Day, etc. – that allow the prioritization of second-person claims over first-person claims constitutive of certain roles to be recognized as such without thereby unduly reversing the priority.

[14] 'Where arrogance is naturally conducive to impatience, lack of self-respect fosters over-waiting. The person who views herself as less worthwhile than other people, sees no reason why her interests should command their attention with either alacrity or efficiency' (Kupfer 2007, 276).

[15] 'The concept of patience describes a person's ability to make prolonged efforts towards future goals, and his or her ability to consider long-term future consequences' (Skog 2001, 207). 'Patience is valuable not for supplying us with goals, but for assisting us in achieving goals. This can be seen in the fact that patience, as with perseverance and resourcefulness, can be instrumental in attaining wicked ends as well' (Kupfer 2007, 277). Adams 2006 and Slote 1992 similarly view patience as a non-moral or only derivatively moral character trait. In contrast, I argue that in patience, the future consequences motivating the agent are those relevant to the three central normative domains constitutive of *eudaimonia* – first-, second-, and third-person claims. Patience embodies a

To be patient, it seems, involves seeing the value of future consequences and being motivated by them in the present.[16] The patient person views the present in terms of future possibilities to be realized through the exercise of self-restraint. She acts now for the sake of something to be realized later rather than for the sake of the more immediately compelling present possibility.

It is for this reason that some thinkers have emphasized patience as essential to having and maintaining a personal identity that persists through time. Patience seems essential to being a unified self that sustains long-term identities – choosing to act now for the sake of the identities constituted by such choices rather than dissolving into a wanton jumble of non-integrated immediate gratifications.[17] Having and maintaining a coherent identity requires that one live in light of who one is striving to be, not simply now but into the future – as opposed to living each moment as unrelated to the next, allowing the immediacy of present frustrations to deter the realization of long-term plans. Thus patience appears to bear an intrinsic relationship to time insofar as it is oriented toward it as a scarce resource that must be allocated well in the long-term projects of self-becoming.

Some have argued that such a temporal interpretation of patience is false, however, rejecting the idea that understanding an agent as a whole – and the way constituent elements contribute to that wholeness – involves any special orientation toward time, particularly toward the future. Indeed, some approaches question the very idea of a self that develops in time at all.

The 'Buddhist' Objection

In his Buddhism-inspired interpretation of patience, Nicolas Bommarito argues that patience makes no reference to either temporality *or* the

---

commitment to balanced responsiveness to these claims in the face of the particular challenge that temporal scarcity poses to realizing this end. As such, it cannot be characterized as a morally neutral skill that can be applied equally to good or evil pursuits. These instrumental and popular characterizations of patience are simply being invoked to highlight how patience involves an essential relationship to the future.

[16] Hurka 2001 notes that this 'temporally impartial division of concern' is sometimes known as *prudence* rather than patience (110). But in patience the agent in some sense *suffers* for her commitment to the future, whereas this is not necessarily the case in prudence.

[17] Rudd 2008 takes up this issue in terms of Kierkegaard's discussions of patience. As Rudd puts it: 'the soul has to be gained in a constant struggle against our tendency to lose it by abandoning our real *telos* for an absolute attachment to merely relative goods' (501). We will discuss Rudd's account in greater detail later.

concept of personal-identity building, since the latter is at odds with Buddhist teaching about the illusory nature of selfhood and the former is not essential to understanding patience.[18] To support this latter claim, he suggests that one can imagine a case in which a person:

> is in a hospital being treated for short-term memory loss. At any moment, she cannot remember anything before a few minutes ago. Again, someone insults her and she responds calmly and graciously. We can rightly praise her patience, even though she does not consciously endure insults for any more than a few minutes – she is patient because of how she reacts in the moment. (2014, 271)

The suggestion here is that patience does not require an agent to have an experience of enduring something for any period of time; her behaviour requires no orientation toward past or future in order for it to count as patience. Patience is not about valuing the long-term over the short-term but about bearing suffering with equanimity and grace, even if only for an instant.

Similarly, Bommarito suggests that one can imagine parents displaying the virtue of patience in their care for a special-needs child without requiring any reference to future possibilities that will be realized by that care. Patience is on display even though they are

> quite certain that there is no possibility of improved functioning or better behaviour. In this case, a person who is patient with the child is not waiting for improvement; they don't expect any improvement to come. They are patient because of how they deal with frustrations in the moment, failing to get angry at a cause of suffering. (2014, 271)

Such cases, he suggests, provide evidence for rejecting the understanding of patience as a stance in which one acts now for the sake of realizing future possibilities. Rather, the people in his examples are focused only on frustrations in the moment, and their immediate ability to avoid anger in the face of those frustrations is a marker of their patience.

But it is not clear that Bommarito's examples succeed in undermining our sense that this virtue is a response to the finite nature of human temporality. Indeed, in the first instance, we might question whether this is a virtue at all. Perhaps the woman's kindness in the face of abuse is in fact evidence of a lack of self-respect. Further, her behaviour could be understood as a habitual residue of a lifetime of genuine patience; i.e.

---

[18] The following discussion brackets the question of whether Bommarito's account is indeed Buddhist and only looks at his account as such.

patient response patterns are part of her character but diminished brain functioning prevents that virtue from manifesting now in its complete form – which involves coping with temporal scarcity in light of the valued future. Thus we might be tempted to deny that this is anything more than a kind of residue of virtue.

Viewing this case as a genuinely virtuous response to human temporal finitude – despite the loss of memory afflicting the agent – requires us to get clear on how temporality is functioning in this example. Bommarito argues that this agent would need to have an experience of herself as enduring the insults for an extended period if her patience were to bear a necessary connection to temporality. But it is not clear that this is true. After all, we could describe her calm endurance of momentary insult in terms of her ongoing project of identity-building and maintenance; i.e. she sees in every particular, isolated episode of abuse a way in which to realize her conception of who she is trying to be and she submits to temporary suffering in the service of that overarching self-conception. She does not need to be able to recall multiple specific episodes of abuse in order to have a sense of herself as committed to the unfolding project of being a certain kind of person. On this account, each discrete instance of abuse – whether remembered in episodic memory or not – is treated as an opportunity to practice her benevolence or forgiveness, and in so doing she is patiently committing herself to developing or maintaining a certain ongoing way of being in the world. A particular self-understanding or way of relating to the world is being enacted and maintained into the future.

The agent need not remember the details of any specific abuse to maintain her commitment to being the kind of person who responds to others with tolerance or kindness. And such commitment need not itself be the result of a specific decision that she might remember – or fail to remember – making. Rather, it is a way of valuing different possibilities of being and ongoingly experiencing oneself as tasked with that purpose. But it is not at all obvious that this kind of 'memory' – i.e. one's commitment to striving to be a certain way in the world – is comparable to the kind of episodic memory that Bommarito's example invokes. Rather, her patient response to that specific event is the way that she acts for the sake of her broader unfolding of identity in time, and commitment to that project does not rely on remembering specific episodic events that may have challenged or triggered that commitment.

Of course, we can imagine cases where the agent has lost all sense of herself *as* committed to being a particular kind of person – all sense of herself as caring about kindness or forgiveness as a possibility to be realized or maintained. But in such cases it is again hard to argue that the behaviour in question could count as genuine patience.

Does Bommarito's other example of patience – the special needs case – succeed in showing that patience bears no intrinsic reference to the temporal domain? Contrary to Bommarito's interpretation, I believe that in such instances patient carers are recognizing particular acts by the special needs child – e.g. feeding herself – as action that embodies the child's understanding of who she is trying to be. And this is the case even if the child never improves on those tasks or builds on them to engage in more complicated ones. The patient parents in this case are giving the child the time to express her own sense of who she is, calmly accepting the time-consuming frustrations of doing so out of respect for that self-expressive striving. They do this despite the fact that the actions will never come to a more complex or productive fruition in the same way that they might with other children. The child's behaviour is nevertheless understood by the patient person as realizing possibilities of agency, regardless of whether those behaviours will build toward a progress that could be recognized as such from the outside. The child's projects are understood already to embody who she wishes to be.

Further, by granting the child time to pursue those preferences, patient carers embody their commitment to being loving parents, occupying and maintaining that more global, long-term project by way of the specific choices that embody it. They understand the immediate frustrations of being patient in light of the long-term good of being in a loving relationship with a person who feels supported in her choices.

Of course, one might object that acting for the sake of the whole – i.e. seeing specific activities through the lens of realizing or maintaining a broader sense of identity – is not necessarily a *temporal* stance. After all, every agent is in some sense a whole now; has an identity now – she will not suddenly transition into having one at some future date. So why should the particular acts constitutive of one's identities be understood as temporally related to the *future*?

As we have seen, the temporally dispersed character of human life is such that *who* one is – kind to strangers, loving toward the disabled, dedicated parent, etc. – is never determined once and for all but only manifests itself as a commitment over time to patterns of being that express those ways of valuing. Such commitment over time requires understanding one's place in the world in terms of possibilities to take up or leave aside – possibilities that more or less embody the striven-for way of being. Though our identities and projects rarely have a distinct beginning, middle, and end, we understand ourselves in terms of the possibility of maintaining and building them into the future – or of letting them die.[19] It is for this reason that we experience ourselves as being *at stake* in what we choose to do. To conceptualize agents in terms of a temporally dispersed process of constant self-becoming via possibilities taken up or abandoned is to recognize that selfhood is characterized by a kind of restless forward movement into the future, an experienced incompletion that we feel ourselves tasked with working to resolve, no matter how illusory the promise of any ultimate resolution turns out to be. Thus even when I am 'in the moment' I experience myself faced with the possibility of doing something other than what I am now doing – a possibility that is weighted both with who I have been and who I wish to be.

Indeed, we can see then how the two tenets of Buddhist thinking in Bommarito's account work together: rejecting any essential link between patience and temporality requires a commitment to the metaphysical claim that there is no such thing as a self that persists across time. Only by denying that there is anything like a temporally constant personal identity can one conceptualize patience as bearing no reference to the realization of future possibilities. Instead, all 'one' is an illusory bundle of time slices, not a self at all.[20] But such a view – which asks us to consider lived moments in abstraction from the experienced sense of being at stake for oneself in how one takes up one's possibilities – and indeed, asks us to view the latter as a destructive fiction – conflicts with first-person experience as it is typically lived. Though it might be *possible* to adopt that view, it is not obvious that doing so is compatible with living lives of human flourishing, since it asks us to renounce the ordinary forms of human consciousness that characterize our everyday lives. As Schechtman puts it:

> Let us grant the possibility of this kind of self-conception for the sake of argument and ask about the individual who achieves it – an individual whose sentience is focused always in the present and never extends – either cognitively or affectively – to the past or future. It should be immediately obvious that individuals who arrange their experience in this way lead lives

---

[19] Such a view is found in Heidegger's account of the self as always acting for the sake of who it is trying to be, and his claim that this orientation to oneself in terms of possibilities is the primordial meaning of the future (1985, 373).

[20] It is beyond the scope of this chapter to fully consider Buddhist views on this issue. As I will argue below, however, at the very least they appear to involve metaphysical commitments at odds with a phenomenological approach aimed at describing lived experience. For a related identity-challenging view, see Parfit 1984: 'Nagel once claimed that it is psychologically impossible to believe the Reductionist View [of the self]. Buddha claimed that, though this is very hard, it is possible. I find Buddha's claim to be true' (280).

exceedingly different from our own. Such individuals do not make plans, engage in long-term commitments, or take responsibility for the past; their subjectivity and their actions are quite different from our own ... it does not seem like an exaggeration to say that the individuals who live such lives are not persons. (1996, 101)

Even if one wishes to hold that personal identity across time is in some sense metaphysically illusory, then, from the first- and second-person perspectives of our everyday lived experience we nevertheless feel that it must be true that there is some 'me' and 'you' that persist from moment to moment. In our everyday lives we experience ourselves as weighed down by the past and at stake in the future even if we should want to say that from an external perspective – philosophical, scientific, or religious – this is illusory.[21] While it may be an 'illusion', it is an illusion that shapes our entire lives and can be escaped only rarely and with great difficulty.

Despite this insistence on the temporal continuity of the self and the emphasis on the futurity of patience, however, there is nevertheless something right about the claim that patience requires one to be 'in the moment' in a certain sense. How so? Think back to the example with which I started this chapter: that of my daughter learning to read. One might object that it seems wrong to say that the patient person has to understand the object of her patience in terms of identities to be realized, as opposed to simply treasuring the value of the current moment for its own sake.

But it is my contention that these are not in fact at odds. Rather, the form that 'valuing the moment' takes in patience is in letting go of one's harried perusal of the alternative possibilities on which this time could also be spent. It involves focusing in on the chosen possibility, allowing other possibilities to fade into the background. But letting go of the urgency of the other unrealized possibilities is not a simple focusing in on an isolated moment. Rather, it is the expression of a deep commitment to the value of enabling this possibility in its temporal unfolding, of seeing this specific event as constitutive of a larger value. The commitment to the valued whole manifests itself as a buffer against the tendency to fixate on the range

---

[21] Schechtman 1996 does a nice job of separating out what she describes as two questions under the banner of the single heading of 'personal identity'. On the one hand, there is the question of reidentification across time: namely, what makes a person at T_1 the same person as the one at T_2? But on the other hand, we also have what she calls the 'characterization question': namely, 'which beliefs, values, desires, and other psychological features make someone the person she is'? (2). Like Schechtman, I hold that answers to the first question do not necessarily produce answers to the second, as is regularly assumed.

of alternative possibilities that are not being realized. By prioritizing the development of one person or one relationship, other possibilities are silenced, thereby enabling the present moment to appear in its simplicity and value. That kind of commitment to the overarching project – of which the specific event is understood as one component – provides a kind of focus that the impatient person lacks.

Being committed to the value of my daughter's literacy for the enrichment of her life can have a silencing effect on the other possibilities crowding my mind and vying for attention. Insofar as they are silenced, they no longer prompt me to view the time-consuming task of helping her read as a long and frustrating interference with tasks on which I might also spend that time. By committing to the valuing of one unfolding aspect of her identity, the now is no longer overshadowed by the other possible uses of that time, and the sense that time is 'running out' abates.

The Kierkegaardian Objection

In contrast to objections that require us to dissolve or deny the self, Anthony Rudd presents a Kierkegaard-inspired account that starts with an account of the person as 'a self-conscious being, aware of itself as having a past and a future' (2008, 495). On this account, 'patience is the virtue of properly orienting oneself to one's future on the basis of one's past' (2008, 496). Human existence is such that we experience ourselves as dispersed across time – which means that the ongoing task of building and maintaining who we are is never complete but only more or less perfectly embodied in the elements of which it is composed. As Rudd puts it: 'it is a process that I am engaged in throughout my life, one that does not issue in secure results on which I can then sit comfortably back, but one that must be renewed in every moment' (2008, 499). As we saw, the consequence is that the structure of human identity is necessarily futural: the ongoing demand for renewal requires an orientation to possibilities that will facilitate this continual unfolding of the self that one is trying to be.

However, this kind of striving to be who one is could seem like 'a Sisyphean task, one which really has no temporal telos (no telos beyond the continuance of the process itself), one which reaches no goal but only an end, in death' (2008, 500). For this reason, Rudd also suggests that it is perhaps wrong to claim that patience is a fundamentally temporal perspective, since a temporal perspective is incompatible with grasping oneself as a meaningful whole; there can be no such perspective on the 'whole' in an eternally incomplete process. But in order for patience to be anything other than an instrumentally beneficial skill – i.e. for it to be a genuine virtue – one must have access to a standard by which one can choose the shape of a good human life as a whole. Since that kind of wholeness and completion is at odds with the kind of incompletion built into our fundamentally temporal mode of being, it appears that we need a standard that exists outside time if patience is to be a virtue. Thus Rudd suggests that it is perhaps better to conceptualize patience as a relationship to the *eternal*, as Kierkegaard did. Understanding how to establish a good relationship between specific uses of time and one's identity as a whole requires turning to God as a source of completion outside time that can serve as a guide and a telos for our intrinsically incomplete self-becoming: 'our understanding of what it is to flourish as a being in time requires a reference beyond temporality'; any 'purely immanent standard' could not 'provide an adequate telos for human life as a whole' (Rudd 2008, 497, 507).[22]

In other words, when it comes to the discrete teleology of specific tasks, we are oriented toward a future completion that can be recognized and assessed as such from *within* the flow of time. We know when we have finished making the sandwich. But when we are speaking of the teleology of a life dedicated to self-becoming as a whole, we must be oriented toward a completion that is unavailable from within the temporal constraints of that life. If we are to recognize and assess it as a whole, Rudd argues, the required grasp of it qua whole can only come from an atemporal orientation to an eternal god, which grants us a kind of external perspective on the ongoing flow. As such, patience – insofar as it is an understanding of the parts in light of the valued whole – cannot be a temporal orientation. Instead, patience solves the problem posed by our temporal finitude by escaping it for the perspective of the infinite.

Thus both Bommarito and Rudd suggest that patience requires a metaphysical interpretation of reality according to which the problem of temporal finitude is overcome or dissolved.[23] In Bommarito's case, the project of human identity creation over time is conceptualized as an illusion, with only the distinct moments mattering. In Rudd's case, an eternal supratemporal power that guides and anchors human identity

---

[22] Rudd suggests that recognition of this fact helps explain Alisdair MacIntyre's and Charles Taylor's turn to theism.
[23] Rudd notes that his conception of patience as a fundamental virtue by which we realize our ultimate end of conforming to God's vision of the world 'requires some metaphysic, that is, some account of the ultimate nature of reality, which would make this claim intelligible' (2008, 498).

beyond its specific temporal manifestations is posited. But this means that the problem of how to view the meaning of specific events in light of the valued whole is 'solved' by avoiding it: by either collapsing the whole into the discrete point of the isolated now or expanding it until it coincides with the infinite. In either case, that for the sake of which the patient person ultimately acts is taken to be something beyond or outside the self-becoming of the individual in time.

But such appeals to metaphysics – wherein we leave behind everyday experience and presuppose a reality outside time or beneath (illusory) personal consciousness – are useful only to those who are antecedently committed to that underlying metaphysics. They are methodologically closed to the phenomenologist who seeks to make sense of human experience from within the boundaries of that experience. We adopt phenomenology as our methodology because we are looking for a general account of human flourishing available to all of us, rather than one that relies on specific metaphysical commitments about the nature of reality that are beyond the purview of everyday human experience. If we discover that patience is in principle impossible from within that perspective, we might then turn to metaphysical stories about eternity and the veil of maya. But we should first see if there is a form of patience that does not rely on them. Thus metaphysical posits of the kind endorsed by Bommarito and Rudd are closed to us, except insofar as we can translate them into features of first-person lived experience – perhaps by viewing them as helpful narratives that the patient person may need to invoke in order to act patiently.

We are left then, with questioning how one can grasp oneself as a kind of whole, despite the fact that that wholeness is an open and evolving movement into an unwritten future. How can that whole be available from the perspective of the one engaged in that ongoing striving?

We can begin to answer this by noting that for the most part we need not be able to grasp the *entirety* of an agent's selfhood in order to engage in the prioritization of the long-term over the short-term and see the immediate action in light of broader identity possibilities. We can all imagine the completed painting, for which the patient person commits to persevering in the face of setbacks. We can all distinguish between loving, reliable relationships and those characterized by hostility and doubt. When we demonstrate patience, we act in light of our commitment to the former kind of possibility.

What Rudd is pointing out, however, is that we need a more global stance of self-assessment if we are to know how to allocate our time so as to live good human lives, not just succeed in one or another long-term project: 'Only if we have a notion of the human good that transcends particular projects can we have a criterion for which projects are worth pursuing patiently. But this, for us, is precisely the problem' (Rudd 2008, 494). But on my account, patience is ultimately motivated and guided by the need to coordinate and respond to claims from the three different normative domains – and for the most part, our understanding of what such an optimal condition of normative responsivity looks like is provided to us by way of the admired other person, who models for us both specific possibilities of long-term accomplishment and examples of good lives displaying normative balance. Indeed, role models can also show us how far we have progressed in this regard – a progress that is often more easily recognized from the outside.

Further, when we think through the nature of patient experience we can see that for the most part our sense of who we are trying to become – and how to understand specific choices in light of that – is almost always shifting and open to question. Typically our understanding of whether we are succeeding in this striving to be who we hope to be is given to us only in rare moments of clarity in which we see the extent to which we have achieved a condition of proportionality and responsiveness to the normative claims that bind us: we see that we have or have not let our loved ones down; we sense that our potential is or is not being fulfilled; our place in the human community becomes clear to us for a moment.[24] The orientation toward these glimpses of the whole is itself futural because they are fleeting; we must always look forward to the next for information about how well we are responding to the norms that govern our struggle to be in the world well. We work continuously toward experiencing such moments because they serve as testimonials to the project of self-realization for the sake of which we continually act. But there is no point – either momentary or eternal – from which one's striving could be experienced as completed or ultimately justified. Rather, all we can hope for are moments of insight in which we can see that our efforts are not in vain, that we are making progress in realizing the person that we hope to be.

---

[24] Such a global grasp of oneself as a whole is theorized under Heidegger's notion of *Angst* and the 'authenticity' to which it can give rise – an account that Rudd contrasts with his own Kierkegaard-inspired approach. Defending Heideggerian authenticity against Rudd's charges would take us too far afield, but suffice it to say that I am sympathetic to Rudd's worries about empty decisionism and the need to provide a more 'substantial normative backdrop' (2008, 507). My account does so with the notion of the three basic normative terrains while avoiding the more substantial metaphysical commitments that Rudd seems willing to take on. McMullin 2013 argues that such an approach is consistent with (a version of) Heidegger's own view.

The patient person understands this temporal structure of agency, viewing the realization of particular projects or preferences as essential constituents of that whole, exercising self-restraint now for the sake of the valued whole in its unfolding – and recognizing, above all, that there is no escaping the open-endedness and uncertainty that comes with being a creature dispersed in time. Patience cannot free us from that condition – by either dissolving the self or giving us access to the infinite – it can only help us cope with this difficult existential fact gracefully.

Impatience and Perfectionism

Indeed, one could argue that both of the above accounts display an orientation characteristic of *impatience*: a refusal to acknowledge the temporal limits placed on human agency. However, in impatience this refusal occurs primarily on an affective level, not a theoretical one: impatient people experience anger and resentment about human temporal limits. This rage and resentment is typically rooted in an implicit perfectionism, which operates with a normatively loaded and unrealistic sense of what self, other, and world can offer temporally finite creatures. For the impatient, ideal or unrealistic possibilities of accomplishment are taken as perfectly reasonable to expect from ordinary people in everyday circumstances. Angry blaming behaviour is the result when those expectations are disappointed. As we will see, the object of this blaming behaviour can be either individual agents or existence itself.

On the one hand, human beings are weak, fallible, and slow. We rarely perform tasks as well or as quickly as we wish or indeed as we are capable of, given ideal conditions – whether for reasons of technical weakness, depleted resources, or moral failing. The impatient person fixates on the fact that these failures could in principle be avoided, emphasizing that the other person's laziness or carelessness is to blame for their inability to complete the task as quickly as humanly possible. Perfectionist impatience of this kind assumes that time is running out not because temporal finitude is an existential fact, but because of careless disregard for that precious resource – disregard arising from the agent's incompetence or failure to appreciate what is at stake.

In impatience one rages against this powerlessness and blames people – self or others – for those limitations. In so doing impatience moralizes temporal finitude, denying that human agency is limited by insisting that things could have been otherwise if actions had been undertaken more responsibly or capably. The impatient agent holds himself or the other person accountable for human temporal limitations by viewing them as the result of avoidable human failures. This often includes an element of contempt for the other person's abilities, sometimes coupled with an implicit judgment that you yourself could do it faster and more competently since you have adopted efficient performance as the norm. Of course, on attempting to perform the activity that *seemed* so easy, it often becomes clear that the exercise of this ability is more difficult and time-consuming than it seemed. Such an immediate realization of the limited nature of one's own agency – coupled with humiliation at being shown up – can lead to further irritation, as is evident in the proneness to destroy or discard the item that has resisted one. In such cases, the impatient person rages at the way limitations on his agency thwart its desired expression. Thus impatient people can also be prone to *self*-contempt insofar as they also hold themselves up to unrealistic standards about how quickly and competently humans ought to be able to perform certain tasks. The inevitable thwarting of those expectations is experienced as licensing outbursts of impatient blame and denial.

Of course, there will be cases where the person has indeed displayed a blameworthy incompetence or obliviousness. Nevertheless, exercising patience typically requires self-restraint and forgiveness for how slow or recalcitrant people can be in gaining or displaying the mastery that they are (at least theoretically) capable of achieving. Though it is *possible* that one will never lose one's keys or react slowly to a changing traffic light, the patient person has a realistic sense of how hard life can be, how unlikely it is that we will always act with perfect, smooth efficiency. Patience accepts this, displaying an orientation to human striving that is attentive to the time-consuming struggle involved in its accomplishment. It is an accommodating grace in the face of human temporal finitude, a refusal to blame people for the way their lack of perfection consumes precious time.

The other target of blame is the fact that all human agency – no matter how competent or efficient – is enacted in a world that regularly thwarts us in ways that are beyond our control. We are at the mercy of the world no matter how good we are or how hard we try. The patient person has a realistic sense of how much the world will bow to our endeavours, how much it will harass and slow us – and he adjusts his expectations accordingly.[25] He refuses to lash out at the world for not more perfectly enabling

---

[25] 'Relevant to questions of waiting and whether patience is at issue is an understanding of how the world works and the amount of time that things usually take. People wait too long or not long enough because they lack such understanding not because they suffer from the relevant vice ... So

his plans and preferences. The patient person endures time-consuming hindrances to human projects with equanimity, acknowledging that giving himself and others the time to express their agency means accommodating this fundamental human powerlessness over the conditions in which we do so, including and especially our basic powerlessness over the temporal structure of human agency itself: the fact that our identity is dispersed across time in a continual process of self-becoming. This temporal dispersal means that our identities are never complete – that we can never fully know who we are and thus must constantly press forward into the endless task of becoming in conditions of temporal scarcity. Impatient people struggle with the anxiety and rage that attends such uncertainty and incompletion: they are angry at existence for the fact that there is never enough time to realize the projects on which their identities and sense of meaning depend, that there is never a point where we fully become who we are trying to be.

The Paradox of Passive Mastery

It seems, then, that the patient person is he who masters countervailing desires for alternative uses of time, silencing them in light of the value of long-term projects and preferences expressive of human agency. This appears to raise a problem, however, since it is difficult to see how this kind of self-mastery could be reconciled with the traditional conception of virtue as a habituated temperament in which self-control is unnecessary. The idea of having to *master* countervailing urges seems to indicate that a truly virtuous patience is impossible.[26]

There is clearly something right about this. As we have seen, the fixation on unrealized possibilities was the mark of the *im*patient person. Patient people do not wrestle with the powerful urge to fly into a rage or push their way to the front of the line. On the contrary, they display calm and restraint despite their awareness of the appeal of spending time otherwise. We must clarify, then, the way in which the patient person understands herself as having the ability to gain some relief by abandoning or renouncing the current possibility in favour of

---

too may ignorance be the cause of apparent impatience. We do not wait a sufficient amount of time because we are not aware that the time being required of us is reasonable or unavoidable' (Kupfer 2007, 270).

[26] See Pianalto 2016b, 148.

more appealing uses of time – but without having to actively fight the urge to pursue those options.

What the patient person recognizes is that such relief would come at the cost of abdicating the long-term agency-enabling behaviour to which she is committed. The ultimate consequence of impatience – the belief that one can abandon any project and repudiate any relationship that does not provide instant gratification – is a failure to develop the long-term identities, relationships, and projects constitutive of genuine flourishing. The patient person recognizes that one can opt out of specific identity-constitutive activities and relationships only so many times before those relationships and that identity are lost. The inability to be bound in one's allocation of time and attention on the basis of commitment to the value of certain ends would prevent an adequate response to any of the normative domains, since it would foreclose self-realized agency, deep relationships, and a community of civility and mutual recognition. Thus even in the cases where it *seems* that one can do otherwise by stopping or repudiating the task at hand, in fact we cannot do so and still maintain the first-, second-, and third-person normative commitments that make us who we are over time. There is only a limited or local sense in which one can choose to do otherwise without losing oneself, without eroding the long-term project of expressing who one is trying to be. Understanding this facilitates a commitment that is not blind to other possibilities but recognizes that the allure of a wide-open field of possibility – the tendency to ask, 'What else could I be doing with this time?' – is ultimately detrimental to the very reason we are gripped by such a question to begin with – the struggle to do a good job at existing by supporting and sustaining the agency of self, other, and community.

Patience is a form of dedicated commitment to long-term projects, values, and relationships, a complex state wherein you are both aware of compelling alternatives that could be pursued but act as if there were not – all while being aware that you yourself are the one who has stipulated that there are none. The patient person sees her power to act on possibilities as operating within a larger field of constraint – the ultimate constraint being the fact that identity is not accomplished once and for all but is an ongoing task for the sake of which one must constantly recommit oneself to agency-defining roles and relationships. The patient person recognizes and accepts the constraints governing not only her ability to realize her tasks, but the very fact that her temporally extended identity- and relationship-constitutive projects can never give her the closure or completeness of identity for which she yearns.

Patience is a refusal to punish ourselves for the limitations placed on us by temporal dispersal and scarcity, either through blame or abdication. Accepting human temporal limitations does not mean abandoning our efforts to improve on the way those limits manifest in our lives. What it means is that one rejects a stance of existential *entitlement*: an insistence that human striving ought not to face so many obstacles to its realization – and therefore that rage, blame, or contempt are justified responses. Patience is not incompatible with an awareness of the halo of other possibilities that one might pursue – and this awareness can produce some suffering or frustration. But the patient person lacks a sense that she is entitled to abdicate on her commitments merely because of the existence of other appealing paths. What the patient person rejects is a sense of entitlement to a limitlessness in which long-term commitments could be realized without short-term suffering, to a limitlessness in which time is a boundless commodity and all possibilities can therefore be realized. Patience helps us to thrive in the face of these temporal limitations, accepting them for what they are: the existential structure of a temporally diffuse worldly agency striving for self-realization.

Thus the orientation characteristic of patience is not necessarily inconsistent with the Aristotelian model of virtue. The patient person does not crush or eradicate the frustration intrinsic to our finitude – rather, she acknowledges a deep powerlessness at the heart of human life, and rather than allowing this to motivate despairing or raging forfeiture of a project, she continues to strive for what can be won in the face of it. At its core patience involves a subtle and wide-reaching understanding of the parameters of human power and a commitment to acting in light of those constraints. It involves holding simultaneously to the pain of our limitedness and the worth of our striving. The patient person accepts, in other words, that commitments sustained through time are the only answer to the problem of temporal finitude.

Overcoming Entitlement through Metaphysics

In closing, I would like to consider the idea that one way to avoid falling into the grip of an entitled refusal to accept human finitude and to maintain agency-enabling commitments is to adopt one of the metaphysical perspectives that we mentioned earlier, which help to normalize and legitimate human finitude.[27] In doing so, they might help to foreclose thoughts of roads not taken and facilitate the necessary acceptance of our temporally limited condition.

Such approaches call for a shift whereby one interprets agent-specific finitude – for which blame might conceivably be appropriate – as a kind of neutral existential fact. They seek to remove us from the terrain of entitlement and blame by adopting an abstract third-personal view on human agency: seeing it as just another event in the universe over which we have no control and which has no particular priority or import.[28] In doing so, it is suggested, one can undermine the entitlement that fuels impatience.

There is much to be said for such accounts. Nevertheless, I wish to close by problematizing any view of flourishing that requires agents to understand their own striving – or the striving of others – through a lens that strips that striving of its meaning or value. We should be wary of any account in which an excellent human life requires one to decouple from what we typically hold to be its constitutive elements: commitment to one's projects, one's relationships, and one's place in the human community.

I do not mean to suggest that Buddhist or Kierkegaardian/Christian approaches do not have answers to these worries – answers that I cannot consider here. I merely wish to insist that any moral theory we provide should be one that ordinary people can understand and feel motivated by without having to commit to a metaphysical system that appears to be at odds with the structure of their lived experience. These approaches all insist that we view ourselves and our relationships through the lens of universal categories that diffuse the power of certain first- and second-person experiences. But without a grounding in first-person care for who we will be – along with second-person concern for the success of the other person's striving to be – it is hard to see why one would be motivated to do

---

[27] These are not the only options. Stoicism, for example, is another theory that can help promote patience (Pianalto 2014, 99).

[28] Schopenhauer similarly engages in this kind of shift from second-person to third-person interpretations of the interactions with other people in order to avoid impatience: 'The art of putting up with people may be learned by practicing patience on inanimate objects, which, in virtue of some mechanical or physical necessity, oppose a stubborn resistance to freedom of action – a form of patience which is required every day. The patience thus gained may be applied to our dealings with men, by accustoming ourselves to regard their opposition, wherever we encounter it, as the inevitable outcome of their nature, which sets itself up against us in virtue of the same rigid law of necessity as governs the resistance of inanimate objects. To become indignant at their conduct is as foolish as to be angry with a stone because it rolls into your path' (1995).

anything at all, let alone act patiently. What we need in order to be patient, then, is a conception of human striving that is realistic in its grasp of what that can be, considering the existential limits that we face.

In this chapter I have argued that patience is a graceful relinquishing of immediate or entitled claims to the limited time we have, displaying, instead, commitment and self-restraint in the service of the value of human self-becoming. Integrating the competing demands of the different normative terrains in conditions of temporal scarcity is at the heart of this central human virtue.

CHAPTER 8

Modesty

When something or someone is described as 'modest', a number of different meanings may come to mind, including inexpensive, sexually bashful, lacking in ostentation, and virtuously self-deprecating. In this chapter we will build on our account so far to explain why modesty should be considered a virtue and account for all of the above dimensions of the word's meaning. We have defined the virtues as stances that respond to specific existential problems that inhibit our ability to answer the three classes of normative demand. Modesty is the virtue that addresses the particular problem posed by different levels of success.[1] It negotiates this problem by simultaneously accommodating (1) an understanding of and commitment to the public norms that determine one's success *as* success, (2) a second-person recognition of the suffering that this success may trigger in others, and (3) a first-person self-understanding that one is the kind of creature that can never be fully defined by such public categories. Modesty, I will argue, is characterized by the correct understanding of the degree to which one's accomplishments ought to be taken as definitive of who one is. The modest person communicates to others his complex self-understanding of the relationship between first- and third-person interpretations of such success through certain behaviours motivated by the second-person desire to ensure that his accomplishments do not cause the other person pain.

Why Modesty?

Recent debates over modesty were primarily initiated by Julia Driver's 'The Virtues of Ignorance', where she argues that the modest person

---

* An earlier version of this chapter originally appeared as I. McMullin, 2010, 'A Modest Proposal: Accounting for the Virtuousness of Modesty', *Philosophical Quarterly* 60: 783–807.
[1] The focus of this chapter will be on the moral virtue of modesty, not the epistemic virtue.

'*underestimates* self-worth' (1989, 374). According to Driver, this underestimation must be unknowing and involuntary in order for it to avoid (vicious) false modesty – in which a person knows exactly how good she is but presents herself as less good. Modesty is therefore to be considered a 'virtue of ignorance' because it is 'dependent upon the epistemic defect of not knowing one's own worth' (1989, 374).[2] It avoids falling into the vice of complete self-deprecation, however, because it is limited in scope: 'the modest person must still think his character and deeds to be of some worth' (1989, 376). What we value in modesty, Driver claims, is the psychological disposition not to 'examine oneself thoroughly in terms of accomplishments' and the consequent alleviation of jealousy in others (1989, 383). As Driver further notes,

> People in general have a tendency to rank and estimate worth relative to others, and this tendency is destructive. The modest person is one who does not spend a lot of time ranking, who does not feel the need to do so, and thus remains ignorant to the full extent of self-worth. (1999, 828)

As commentators have pointed out, however, if we characterize modesty as unknowing and involuntary, it cannot be understood as a virtue that we can cultivate.[3] Furthermore, one can be ignorant of or underestimate one's accomplishments while still being a loud-mouthed braggart.[4] The connection that Driver draws between self-ignorance and socially beneficial behaviour, then, is hardly a necessary one.[5] As G. F. Schueler points out:

> Ranking oneself lower than one deserves is not the same as not ranking oneself at all and is perfectly compatible with ranking oneself pretty high, and hence compatible with the sort of boasting and the like that exacerbates, rather than lessens, feelings of envy and jealousy. (Schueler 1999, 836)

Thus Driver's claim that modesty is equivalent to being ignorant about one's accomplishments – and having the tendency to remain so – cannot fully account for why this trait should be considered a virtue.

---

[2] Driver argues that such 'virtues of ignorance' demonstrate why some virtues can be separated from the Aristotelian requirement of *phronēsis*.
[3] See Flanagan 1990; Smilansky 2003; Statman 1992.
[4] See Schueler 1997 and 1999.
[5] For this reason, several accounts have argued that modesty is not a tendency to *under*estimate one's accomplishments, but the tendency not to *over*estimate them. See Flanagan 1990 and Richards 1988. But not overestimating my successes does not guarantee that I won't be a braggart. If I am genuinely excellent at something – and understand just how excellent I am – I may be an offensive boor about it without having to overestimate my abilities. See also Schueler 1997, 472.

In contrast, Schueler has argued that modesty involves not ignorance of one's successes but a lack of desire 'to impress others with one's accomplishments' and that this is a virtue 'because of what it reveals about the person who has it, namely, that her goals and purposes come from herself, not from others' (1999, 838, 839). Though there is something appealing about this characterization, Schueler nevertheless fails to articulate adequately what it means to be a person 'whose direction in life is generated from herself' (1999, 838) and why this is to be considered a virtue, particularly insofar as it does not sufficiently differentiate between the modest person who fits this description and the sociopath who is completely indifferent to the norms of social life.

While Driver characterizes modesty as ignorance of oneself, Schueler characterizes it as a type of indifference to the estimation of others. In both cases the emphasis is on undermining either the knowledge or the legitimacy of public norms of success in favour of a kind of detachment from them. But understood in this way, both cases seem to misrepresent the nature of modesty, at least if we are to continue to think of it as a *virtue* – i.e. as a both cultivatable and admirable quality. Indeed, I will argue that modesty is in a way the *opposite* of what both Driver and Schueler have claimed: it is in fact a heightened awareness of self in light of the esteem in which others may hold one.

Modesty's Other-Directedness

Turning to another meaning of modesty may provide a clue to such an account. As we noted above, a traditional meaning of modesty is that of sexual bashfulness or a desire to hide one's body. Such stances do not arise from an ignorance of one's sexual nature or indifference to the judgments of others – children and animals are not sexually modest. Rather, the modest person seeks to hide so as *not to give offense* to the other person. As Havelock Ellis notes in *Studies in the Psychology of Sex*, modesty is the disposition to turn away from the gaze of the other person primarily for 'fear of being disgusting' or causing offense (1929, 58). This dimension of the meaning of modesty can clarify the virtuousness of this disposition, understood not only in its traditional sexual sense, but *tout court*: modesty involves an other-directed recognition of the fact that how one appears as an object of the other person's experience may cause harm or offense. Sexual modesty is the response to the shameful thought that one will appear to the other person as vulgar – either in terms of one's mere physical presence or because of how this presence might violate sexual mores (e.g. by being viewed as flaunting oneself sexually or inviting inappropriate sexual interest). One can see then why modesty is a traditionally 'feminine' virtue insofar as the enforcement of sexual self-concealment and passivity in women is rooted in deep-seated notions of the proper relationship between sexual appetite and femininity – hence the idea that it is offensive when women demonstrate their sexual desire or agency. The more general sense of the virtue of modesty similarly involves the awareness that one's presence may give offense or be harmful – but there the concern is focused on how one's successes will be experienced by the other person. The modest person is not ignorant of his successes – on the contrary, he is aware that his accomplishments may be experienced as a source of pain by those who are not so accomplished, and he responds to such a second-person claim by attempting to prevent or alleviate this pain in others.[6]

A fundamental characteristic of modesty, then, is the fact that it is not simply a self-regarding attitude but is instead a profoundly other-regarding stance. Though it involves a heightened mode of self-awareness, it is a type of awareness that is accessible to me only through (1) the recognition of how I am being experienced in the eyes of the other person and (2) a desire to alleviate any suffering that this may cause. Modesty necessarily involves a type of second-person acknowledgment of the other person, then, because it is an experience of the self as a particular type of object for the other person's observation and judgment, coupled with the motivation to mitigate any suffering that this might cause. Without the presence – or potential presence – of another person, one would have no reason to act or feel self-deprecatingly in the way that modesty prescribes.

This concern not to harm other people means that – contrary to *im*modesty – modest behaviour does not demand a high social cost. The modest person does not demand that his success be acknowledged at the cost of the other person's well-being. This lack of social 'cost' helps explain another meaning of the term. When we describe a house as modest, for example, we are clearly not referring to its form of self-assessment; we are indicating, rather, that its presence is not vulgar or excessive in its presentation. A house that presents itself as average in its *economic* cost is described as 'modest' because it does not come at the high *social* cost of

---

[6] Indeed, both of these meanings of modesty indicate why it has always been considered a feminine virtue. Women have traditionally been required not only to conceal themselves sexually but also to subsume their accomplishments to those of their male counterparts. For a classic examination of how men and women have traditionally been evaluated by different moral norms, see Beauvoir 1952, 203–210.

causing offence or harm through its ostentation or pretentions to wealth. It is not demanding to be noticed or admired. This dimension of modesty's meaning helps explain Jonathan Swift's choice of the title 'A Modest Proposal': the satirical nature of the work is highlighted by referring to such excessive, vulgar, and offensive content as 'modest'.

The lack of social cost dimension of the meaning of modesty is evident in how the modest person expresses his concern for the well-being of others: by downplaying or de-emphasizing his accomplishments or high standing in a particular way. We will be returning to the behavioural manifestations of modesty in further detail later, but at this point it is enough to note that although this self-deprecation may appear as ignorance or underestimation of one's gifts or accomplishments, the modest person must in fact know what it is that he is being modest about – or else he would not know what to deflect attention away *from*. Were this not the case, modesty could not be differentiated from the innocence of children. Modesty is not ignorance of the self or indifference to others but an orientation toward protecting the other person from the hurtful lack or loss in feelings of self-worth that may arise from the experience of having a 'lower rank'. Contrary to Driver's account, this orientation arises precisely in response to the modest person's self-knowledge regarding where she stands in terms of social ranking. If one did not realize how one's accomplishments and successes might be painful to the other person, one would have no reason to seek to downplay them but would, on the contrary, simply *enjoy* them.[7] And contrary to Schueler's account, indifference to esteem cannot be the mark of modesty, since modesty requires one to recognize that this esteem may cause the other person pain. Schueler is correct that the modest person cannot desire social esteem 'too much' – but he leaves this 'too much' unexplained.[8] It now seems clear, however, that the modest person cannot be so desirous of social esteem that she will accept it *at the cost of the other's pain*.

This tendency must be limited, however, if it is to remain a virtue. As I will discuss further later, it must be a type of mean between the vicious extremes of arrogance and self-abnegation. One cannot forfeit certain

---

[7] Even when the successful person cannot enjoy her successes because she is too focused on improving herself further – as suggested by Brennan 2007 and Smith 2008 – this would still not account for the modest person's tendency to protect the other person from the pain of his inferior rank. It is for this reason that the other-directedness of modesty must be emphasized.

[8] Ridge 2000 argues for a similar approach: the modest person cannot desire esteem either too much or too little – but like Schueler he leaves the sense of 'too much' largely unexplained.

forms of acknowledgment for the sake of the other person without sliding into the latter extreme.[9] One should also not be concerned to protect people from hurt if they are fundamentally opposed to recognizing *any* of your successes because they refuse to acknowledge you as having equal social standing – for example, white supremacists will always experience the success of people of colour as 'hurtful', but the latter clearly have no moral obligation to shield white suprecists from this hurt.

Despite the richness of the other discussions of modesty, few of them to date have sufficiently emphasized the central role that this second-person other-directedness plays in explaining what it is. Though other accounts are correct to note that modesty involves a particular kind of self-assessment, they fail to acknowledge the degree to which concern for the other person must be what motivates it. For example, though Ridge (2000) and Statman (1992) also argue that modesty must involve a tendency to present oneself to others in a particular way, neither recognizes that concern for the other person must be a fundamental motive if this behavioural tendency is to count as modesty. Similarly, Driver acknowledges modesty's socially beneficial consequences, but on her account modesty is not *motivated* by consideration for the other person. As we will see below, Brennan's Adam Smith-inspired account recognizes the role that the modest person can play in the moral development of others, but unlike my account, it does not hold the view that modesty must be *triggered* by concern for the well-being of others. And though the so-called egalitarian view seems to avoid the problem of being too self-directed, we will see that it does so on the basis of problematic assumptions about the beliefs necessary to sustain the modest stance.

What differentiates my account of modesty, then, is that (1) the modest person deflects or refuses certain forms of public esteem out of second-person concern for the other person, (2) this tendency arises *despite* knowing that the esteem is deserved according to third-personal measures of success, and (3) it can be deliberately cultivated. Modest people do not seek or demand legitimate recognition from others because they value the other person's well-being more than they desire having their own success acknowledged or celebrated.[10]

---

[9] See Statman 1992, 424 on this point.
[10] Kant similarly notes – but does not examine in any detail – the fact that the 'willing restriction of one's self-love in view of the self-love of others, is called modesty' (1996, 209).

False Modesty

Is the modest desire to protect the other person's feelings of self-worth simply a condescending response to his 'lesser' status? In other words, is there a real distinction between modesty and *false* modesty? To answer this question, we must take a closer look at what type of self-understanding encourages the modest person to de-emphasize her accomplishments for the sake of the other person.

Genuine modesty is the attempt to communicate to the other person that one does *not* in fact believe that he is 'lesser' – despite recognizing that one ranks higher on the particular standard of value in question. False modesty, on the other hand, is the dishonest and patronizing attempt to communicate to the other person that one does not believe one's success to be definitive evidence of being better than he, when in fact one *does* believe it. Understood as such, we can recognize false modesty's relationship to arrogance, which is perhaps best understood as the belief that a particular social ranking *does* provide evidence of one's higher worth – coupled with the desire to have this status publicly acknowledged, despite (indeed, sometimes because of) the pain that this acknowledgment will cause others.[11] False modesty, then, is a sort of quiet or surreptitious arrogance; one believes oneself to be better than others but does not want them to know it. False modesty – in contrast to arrogance – *could* therefore involve the sympathetic desire to conceal this belief in one's superiority from the other person out of a desire not to hurt him, though it more often seems to involve the selfish and strategic desire not to be deemed immodest.

It is for this reason that concern for the other person and tendencies toward self-deprecation are necessary but not sufficient conditions for modesty. An adequate account of modesty must be able to distinguish between the agent who successfully conceals her superiority complex and the agent who lacks one in the appropriate way. Modesty must not only involve the desire to save the other from pain – since this alone could be motivated by purely strategic reasons or enabled by lies. Rather, it must also involve the modest person's belief that she is *not* fundamentally better than the other person, despite her awareness that in another sense she *is*.

---

[11] Further helpful discussion of arrogance can be found in Tavani 2007 and Tiberius and Walker 1998.

Accomplishment and Worth

How is it possible for one to both recognize oneself as 'better' according to social standards of success and to nevertheless believe that one is fundamentally *no* better than those above whom one is ranked? Daniel Statman (1992) and Aaron Ben-Ze'ev (1990 and 2003) argue that such belief structures demonstrate that modesty is essentially a commitment to egalitarianism: the immodest person believes that his successes indicate that he is fundamentally better than others, while the modest person recognizes that we are all of equal moral worth.

Like my own account, then, the egalitarian view emphasizes that modesty is characterized by an other-directedness in which concern for the other person is prioritized over certain kinds of social esteem. Nevertheless, the egalitarian characterization of modesty suffers from several difficulties that prevent it from being a completely compelling account. The egalitarian view is in danger of substituting a more general account of moral commitment to the equal moral worth of all persons for a discussion of the specific virtuousness of *modesty* – one particular way in which this type of moral commitment might manifest itself in specific circumstances. Since the specific circumstance is one in which the equality of persons is challenged by inequalities of success and accomplishment, the egalitarian view must be able to account for how conflicting beliefs about one's worth can be reconciled in modesty. In other words, the existential problem posed to modesty is recognizing the legitimacy of both public norms of success that deem some people better *and* the fundamental moral equality of all persons.

Egalitarian accounts attempt to solve this problem not by claiming that modest agents are *ignorant* of the degree to which they surpass others on public measures of success; they claim, rather, that the modest agent must not *value* these successes because they interfere with a commitment to moral equality. In order to explain how one can maintain this evaluative stance, the egalitarian view holds that the modest agent must subscribe to certain beliefs. As Ben-Ze'ev puts it: 'This evaluation rests on a belief in the common nature and fate of human beings and on a belief that this commonality dwarfs other differences' (1990, 237). In other words, human similarities vastly outweigh any differences between us, revealing such differences to be ultimately irrelevant when it comes to understanding our respective worth. Indeed, Ben-Ze'ev argues that modest people do not even 'compute their comparative advantages ...

because in their evaluative perspective such a computation is insignificant in light of the basic common nature and fate (say, death) of all human beings' (1990, 237). On the basis of this type of belief, egalitarians argue, the modest agent keeps her accomplishments 'in perspective' such that egalitarian feeling can be maintained in the face of obvious superiority in other regards. What this amounts to is that the modest agent overrides evidence of superiority according to certain public norms by adopting an interpretive stance according to which such differences in accomplishment and ability can be experienced as negligible. One does this by encouraging a perspective according to which all human accomplishments are experienced as insignificant (e.g. the perspective of death). Such an approach is also evident in Owen Flanagan's claim that modesty might involve one recognizing that any of one's accomplishments – including curing cancer – are 'not so important *sub specie aeternitatis*' (1990, 425).[12]

Though the egalitarian view rightly characterizes modesty as motivated by moral concern, then, it appears to require that we 'keep things in perspective' by adopting a stance whereby all standards according to which one agent is ranked superior to another are discounted. In the face of God, eternity, or mortality human accomplishments are small indeed – but it is hard to see *why* one should look at one's accomplishments only from such a perspective. These human standards ought to meaningfully apply to us even when we are viewing others as moral equals. Further, such an approach seems to involve another version of false modesty. If one were to *publicly* apply this type of interpretation to one's accomplishments in order to downplay them and affirm one's commitment to egalitarianism, those ranked lower might be insulted by the implicit condescension. An intelligent person pointing out that we are all equally stupid compared with God is small comfort to the cognitively deficient. Most importantly, however, such an account appears to directly contradict the experience of being modest, which does not seem to involve applying a theory of human insignificance in order to remind oneself not to experience one's own high ranking *as being* a high ranking. Indeed, the need to appeal to God or eternity in order to maintain the proper perspective on one's excellence seems to indicate that one's character is marred by a kind of deep arrogance

---

[12] Richards 1988 and Statman 1992 show how such evaluative standards typically occur only within a religious framework where human accomplishment is nothing before the glory of God. See also Cooper 2002.

that can be kept in check only through a spiritual exercise whereby human measures of accomplishment are delegitimized in order to be able to recognize the other person's moral status.

The truth at the heart of the egalitarian account, I contend, is its implicit recognition of the fact that there are distinct normative domains at work. Individual dignity and moral standing are experienced, on my account, in the second-person perspective, a stance wherein one experiences an immediate recognition of the other's moral authority in a way that cannot fully be captured by general categories. The egalitarian view is essentially specifying that modesty requires a shift from the third-person to the second-person perspective, to seeing others as persons whose presence makes an immediate moral claim as opposed to just competitors on the various public measures of success. But it is not clear that we must denigrate one arena of normative claim in order to respect the other, that we must undermine public measures of success in order to experience the moral standing of the other person as such. Though doing so might be a helpful tool for people who have a particularly hard time recognizing that moral standing, it is a not a fundamental feature of modesty as such.

Indeed, one might worry that the egalitarian suggestion that this is necessary arises because of its tendency to think of second-person moral recognition in implicitly third-personal terms, a problem we examined in Darwall's account of the second-person perspective in Chapter 2. Namely, by conceptualizing this moral recognition in terms of equality (and not, say, authority or claim), the suggestion is that the other's moral dignity is a category whose value can be recognized only by first delegitimating third-person categories with which it is taken to be in competition. As we have seen, this delegitimation work takes place by showing that any differentiation via public norms of success is meaningless in the face of the absolute difference of God or death. But such a competition model is at odds with my view that agents can and must simultaneously hold to the legitimacy of all three normative perspectives at once: acknowledging the other person's unique moral standing, recognizing the legitimacy of standards of success that measure our differential public worth, and, as we will see further in the discussion, pursuing one's first-person project of self-becoming in response to those public standards of success. Though the egalitarian approach is on the right track, then, by distinguishing between the different normative perspectives we can get a clearer picture of what modesty involves.

The 'Double Standard' Account

A number of recent accounts have offered other ways to think about the idea that modesty involves keeping one's accomplishments 'in perspective' in the correct way. Nicholas D. Smith, for example, has argued that the modest person must recognize an appropriate *hierarchy* of accomplishments. Thus the champion chess player is modest about this form of excellence – even if she knows just how good she is and values the standards by which this is assessed – because she realizes that it is relatively low on the list of human excellences.[13] On this view, the modest agent is modest because she realizes that her particular accomplishment is insignificant compared with many other forms of publicly assessable human excellence. Modesty is not about recognizing human equality by downplaying the import of human accomplishment, but about distinguishing between higher and lower goods and measuring oneself against the former.

This account has the unfortunate consequence that the greater one's accomplishments, the less one can be modest. The person who cures cancer either cannot be modest or can be so only if she assesses her accomplishments according to a standard that is essentially impossible to meet.[14] On this account we are forced to reach the counterintuitive conclusion that the more one has to be modest about, the less one can succeed in being modest.

In response, some have argued that even the highly accomplished modest person can keep this perspective by always measuring herself against the human *ideal*, not against *average* measures of success. Adam Smith was one of the first to argue that modesty relies on there being two different standards against which we might assess ourselves – the real or average standard and the ideal standard:

> In estimating our own merit, in judging of our own character and conduct, there are two different standards to which we naturally compare them. The one is the idea of exact propriety and perfection, so far as we are each of us capable of comprehending that idea. The other is that degree of

---

[13] This example is from Smith 2008, 26.
[14] Statman 1992 notes that 'keeping things in perspective' in such cases seems impossible – or bizarre, at the very least – because 'From the perspective of all ordinary people this person is an extraordinary character; and, indeed, he *is*' (427). See also Richards 1988, 253.

approximation to this idea which is commonly attained in the world. (Smith 1976, VI.iii.23)[15]

Modesty, then, is a matter of applying the correct standard.[16] The modest person measures herself against the ideal of human perfection – and therefore always finds herself wanting, even if she has cured cancer. The immodest person, on the other hand, always measures himself against the degree to which that ideal is accomplished in reality – and therefore often feels smug self-satisfaction. On this view, the appropriate stance involves a type of double standard: always measuring *oneself* against the ideal and *others* against the average instantiation thereof – ensuring, thereby, that one will not judge others too harshly and oneself too leniently, as is the human tendency (Brennan 2007). Note the similarity with the egalitarian view in this regard: what I am calling the double standard view claims that we ought to apply a different standard to self and others in order to more closely approximate an egalitarian assessment of all parties. The more demanding standard thereby ensures the 'proper perspective' on one's success. Just like the *sub specie aeternitatis* stance, then, the *sub specie idealis* stance ultimately requires one to apply an evaluative framework according to which one's accomplishments are not experienced *as* accomplishments worthy of note.

But characterizing modesty as a tendency to use one standard for oneself and another standard for everyone else oversimplifies things. Though Brennan is correct to note that measuring oneself in terms of the ideal and others in terms of the real serves to counteract our tendency to be harsher with others than ourselves (2007, 122), the modest person must nevertheless continue to simultaneously apply *both* standards to himself and others. Only by doing so can he avoid the dangers that such either/or thinking poses. Adopting a selective focus whereby I highlight only my own failure to accomplish the ideal and the other's success in reaching the average standard is essentially the flip side of the immodest person's selective focus on her own success and the other's failure. Adopting this opposite attitude may serve to correct a self-favouring imbalance, but it

---

[15] I am indebted to Brennan 2007 for bringing Adam Smith's account to my attention. Nicholas D. Smith similarly argues for two different standards: (1) a single vertical standard versus (2) what he calls 'aspirational' standards (2008, 30).
[16] Though this emphasis on different evaluative frameworks is structurally similar to the egalitarian accounts, it differs insofar as the double standard account involves two distinct normative standards according to which one can measure degrees of success or failure. On the egalitarian view, the assessment of the other person as a being possessing moral worth is not a matter of degree. One is reminded of Darwall's distinction between respect for meritorious persons and respect for persons as such (2004).

does not address the underlying issues that result in immodesty: namely, a misunderstanding of the nature of these standards and a failure to accomplish an appropriately complex application of them. As a result, the double standard's suggestion that one adopt the opposite selective focus – whereby one glosses over one's own successes and the other person's failures – can produce the opposite difficulty: the failure to value oneself sufficiently. In the following sections, I will argue that modesty does not require such selective focus but demands, rather, a simultaneous assessment in terms of both standards at once. Such an understanding is accomplished by understanding the meaning of these standards from both the first-person and third-person perspectives. From the former we are oriented toward the task of individual self-becoming and hence focused more on the ideal. From the latter we are oriented toward understanding ourselves as public objects in a shared world, and hence focused on comparing ourselves with others in terms of shared norms.

Complicating the Picture

A person is always capable of taking multiple stances toward herself: viewing herself, as we have seen, from the first-person, second-person, and third-person perspectives: namely, experiencing herself as a being entrusted with the project of her own self-becoming, as the recipient of moral claims from others, and as one among many tasked with establishing a shared world. Modesty helps us to negotiate our responses to the different normative claims that arise from these stances in the face of differential levels of accomplishment that can prompt us to resist doing so.

As we have seen, the third-person perspective involves understanding oneself in terms of objective categories that arise out of the work of intersubjective world-building. Viewed in this light, human beings can understand themselves as public objects defined by various third-personally ascribable facts. This status as public object available for categorization and assessment encompasses all of the constraints and determinations embedded in the concrete contours of one's situation – including the existing social roles and norms that one does not create but to which one must nevertheless respond.[17] Like other objects in the world, certain objective facts will be true of each of us – and by adopting a third-person perspective on myself I understand myself to be defined and measured according to these publicly recognizable categories and norms.

---

[17] See Chapter 6 for discussion of our relationship to these public norms.

Because I am constrained by the worldly conditions in which I find myself, it is never simply up to me to decide what I am. Different norms will have different levels of definitiveness, of course – though my height is a public fact that is open to very little in the way of controversy or interpretive spin, my sense of humour is much less so since the public standards by which humour is assessed are shifting and open to disagreement in a way that standards of height are not. Nevertheless, we can and do make publicly recognized distinctions between better and worse, more and less accomplished, even in those domains. Because our identities are constrained by these social-material conditions in which we happen to find ourselves, the average standards of assessment entrenched in them will always determine who we are. We are all public objects, and the public is engaged in the game of categorization and measure.

Though we can never fully escape these external assessments, neither are we fully defined by them. We are not merely public objects determined by average measures and external constraints – we are also subjects whose first-person self-givenness complicates this third-person understanding of the self. The fact that we are capable of assessing ourselves in terms of a vision of the possible essentially involves our freedom to refuse to accept that these public determinations or average assessments fully delimit who and what we are. This transcending of the given toward that which is 'not yet' does not occur simply when we compare ourselves with this or that particular ideal, however. The capacity to make these specific self-comparisons is a function of the general human ability to understand oneself not simply as a third-personally measurable fact but also as a first-personally self-aware agent tasked with defining the course and meaning of her own life. I am related to the beliefs and qualities that define me not simply as neutral information but as the very content of the identity to which I am committed.

My first-person relation to the public facts that define who I am enables me to not only know myself but to take a stance on who I understand myself to be. Insofar as I can be aware of the facts that are third-personally true of me, I am never merely identical with them – I am always free to exceed or transcend these determinations. The consequence is the ability to imagine oneself otherwise and to strive to become it. First-personal self-awareness is characterized by the capacity for a kind of free stance-taking that allows one to reinterpret and overcome one's factic conditions in light of a different understanding of what one can be.

Another consequence of such first-person freedom, however, is a pervasive indeterminacy whereby who I am is never fully or finally established – my identity can always be surpassed by a new self-understanding.[18] Who I am depends on this constantly renewed activity of self-interpretation such that I never straightforwardly *am* these third-personally ascribable facts but am always *striving to be* – or not to be – them. Though it is true that one simply *is* a woman, a sailor, a Buddhist, etc., the meaning of these social categories must always be taken up and interpreted. Being aware of who I am means that my identity is not an established fact but requires me always to take responsibility for committing myself anew to understanding what it means to be who I am.

These different stances we can take toward the self help explain the 'double standard' account. We are capable of applying two different types of standards – the real and the ideal – because of these two fundamental ways in which we can understand ourselves. As a result, who I am always both *is* and is *not* defined by the external standards of assessment according to which I am deemed a success.[19] When I consider my identity as a type of third-personally accessible established fact, these external standards do indeed define who I am in the world. But when I consider myself as a first-person self who is free to make herself otherwise than what she is, these measurements are suspended and problematized – though they do not thereby cease to apply. One is always simultaneously claimed by both possible self-conceptions. Understanding the appropriate stance to take toward one's success, then – especially when claimed by a second-person recognition of the pain that this success may cause others – is far from simple.

The double standard account recognizes that two different self-assessments will result if one aspect is emphasized over another. But unlike my account, the double standard approach endorses this either/or stance: emphasizing the ideal – one's freedom to be other than one is – when assessing one's own accomplishments and emphasizing the real – objectively measurable facts about success and failure – when assessing others. On my account, in contrast, the modest person must recognize self and other as simultaneously factic and free, continuing to apply both standards at once. To be modest I must recognize both that these rankings

---

[18] We discussed this in Chapter 7 in terms of the temporal dispersal problem.
[19] We saw in our discussion of egalitarianism that the same is true in our relationships with other people: we can see them simultaneously in terms of their second-person moral standing and in terms of their third-person public status.
This section was inspired by Sartre's notion of 'bad faith' in *Being and Nothingness* (1992).

are true and that they are incapable of simply defining me such that I can judge myself to be 'better' than others in the same way we judge one table to be bigger than another. In contrast with the other accounts, then – which ruled out experiencing one's accomplishments *as* accomplishments – on this account the modest agent continues to experience her successes as such, but she acknowledges that they are not entirely definitive of who she is. Insofar as she is aware of them – and she must be aware of them if she is to demonstrate concern for the well-being of the other person in the face of them – she is not identical with them and will refuse to accept the admiration that only simple identity with her successes could make legitimate.

Modesty and Responsibility

How does the modest person accomplish a condition in which the tension between these two stances is reconciled, and what inhibits the immodest person from doing so? In the face of hierarchies of success, the temptation is to selectively apply one mode of self-assessment rather than the other – depending on which self-understanding will better serve one's desire to avoid the type of responsibility and honest self-assessment that coordinating these dimensions would entail. As we will see later, the immodest person tends to selectively acknowledge first- or third-person claims depending on how well they fit with his particular agenda. The immodest person fully endorses public facts about who he is when these denote his success, but emphasizes his freedom for self-overcoming when he wishes to distance himself from any poor rankings that these facts might reveal. This either/or tendency is motivated by the fact that acknowledging himself to be both simultaneously involves facing the exhausting realization that he will never be able to just relax into being who he is. Rather, he will always face the twin constraints of having to constantly *make* himself who he is and having to face this responsibility in conditions that are constrained by the structures of the shared world. Because one must make choices despite this uncertainty and powerlessness, the temptation is to avoid the burden of responsibility that such a condition involves.

There are two characteristic ways in which one can attempt to do so, depending on whether one tries to understand oneself solely from a third- or a first-person perspective. Both types of either/or thinking map onto two modes of immodesty: arrogance and a type of otherworldly perfectionism.

Facticity and Arrogance: Prioritizing the Third-Person Perspective

To avoid coming to terms with the complexity of being creatures who are both factically conditioned and free, we often attempt to think of ourselves as having the same type of settled, complete existence as things do. In this type of either/or thinking, one attempts to understand oneself strictly as an object determined by the publicly recognizable attributes that currently define one. By interpreting one's identity as if it were an established fact, one can essentially evade all responsibility for it. Through such an either/or self-interpretation, one can flee into the settled parameters of a social role or category in the attempt to make oneself into it without remainder. Thus I *must* send these people to the gas chamber because I *am* a Nazi and that is what Nazis do. Such a self-understanding consists in the refusal to accept that these roles and categories involve standards to which one must choose to conform – they are not *simply* facts that require nothing in the way of responsible self-interpretation and creation.

The attempt to avoid the responsibility of one's freedom by thinking of one's successes in purely third-personal terms is the mode of self-understanding operative in arrogance. Arrogance is essentially the belief that one just *is* one's excellent social standing in the same way that a stone is heavy. In the face of facts about his own success, the arrogant person simply accepts them as valid evidence of his own excellence and avoids recognizing that such facts are never entirely definitive insofar as his first-person response to these facts – how he freely takes them up and gives them the meaning that they have in his life – is also determinative of who he is.

It is clear that this same kind of self-understanding also characterizes the person who takes her *failures* to be entirely determinative of who she is. Such negative self-regard or low self-esteem is the opposite of arrogance in terms of substance but identical in terms of form. The person consumed with negative self-regard treats her failures as if they were irrefutable objective evidence of her status as worthless, while the arrogant person identifies himself entirely with his social successes. Both avoid the thought that they are constantly more – or *less* – than their past accomplishments or accumulated social esteem. This allows the arrogant person to ignore the fact that he cannot simply relax into being a good father, a great physicist, a loyal friend – even though he is one. These standards of success must always be met again in the future because each person's responsibility for their interpretation and implementation is never overcome but must be constantly renewed. The failure to accommodate the claims of the first-person stance – relying solely on the third-person stance in one's self-conception – is characteristic of this kind of immodesty.

Freedom and Perfectionism: Prioritizing the First-Person Perspective

A similarly destructive kind of either/or thinking is also evident in the opposite tendency: namely, the refusal to recognize that these determinations of the self *are* evidence for who and what one is:

> If I were only what I *am*, I could, for example, seriously consider an adverse criticism which someone makes of me, question myself scrupulously, and perhaps be compelled to recognize the truth in it. But thanks to transcendence, I am not subject to all that I am. I do not even have to discuss the justice of the reproach. (Sartre 1992, 99)

One can flee into the comfort either of facticity or of freedom – and in the latter case, one avoids or denies the ways in which certain assessments do in fact define one. The person who refuses to believe that she is a liar – despite her many lies – can succeed in maintaining this attitude only by focusing strictly on her freedom to be other than the way public categories define her. She denies the public facts that define what she is by thinking only of her freedom to be otherwise – of the clean unwritten future.

This refusal to acknowledge the third-person claims of the shared world allows one to avoid taking responsibility for facts about oneself by taking comfort in the distance that always lies between the public object that one is and first-person conceptions of who one understands oneself to be. As a result of this type of refusal to acknowledge the plurality of demands, an agent can refuse to recognize those ways in which she is genuinely failing to live up to public standards of success – being 'pure freedom' means that she can choose, instead, to disengage from those aspects of herself that do not meet an inflated self-understanding. And even if the agent *is* successful, this kind of either/or thinking can encourage the immodest person to blithely flaunt her goods or successes with the dishonest sense that who she is could *never* be legitimately assessed by the standards that apply to everyone else, and as such she need not be concerned with how those successes – and the privileges they provide her – might be experienced by others. One can perhaps think of a case in which a blind idealist – one focused only on the fundamental equality of all persons or on the moral ideal – can do a good deal of damage through her obliviousness to the manner in which her wealth or success or race privilege create negative feelings in those she wishes to help. Her position in certain public hierarchies – unless recognized as having a certain kind of status in shaping and defining her life – can inhibit her capacity to respond well to second-person claims. Such obliviousness describes an immodest person who fails to recognize how her facticity – the fact that she *is* defined by these goods and successes – may be experienced as painful to others. Since such an understanding is necessary if one is to display the appropriate concern for the other's well-being, avoiding this second kind of either/or thinking – in which first-person resistance to the legitimacy of public measures is emphasized – is also a necessary condition for modesty.

In both cases of immodesty one fails to acknowledge that one is simultaneously defined by and irreducible to one's social status – and one tends to do so by focusing on only one or the other type of self-understanding, prioritizing either the first- or third-person perspective and ignoring the claims of the other normative stance. Such an either/or understanding of oneself is a common and convenient way to avoid the negotiation work and responsibility required for living well as creatures claimed simultaneously by multiple normative domains – an avoidance motivated, in this case, by the complicated normative terrain into which different hierarchies of public success force all of us who face this existential problem.

Philosophical Varieties of Either/Or Thinking

It is my contention that many of the characterizations of modesty examined above tend to slide into this kind of either/or thinking – particularly the latter variety in which a kind of first-person freedom (and not the third-person facts that constrain it) is the primary focus. This is evident, for example, in Driver's requirement that the modest person not even *know* how he measures up to certain standards. Like the person who avoids seriously considering the criticisms being leveled against him, the modest person on Driver's account requires a certain obliviousness to one's place in the world. Despite the obvious social facts with which such a person is confronted, he remains ignorant of his own social standing – and therefore of the way in which this standing can be hurtful to others. But it is hard to understand why such obliviousness should be deemed a virtue. Indeed, one could argue that such obliviousness in adults must on some level involve a type of *refusal* to recognize these public facts about oneself – or the responsibility that they entail. Though other accounts attempt to present this indifference or obliviousness to worldly standards as an inherently virtuous stance, it is hard to distinguish from a kind of irresponsible and otherworldly obtuseness. Thus Schueler argues that the modest person's self-interpretations must come entirely from within and not from social assessment – a position demonstrating the latter variety of either/or thinking insofar as the entire focus is on the freedom of first-person self-interpretation and not on the public context in which that freedom must be exercised.

Despite their seeming improvement on the Driver and Schuler accounts, the egalitarian and 'double standard' approaches also seem to be characterized by this same type of either/or thinking insofar as they require one to focus on one normative perspective while ignoring or downplaying the other. As we can recall, maintaining one's commitment to egalitarianism essentially involves an orientation toward self and other that focuses not on the (non-egalitarian) fact of one's successes and accomplishments but on an equal free personhood for whom such social hierarchies show up as irrelevant or meaningless. Though less noticeably so, the double standard's suggestion that the modest person measures himself only against the ideal is also in danger of sliding into this type of either/or thinking. Measuring oneself almost exclusively against an ideal indicates a tendency to define oneself solely in terms of the first-person norms of self-becoming – what I *can be* – at the expense of third-personally established categories and facts about how I fall into them. Brennan is no doubt right to point out that when we are faced with our own accomplishments, our tendency is to fall into the mode of either/or thinking whereby we simply accept our successes as definitive evidence of our own superiority.[20] It is therefore likely that some emphasis ought to be placed on the fact that we are never simply equivalent to our accomplishments. Nevertheless, it is clear that human beings are also prone to varieties of destructive self-loathing and negative self-regard in which they denigrate all that they do as worthless. Though Smith and Brennan recognize that focusing on the ideal cannot result in this kind of self-abnegation if it is to be considered virtuous, their demand that the modest person assess himself (almost) exclusively in terms of the ideal opens their position to this danger.

---

[20] Flanagan points out findings in cognitive social psychology demonstrating that people are much more likely to straightforwardly believe positive assessments of themselves than of others (1990, 426–427).

Indeed, though it may be harder to see how measuring oneself against the ideal could be considered an inappropriate way to express one's first-person freedom to be otherwise than what one is, such a tendency can indicate a type of false modesty in which someone is willing to measure himself only against the ideal because he believes his 'talents call for a higher standard of judgment' (Richards 1988, 255). Though it *seems* such a person is focusing only on his failures, then, he may do so in light of an overarching commitment to his own superiority, to his own exceptionalism when it comes to shared public measures and meanings. Even when this is not the case, however, understanding oneself solely in terms of the ideal can be a back-door responsibility-avoidance technique: by holding oneself up to a standard that one *knows* one cannot meet, *all* failures are surreptitiously justified insofar as they are equal in their failure status. By understanding oneself only in terms of an unrealizable ideal, the agent not only uses an inappropriate standard for assessing his own life, but he does so in such a way that provides him with the opportunity to excuse all of his failures insofar as everyone fails when measured against the standard of perfection. By relinquishing the task of taking an honest measure of one's success, one also evades the burden of recognizing the degree of one's failure. One thereby rules out the possibility – and the responsibility – of identifying precisely what one needs to improve and whether or not continued struggle toward improvement in this or that domain is a healthy or appropriate activity.[21]

Such an orientation toward the ideal can therefore signal a distorted calibration in one's standard for assessing what counts as a good or successful human life. Refusing to recognize success *as* success because the standard one has chosen for measuring it cannot be met seems a pathological misunderstanding of the meaning of success.[22] Though a person focused solely on eternity or the ideal will not abuse his freedom by refusing to focus on the insignificance or failure that defines him, by focusing primarily on this he can also develop a false self-conception. Such a stance interferes with the development of a realistic understanding of how to negotiate the complex normative terrain within which we operate,

---

[21] Though several of the 'double standard' accounts attempt to protect against this by forbidding 'standards or aspirations that are literally *inhuman* or inappropriate for our position in the grand scheme of things' (Smith 2008, 33), insufficient attention is paid to the fact that developing such 'realistic ideals' is possible only if an agent learns (1) to apply *both* standards at once and (2) to acknowledge the nature of these standards so that their simultaneous application is coordinated properly.
[22] Smilansky makes this point (2003, 106).

producing, instead, a type of selective and distorted sense of responsibility in which one does not allow oneself to take credit for successes but only for failures. The consequence can only be low self-regard or indifference to a failure that comes to be seen as inevitable. Though we are perhaps right to assume that our major concern is to guard against arrogance – and thus that we should be diligent in our application of the ideal as a standard for self-assessment – we must also guard against destructive forms of unrealistic perfectionism.

The truly virtuous stance must protect against both forms of either/or thinking. The appropriate form of self-assessment involves a constant struggle for harmony between accepting *and* striving to be greater than what one is according to public standards of success, while demonstrating concern for those we recognize to be both lesser *and yet* always irreducible to those rankings. Modest people keep things in perspective – they achieve a kind of complex and plural normative stance – by constantly negotiating between the temptation to understand themselves solely in terms of a first-person or a third-person perspective on their successes. Such coordination can be accomplished only by both recognizing external evidence for how well one's struggle for excellence is succeeding *and* simultaneously refusing to take this evidence as conclusive.

Behaving Modestly

We can see this impulse in the modest person's typical response to those who draw attention to her accomplishments; she tends to deflect attention from or recharacterize these accomplishments such that they cannot be interpreted as simply *definitive* of her – and thus of her and the other's respective 'worth'. She typically does so by contextualizing the accomplishment against the background of other social roles that one may play – 'Well, physicist is just another job to be done' – or against the background of other roles that she does play – 'Yes, but you should see me play tennis' – or against the context of those roles in which she may have failed as a *result* of her success – 'I may be a great physicist, but I spend so much time in the lab that I'm a lousy parent.'[23] Such 'contextualizing' communicates to others the modest person's belief that while she recognizes that the roles and rankings under consideration give *evidence* of her worth, this evidence is only

---

[23] Smith 2008 emphasizes the important role that contextualizing one's success plays in modesty.

ever incomplete, context dependent, and open to revision.[24] She highlights the complexity of her agency and the manner in which it resists being defined simply along a single axis. In cases where such 'contextualizing' is impossible because the modest agent is simply excellent across the board, modest behaviour typically involves deflection away from the success toward another topic. In the rare case that one just is a superb parent, physicist, artist, athlete, *and* friend, this modest deflection away from one's own excellence and toward another topic does not demand that one be ignorant of these successes or interpret them as insignificant. It indicates, rather, that the modest person is unwilling to *equate* herself with her accomplishments despite her recognition that from a third-person perspective they do define her, and this unwillingness is motivated by concern both for the truth and for the other person. By making herself responsive to both first- and third-person claims simultaneously – while also responding to the second-person awareness of how her successes might cause the other person to suffer – she negotiates the plurality of normative perspectives in a way constitutive of flourishing.

The modest person's tendency to alleviate the other person's pain must be balanced by the recognition that allowing the other person to continue to feel the pain of inadequacy in comparison to one's own success may in some cases be necessary to motivate him to improve himself. Modesty that is truly sensitive to the second-person claim will strive to alleviate the other person's suffering in a way that does not undermine the self-awareness and self-responsibility that is necessary for his genuine flourishing. If Mary is a successful novelist and Bill's laziness interferes with his success in this arena, Mary's modest behaviour should deflect attention away from her successes in such a way that nevertheless evokes a self-understanding in Bill that will conduce to his own flourishing. She might mention the long hours spent revising and all the failed drafts in order to communicate that her success is not simply a gift of her genius but the fruit of hard work. By shifting the attention in this way – and not, for example, by suggesting that the accomplishment is not in fact an accomplishment ('It was nothing') or pretending that it was mere luck and therefore bears no connection to her identity – Mary communicates that she does not think herself to be fundamentally better than Bill while

---

[24] Similarly, several accounts speak of the modest person's tendency to recognize all of the other factors – help from others, moral luck, etc. – that went into her success. See Flanagan 1990; Nuyen 1998; and Smith 2008.

nevertheless encouraging him to take responsibility for the ways in which he could improve himself according to standards of success that do in fact matter.

The modest person's honest self-understanding and benevolent attunement to the other person illuminates for those around her what it means to live the human condition of normative complexity well. In acting modestly, she demonstrates the appropriate degree to which success should be taken as definitive of the self, occupying the middle path between destructive either/or understandings of the meaning of such success. In doing so, she models a life that resists the temptation to indulge in glorying in success or wallowing in failure. This is communicated to others not by dismissing the possibility or importance of achieving human excellence but by displaying a deep understanding of the role of such success in genuine human flourishing.

Like the other virtues, then, modesty contributes to human flourishing insofar as it solves a particular existential problem that threatens one's ability to respond adequately to the three terrains of normative claim, namely, inequalities of success or accomplishment. It does so by resisting modes of self-understanding that unduly emphasize either the openness or closure of one's identity to definition and it is motivated to do so by a second-person concern for the other person's welfare.

CHAPTER 9

Courage

> Why should we honour those that die upon the field of battle? A man may show as reckless courage in entering into the abyss of himself.
> – William Butler Yeats, 1909

Courage seems to be a virtue more appropriate for an era of warfare and chivalry than for the soft lives that most of us typically lead. Indeed, for Aristotle, courage is a virtue that can be displayed only in the face of death – and not just any death, but death in battle (*NE*, III. 6 1115a25–26, 30–31).[1] When we discuss the virtues we often turn to Aristotle for help and guidance in understanding these different modes of human excellence, but when we consult 'The Philosopher' on the virtue of courage, it seems that he may have let us down. After all, we want to believe that courage is not limited to conditions of warfare: for example, that the man who presses forward in caring for his children after the death of his spouse displays a kind of courage, despite the fact that his death – let alone his death in battle – is not on the line. We do not want to relinquish this virtue to a highly select military few. But neither do we want to lose the distinctive features that differentiate courage from fortitude, endurance, or hard work. As William Miller puts it, when defining courage, 'Some impose so rigorous a standard that Homeric heroes have a hard time qualifying; others are so absurdly soft on admission to the club that just about anyone who sticks to a diet qualifies' (2002, 5). We need an account of courage that makes this virtue a form of excellence applicable to every human life. Despite the fact that its militaristic tenor initially leads us to believe that Aristotle's account of courage cannot help us with this task, in this chapter I will argue that he is in fact right to say that courage is a virtue restricted to situations in which one faces death in battle. In order to

---
[1] It is not clear that Aristotle himself had a principled reason for focusing on martial courage – it may simply have been most appropriate for his audience.

do so in a way that does not unduly limit the instances of courage to the dangers of war, however, I will need to provide interpretations of 'death' and 'battle' that have a somewhat different meaning than their straightforward senses of physical demise and firefights in the trenches. Nevertheless, I hope to show that these expanded meanings maintain enough similarities with those literal senses to warrant keeping the terms. In particular, I will show that courage arises in conditions of crisis in which one's way of being is experienced as at risk. This may occur whenever central relationships, roles, individuals, or communities are experienced as being at stake in a particular situation of choice. Courage is the virtue in which one chooses one's better self – i.e. one responds to the central normative claims at stake in a particular situation – despite the costs and risks associated with doing so.

Existential Death

What can it mean to talk of 'death' if we are not referring to the moment we shuffle off this mortal coil? What kind of 'death' must one face in courage if it is not physical perishing? The answer, I suggest, can be found in Heidegger's famous distinction between mere 'demise' and what can be called *existential* death.[2] Heidegger's discussion of death takes place in the context of his attempt to characterize human life in a way that does not presuppose an ontologically inappropriate characterization of what we are. In other words, Heidegger rejects our tendency to think of ourselves as objectively present things and thereby obscure the mode of being specific to us. When we take the time to think clearly about what we are, we realize that we are best understood as 'being-in-the-world' – a mode of being in which we are immersed in the worldly roles and activities and contexts of meaning by which we understand who we can be. That is what life is for human beings when they are understood primarily as persons and not as mere biological phenomena. In keeping with this reconception of the human, any conception of death must be correspondingly resistant to ontologically inappropriate characterizations. As a result, Heidegger separates the notion of perishing – the moment one's body becomes a corpse – from the idea of death as the ending of one's being-in-the-world. Existential death, then, means going out of the world – losing one's status as being-in-the-world.

---

[2] Heidegger discusses the existential conception of death in 1985, §§46–53. See also Lear 2006 and Nagel 1979.

The import of this suggestion is that it is possible to die without perishing[3] – a consequence of his view that will be important for our interpretation of courage and its virtuousness, since it expands the number of instances in which one can be said to 'face death'. In order to see why, we must clarify further what exactly it can mean to 'die' without perishing. Heidegger characterizes death as the omnipresent possibility of one's absolute impossibility (1985, §53). In facing death, we face up to the existential condition of our radical finitude and contingency – the fact that the self that I am is in danger of ceasing to be. Heidegger speaks of this primarily in terms of a kind of global breakdown that occurs when one is gripped by an anxiety that causes all of one's practical identities to fall away.[4] Unlike most affective orientations, which attract or repel us from certain features of the world, anxiety *nullifies* our relation to worldly things; the roles and activities that typically define us lose their grip on us and we find ourselves totally indifferent to their being. The result is a kind of global collapse of one's worldly identities. Since nothing in particular matters to me in this moment, I cannot grasp myself in terms of some worldly role. When this occurs my everyday self 'dies' because I have momentarily decoupled from its defining commitments. This is existential death – the possibility of the impossibility of existing as the person that I understood myself to be. As Heidegger puts it:

> Death, as possibility, gives Dasein [the human person] nothing to be 'actualized', nothing which Dasein, as actual, could itself *be*. It is the possibility of the impossibility of every way of comporting oneself towards anything, of every way of existing. (1985, 307)

In such a condition one is paralyzed – spinning free from the practical projects through which one normally experiences the meaning of the world. Thus existential anxiety corresponds to existential death because one disengages from the world as the framework of meaning in which one can be who and what one is. Indeed, we could argue that our terror at the thought of physical demise is rooted in our sense that it will be a permanent loss of significance and meaning in this way. In other words, fear of physical death is rooted in fear of existential death.

---

[3] Not everyone agrees that existential death and physical death can be separated in this way. For a more thorough defense of this claim than can be offered here, see Burch 2010. See also Thomson 2009.

[4] For Heidegger's main discussion of anxiety, see 1985, §40.

Heidegger goes on to demonstrate the many features that existential death and physical death have in common – the fact that both are individualizing, inescapable, and able to strike at any time (1985, §53). Here I wish to point out an important way in which they differ, however: namely, the fact that physical death is global, whereas we can understand a more localized sense of existential death. A 'localized' death occurs when a foundational role or relationship ends or is brought radically into question; as a result, the self that one was can no longer be in the world in the same way. Such partial deaths can be legitimately characterized as 'deaths' because they bring to an end a grounding identity: a central way in which one has been answering the question 'Who am I?' In so doing they show up the radical contingency of our identities and relationships, the groundlessness underlying the struggle to define our existence. The end of a marriage, the loss of a career, the death of a child – these are not simply painful or traumatic events – though they are surely that – but they are breaking points revealing that we cannot go on being the selves that we were. They represent for us encounters with the possibility of the impossibility of being the person we understood ourselves to be. And in the face of such loss, we must find a way to go on – in other words, we must find new ways in which to understand the self that we have been, new answers to the question 'Who am I?'

To say that courage occurs in the face of existential death, then, is to characterize courage primarily in terms of facing up to challenges to one's identity. This allows us to make sense of Aristotle's somewhat puzzling claim that the mercenary does not typically show courage, despite the fact that he usually does not run away from battle. Aristotle points out that mercenaries only *seem* courageous from the outside. Their experience with many battles means that they are rarely in any real danger – and they are in fact the first to run away when the risk becomes real. Further, the mercenary's decision to fight is not motivated by the thought of the noble (an issue to which we will return later) or because a grounding identity is on the line. Rather, the mercenary fights because of external benefits that may accrue by sticking around. For the citizen-soldier, on the other hand, the threat to a foundational existential identity – their honour and their status as a free citizen – trumps even genuine threats to life itself. Citizen-soldiers experience their identities as being at stake in the choice to run or fight; they would rather die than save their lives at the expense of their honour (*NE*, III. 7 1116b17–25). The mercenary's regular exposure to physical death on the battlefield therefore only *appears* courageous, a case that highlights the underlying structures necessary for distinguishing acts of true courage.

In contrast, consider the case of Jane Eyre. Jane finds herself in a situation where her sense of self is being called radically into question; the man she loves has been revealed to be a liar who seeks to lure her into a morally dubious arrangement. Rather than succumbing to the temptation he poses, she courageously flees into the wild on her own, refusing to allow her moral integrity to be compromised or destroyed. This is an opportunity for courage because a fundamental aspect of her identity is threatened with the possibility of death, forcing her to choose how to proceed in the face of a recognition of its contingency. Note that the action displaying courage here – running away – is the opposite of the action appropriate for the courageous person on the battlefield. Nevertheless, we can notice that in doing so Jane forsakes the safe and happy self that she has been, choosing to face tremendous pain and fear for the sake of her better self. Her courage is structurally the same as that displayed by the courageous warrior on the battlefield, though the threat of death comes in a radically different guise.

Using Jane Eyre as an example of courage prompts us to note that historically, courage was a virtue attributed only to men. Indeed, in many languages the word itself shares the same root as the word for man (Miller 2002, 13). Though the reason for this is obviously the fact that courage was traditionally equated with excellent acts of war in conditions of great physical danger, we might also think of it in terms of the relative lack of existential flexibility historically available to women. In other words, women rarely faced death of either the physical *or* the existential variety. After all, a woman's grounding identities were taken to be givens of her biology and as such she would rarely – if ever – be in conditions where such identities could be recognized as *at stake* for her. Or, more accurately, there was taken to be only *one* arena in which her identity could be recognized as being at stake: the arena of sexual morality – the choice between mother and whore, wife and mistress. Thus historically the feminine virtue par excellence – the female counterpart to courage – was chastity.[5] In contrast, men were regularly faced with situations in which their public and political identity was at stake – most obviously on the battlefield where the choice of noble death or shameful life was on the line.

---

[5] See Miller 2002, 232–253. One might argue that when a woman faced the dangers of childbirth she had an opportunity to display courage or cowardice – since women would regularly die on that 'battlefield' – but since it was a danger from which women could not flee, it does not obviously display the same structure of existential choice as is evident in conditions of war. We will return to this later.

Entering the Fray: The Moment of Crisis

It is this understanding of existential death that must be operative in our characterization of the virtue of courage as appropriate choice in the face of death. Courage can be displayed only in a condition where one's grounding identities are at risk of death – this is the existential problem that this virtue allows us to face with excellence. Courage is the virtue that the flourishing agent displays in situations where who she will be is in some sense on the line. To make better sense of this claim, let us look to the second part of Aristotle's seemingly anachronistic definition of courage, namely, the claim that only the danger of death *in battle* provides an occasion for courage (*NE*, III.6.1115a28–31). We can understand this in an expanded sense by saying that courage is only possible when one faces a condition in which one's action will in some sense be *definitive* of whether the self that one wishes to be lives or dies.

We can think here of T. S. Eliot's *Prufrock*: 'And indeed there will be time/ To wonder, "Do I dare?" and, "Do I dare?" / ... Should I, after tea and cakes and ices / Have the strength to force the moment to its crisis?' (1920). The idea of having to act in a moment of crisis – a condition of risk that is both sudden and decisive – is a defining feature of courage. For courage to be a possibility, some essential way of being must be *on the line*. This can be seen quite easily in cases of literal battle, particularly when read in terms of world historical narratives regarding the clash of civilizations and the possibilities of identity that they represent. Will I be a free Athenian citizen or a Spartan slave? Such moments of crisis bring one face to face with the existential question: 'Who will I be?' but they do so in such a way that the import of the choice cannot be ignored. My actions here and now in this moment of crisis will determine the answer in an explicit and irrevocable way.[6]

The sense that courage appears only on the battlefield allows us to distinguish between courage and mere hard work or endurance. After all, when I dedicate myself to my writing as opposed to my TV-watching, I am in a certain sense making a choice regarding the self who I wish to be. With every hour spent at the computer I am affirming my writing self – a self that is at greater risk of withering away with every hour spent on the sofa. But such cases of endurance and gradual transformation are not the stuff of courage. Rather, we should describe them as perseverance or fortitude – also virtues, no doubt. But Aristotle is right to say that courage is the virtue

---

[6] 'You are going your way to greatness: here nobody shall sneak after you. Your own foot has effaced the path behind you' (Nietzsche 1995, 153).

of the battlefield in the sense that it is the mode of excellence displayed in conditions of immanent and pressing attack on the self and what it values. Will one fight or run away? Will one take the job, or not? Will one stand up to the bully or continue to be abused?[7]

What counts as an immanent and pressing attack will surely differ for each of us. We can see this when we recognize that there will be cases of existential death where courage is not really the appropriate or most relevant virtue. Consider, for example, a time when a self that one has been will be irrevocably lost: the death of one's parents. In such a moment, the understanding of oneself as a son or a daughter is an identity that is henceforth forever closed (or at least radically attenuated). Though such an event is a kind of existential death, the appropriate response − for most of us, at least − is not courage but fortitude, since what is required is not the dramatic choice or renunciation of an identity but an ability to continue maintaining oneself despite the pain of the loss. In other words, the loss is not experienced as an immanent and pressing attack. For others, however, such a loss could succeed in pushing the moment to a crisis, for example, if one's identity as son or daughter is serving such a foundational role that its loss could derail the self that one is struggling to be. Imagine, for example, that heroin addiction has been kept at bay through the relationship that one has with one's parents − through their support and faith in one's better self. Their demise is thus not only a moment of existential death for one particular grounding identity − namely, daughter or son − but is also a moment in which one faces the threat of further death − the threat of also losing one's life as a sober person. In this sense the addict is facing death on the battlefield; she is thrust into a moment of crisis in which the question 'Who will I be?' must be answered now and answered in a way that will have irrevocable repercussions for the self that she can be. Courage is the virtue in which the addict, like the soldier, chooses to fight on in the moment of crisis. She chooses her better self despite the seriousness of the stakes and the pain she must endure to accomplish the identity she chooses.

---

[7] Miller 2002 notes that in conditions of extended periods of trench warfare it became evident that the men (excepting the psychopaths in the group) could not sustain the courageous stance but became increasingly jittery and frightened over time, before lapsing into a kind of deadened state of emotional exhaustion. Miller's observations here are in keeping with the interpretation that the courageous cannot maintain this stance for extended periods because in such conditions the crisis has become disengaged from the resolution or transformation that was its purpose to bring about. In conditions of modern warfare (as opposed to the contained battles of Hoplite war, for example), each battle seems to bring soldiers no closer to the end of the war or the attendant transformations of identity that it would precipitate, but merely exposes them to an unending series of horrors with no discernible purpose (59–65).

Though such moments of crisis are obvious in cases of war, their existential counterparts are present throughout our lives, though they may not always appear as such from the outside. Consider another example. A straight man recognizes that his gay coworker is being excluded from the group, and when presented with the opportunity, he chooses to make a deliberate gesture of inclusion despite potential hostility from that group. In such a situation the man is faced with a choice: he can continue tacitly endorsing the exclusion of his coworker or he can risk his own ostracism to take a stand on the self that he wishes to be – i.e. one who does not coast on heteronormative privilege but strives to implement conditions of social inclusion and justice. He experiences the moment as one of existential crisis demanding courage. Though on other days he may have been preoccupied and failed to notice the dynamic, today he sees the moment as being forced to a crisis. In that moment of crisis he displays courage by explicitly including his co-worker and calling out those members of the group who are facilitating the exclusion. Such an example is not the stuff of epic poetry, granted, but such a mundane example can nevertheless be an instance of courage – evident in the sense of an identity at stake: the man risks the ease and comfort of his in-group status in order to be the self that he wishes to be by responding to this central normative claim despite the risks he faces in doing so. Of course the relatively minimal stakes of such a choice allow us to note that the degree of courage that one can show in any given instance will be proportional to the centrality of the identity being risked or claimed and the danger and suffering that one faces in doing so. Nevertheless, the structure of courage is evident even in such minimal instances: namely, the choice of a higher identity is made in conditions of crisis at the risk of pain and loss of some kind.

The idea that one can *choose* to see a situation as a point of existential crisis in which a core identity is at risk raises some interesting questions. As Amelie Oksenberg Rorty points out in 'Two Faces of Courage', one might worry that courage is a dangerous virtue insofar as it may promote a tendency to view or even create situations characterized by such conflict and crisis.[8] In other words, the worry might be that a person comes to thrive on the danger of existential death, seeking out opportunities where her grounding identities are threatened, an existential adrenaline junkie of sorts.

---

[8] Rorty 1986 speaks of this in terms of the 'magnetizing' quality of the virtues: 'dispositions to gravitate towards, and sometimes even create the conditions that predictably elicit the exercise of systematically linked dispositions' (154).

Though such a personality type is certainly a possibility, I think it is best understood as both pathological and rare. The reason for this becomes clear when we recognize what a grounding identity is. A grounding identity refers to a set of interrelated activities, relationships, and systems of reference in terms of which one understands who one is. Identities can be more or less peripheral to one's sense of self – grounding identities are those that form the core. Because these central identities provide the bedrock in terms of which the world is meaningful, to lose them or risk losing them is for most people a terrifying and in some cases almost inconceivable prospect. And as Heidegger points out, it is for the most part not up to us when we are thrown into conditions where the contingency of these ways of being is revealed to us. Thus the typical condition requiring courage will be one where a situation arises through no choice of our own, a situation that *demands* courage of us because it reveals a core practical identity to be at stake in some risky or painful choice – whether we like it or not (usually not).

Of course, one can imagine a personality type whereby risk-taking itself becomes a grounding identity. In such a case one can indeed imagine that one seeks out conditions of danger – but as we will see in the final section of the chapter, action that overcomes danger and fear is genuine courage only if it is undertaken for the sake of the noble and not for the mere thrill of an adrenaline high. Like the mercenary, then, the adrenaline junkie is not truly courageous because she does not endure pain and danger for the sake of a *better* self.[9]

Nevertheless, one might push the idea that courage has imperialistic tendencies by noting that one can indeed *choose* to see the situation as one of crisis. Such cases are legion: Rosa Parks's refusal to give up her seat on the bus helped trigger the civil rights movement because she chose to see the events of December 1, 1955, *as* a moment of crisis. Despite the long series of racist indignities that she had endured throughout her life, on that day she refused to tolerate another. One might say that she had the strength to force the moment to its crisis, seeing the choice as definitive for her identity and facing up to the suffering that would result because of her commitment to that identity. What role does courage play in such a choice? Can every moment potentially be 'forced to its crisis'?

---

[9] We can similarly reject moralizing types who tend to view every situation as a potential test of virtue. Moralism can be defined as 'treating moral reasons as more pervasive than they actually are' (Driver 2005, 138). Thus the tendency to view *every* moment as a crisis or a potential crisis – i.e. as bearing extreme moral implications for one's identity – can be viewed as a variety of moralism. See also Diamond 1997.

It seems that in such instances one sees the symbolic import of a moment or event; it stands out from the background of ordinary life to take on a kind of exemplary significance. One experiences that instant as a crossroads, a turning point between two selves whose paths will irrevocably diverge from that point forward: in the case of Ms. Parks, the self who demands respect for her human dignity versus the self who allows that dignity to be denigrated. One might think of this kind of crossroads moment in terms of Heidegger's notion of the *Augenblick* – the moment of vision, the blink of the eye.[10] '*Augenblick*' translates the ancient Greek *kairos* – a kind of supreme or definitive moment. The term is sometimes used to refer to the *phronimos*'s moment of insight into what practical wisdom demands: it is the time of appropriate skillful action made possible by seeing the moment in the 'fullness of its possibility' (Kisiel 1993).[11]

The notion also has profound religious connotations dating back to St. Paul's characterization of the resurrection of the body.[12] This concept has played a major role for thinkers like Luther and Kierkegaard and their idea of religious conversion, as well as for Nietzsche and his secularized version of such conversion or self-overcoming. Heidegger's own use of the concept appears to be an attempt to combine the notion of practical wisdom with the quasi-religious connotations of conversion. This hybrid understanding of the *Augenblick* can be useful for our account of courage.[13] Namely, I take it to refer to 'those moments which stand out from the ordinary run of time' with a kind of decisive significance for who one will be (Ward 2008, 7). It refers to a condition in which one sees the moment not as another undifferentiated point in the unending flow of time but in terms of the symbolic or ideal import of this instant and the

---

[10] McNeill 1999 discusses the concept of the *Augenblick* in terms of the traditional philosophical prioritization of vision.
[11] See also Dreyfus 2000, 163. Heidegger touches on the Aristotelian dimensions of the concept (2003, 100 and 1982, 288). Aristotle himself only seems to use the term *kairos* in this regard when he is discussing the imprecision of practical thinking (*NE*, 1104a8) and the notion of 'mixed actions', which are neither simply voluntary or involuntary but are choiceworthy in the specific situation (*NE*, 1110a14). I am grateful to David McNeill for bringing this to my attention.
[12] Corinthians I, 15:52: 'We shall all be changed in a moment, in the twinkling of an eye.'
[13] There is some debate on how Heidegger understands the relationship between the Aristotle-inspired notion of a decisive moment in practical wisdom and the theological notion of the instant of conversion or self-grasping. 'Heidegger seems to be distinguishing Dasein's primordial understanding of the current Situation from Dasein's experience of its most primordial way of being and yet trying to subsume them both under the *Augenblick*' (Dreyfus 2000, 165). See also Van Buren 1994: 'Following St. Paul, as well as Aristotle, Heidegger stresses that particular *kairoi*, situations, are always "new creations" that come "like a thief in the night"' (283).

choice it represents for one's identity. Such a moment bears existential significance, revealing in a heightened form the weight that one's choices play in determining who one will be. Such moments therefore involve a kind of explicit existential awareness – they require a shift in point of view whereby one is no longer simply acting through one's identities but seeing them *as* one's identities, as the normative constructs in terms of which one answers for oneself. In such a moment, one can recognize that one *cannot go on* in the life that one has been occupying. It is not simply to experience one's choices as having a bearing on one's identity – as they always do – rather, it is to feel that this specific choice has taken on a kind of symbolic or outsized significance for determining who one will be, and as such one is motivated to endure the pain and suffering associated with choosing it.

One can see, then, why Heidegger regularly links the concepts of authenticity, the *Augenblick*, and courage or 'daring'. Simply put, authenticity requires ontological self-awareness; it is the ability to see and take responsibility for the kind of being that one is, namely, a finite being who is attempting to answer the question 'Who am I?' through the worldly roles and relationships that it endorses. Moments of crisis occur when one recognizes that these worldly identities can collapse or conflict or fail to express the self that one is struggling to be. Courage is the mode of excellence whereby one seizes on the right choice in the face of such crisis despite the risk of suffering and loss that this choice brings with it. As such, it displays the distinctive structure of the virtues as problem-solving stances that allow us to respond well to the normative claims by which we are addressed. In courage, we see a virtue that allows the central normative claims addressing us in a given situation to override the fear that can prevent us from acting on them.

There is obviously a great deal more that could be said about the relationship between courage and authenticity, particularly insofar as it manifests in what Heidegger refers to as 'resoluteness' – a stance of responsibility in which one lives in light of the possibility of existential death. For our purposes here, however, it is enough to say that courage seems to demand that one experience a particular event as representing a choice between two fundamentally different possibilities of being. Doing so need not require the kind of global and relatively explicit awareness of oneself that seems to characterize full-blown authenticity, however. Understanding the symbolic implications of the moment need not and in most cases will not occur on an explicit cognitive level. Rather, the existential weight of the choice will be felt in a pre-theoretical and unthematized way. This need not rule out the possibility of abstracting from this implicit awareness in order to deliberate about identity-founding projects, as we saw in Chapter 6. But the truly virtuous person – for the most part – will simply see the situation as making certain kinds of claim on her, and she will respond well to those claims despite the suffering that this may entail.

Courageous Passions: Fear and Confidence

The idea of threat is therefore essential, since courage is by all accounts the stance that the virtuous person takes in the face of *fear*. There is some debate about exactly what role fear plays in the courageous person's character, however. To be courageous it seems that a person must not be fearless but must instead feel the level of fear that is appropriate to the terrifying and terrible thing that threatens her. She must feel that fear *and yet* find her way into performing the appropriate action despite it. Or as Aristotle also puts it, she must feel fear and yet also feel the confidence necessary to endure and act despite the terrible things that threaten. Thus Aristotle argues that courage has a more complex structure than many virtues because it demands avoiding excesses and deficiencies in terms of *two* characteristic passions: fear and confidence.[14] Aristotle defines fear as pain at the thought of an immanent evil (1984a, II.5 1381a22–23). In the *Rhetoric* he defines confidence as the opposite of fear (1984a, II.5 1381b13–16). Thus confidence can perhaps be understood as pleasure at the thought of an immanent good.[15] Courage demands that one adopt the appropriate relationship to both fear and confidence – a demand that again can be illuminated by transposing the Aristotelian discussion into the Heideggerian framework that we have introduced. In other words, if courage is the stance required in conditions where a central practical

---

[14] As Young 2009 points out, the *Eudemian Ethics* has a simple account: courage simply lies between rashness and cowardice. The *Nicomachean Ethics*, on the other hand, has a more complicated story involving three vices, all of which appear to be excesses: excess in fearlessness (nameless vice), excess in cheer/confidence (rashness), excess in fear (cowardice). The account is more complicated in the *NE* because it breaks the link between excess of confidence and deficiency of fear – they are treated as two distinct vices as opposed to flip sides of the same vice. It does not seem that Aristotle is always consistent on this, however. 'In allowing that fear and cheer can vary independently of one another, the *NE* raises a question about the unity of courage as it conceives of that virtue. For it would seem that courage involves *two* mean states, one relative to fear – call it *fortitude* – and another relative to cheer [confidence] – call it *discretion*. Why, then, does Aristotle not regard these apparently distinct mean states as two distinct virtues?' (443). We are not in a position to solve this problem here. For further discussion, see Ross 1995.

[15] See Young 2009 for a discussion of this conclusion.

identity is at immanent risk, one can understand confidence as pleasure at the thought of a new or perfected identity and the life that it enables, pleasure that motivates one in the face of threatened loss. The confidence at the heart of courage is essentially the ability to envision and desire the better self that the courageous act will allow one to be. This is not always easy: pain and fear of pain can easily drown out hope for the good.[16] Courage requires both coping with appropriate fear and displaying sufficient confidence, both mourning the lost self and celebrating the possibility of a better one. Indeed, with the notion of celebration we can make room for the possibility of joy accompanying this event, joy in an existential rebirth whose labour pangs are painful and terrifying but whose fruit is the transfigured self.

In contrast to the virtuous harmonizing of fear and confidence that occurs in courage, it is of course possible to act inappropriately due to excess fear – i.e. display cowardice – such that one is unable to face the costs associated with becoming the self that one is trying to be. Excess fear in conditions of existential crisis means that one is inappropriately clinging to the self one has been for fear of the pain that change might demand, choosing to avoid that potential pain rather than working toward realizing a higher good. Excessive fear is regularly accompanied by a deficiency of confidence, but Aristotle insists that it is the former that is the true mark of the coward. The coward clings to her old identity out of fear and refuses to embrace the possibilities of goodness that the courageous choice offers.

Aristotle suggests that there are two vices displaying *excess* confidence – one coupled with deficient fear, sometimes called rashness, and one coupled with excessive fear. In both cases the presence of excessive confidence indicates an inappropriate degree of hope, an inability to recognize that the choice being demanded is indeed an existential risk.[17] The rashness characteristic of excessive confidence is best understood as a refusal or an inability to acknowledge or understand the stakes – that the self one has been might die with no guarantee that the new identity formulation will be capable of successfully grounding one's future sense

---

[16] 'Yet the end which courage sets before it would seem to be pleasant, but to be concealed by the attending circumstances, as happens also in athletic contests; for the end at which boxers aim is pleasant – the crown and the honours – but the blows they take are distressing to flesh and blood, and painful, and so is their whole exertion; and because the blows and the exertions are many the end, which is but small, appears to have nothing pleasant in it' (Aristotle, *NE*, III.6.1117a30–b6).

[17] In the *Eudemian Ethics* Aristotle talks about how children and madmen seem brave because their ignorance causes them to do foolish things such as grasp snakes (2011, 1229a18). We have already seen that those who are experienced in battle – like the professional soldier – seem to be courageous but are in fact not, since they do not believe themselves to be in any danger (2011, 1230a 13–15).

of self. Such excess confidence is often combined with deficient fear, which similarly involves a failure to recognize the danger as such – in this case, because one is unwilling or unable to recognize the risk of suffering or lost physical or existential life.

It is hard to understand how one could simultaneously display excessive fear and excessive confidence, but we can see Aristotle wrestling with this possibility when he suggests that rashness often turns out to be cowardice. The suggestion is that rash or foolhardy people are in fact cowards who conceal this fact from themselves: such a person is a 'boaster and pretender to courage' (*NE*, III.7.1115b28). Such people do not seem to have fully acknowledged the reality of the pain and loss that threaten them. Their bravado and excessive confidence is based on blindness to the enormity of the choice facing them – a blindness, I would argue, that is in some cases perhaps *motivated* by excessive fear. In other words, in some people rashness may be grounded in a kind of self-deception – an unstable combination of excessive fear and excessive confidence that produces the illusion of fearlessness. In essence, we could say that such people refuse to face the fact of moral luck in Bernard Williams's sense – the recognition that one can gamble and *lose*, that one may make a choice that one's future self cannot recoup or experience as justified (1981, 20–39). The risk characteristic of conditions in which courage is called for is predicated on the openness of the future, the uncertainty about what courage demands, and the very real possibility of failure. To act courageously demands that one take action in the face of the unknown in light of a vision of a future good. The rash person's excessive confidence in the realizablility of that future good means that he does not sufficiently acknowledge the genuine risk that the life he has gambled will not be replaced by a truer or higher self and thus might only be the object of grief and regret. Foolhardiness often reveals itself only retrospectively from the viewpoint of failure, through the fact that one has not accomplished a new or more perfectly realized version of oneself, but simply lost or damaged an old one. The open-endedness of the future and the impact of the existential choices that shape that future mean that it becomes very difficult to assess the wisdom of the transformation that one is facing pain and fear to undergo. Assessment prior to the choice cannot discern whether the identity will be accomplished – a fact concealed by excessive confidence.[18]

---

[18] But assessment *after* the choice occurs from the perspective of the successful or failed gamble: 'The standpoint of that retrospective judge who will be my later self will be the product of my earlier choices' (Williams 1981, 34–35). The role of acting for the sake of the noble becomes important

Despite displaying endurance in the face of fear and danger, then, foolhardiness fails to be courage because its excessive confidence demonstrates that it is not appropriately rooted in a recognition of the contingency of the grounding identities that are at stake in the choice. To show courage requires that one not give in to the fear that inevitably comes when one fully recognizes that one's most basic sense of self is on the line.

Self-Control?

A major puzzle that afflicts the literature on courage relates to the question of how the courageous overcoming of fear can be anything other than self-control, as opposed to the kind of habituated expression of appropriate passions characteristic of genuine virtue. As we have seen, on Aristotle's account the virtuous person does not struggle against strong temptation but exists in a condition whereby her desires and her considered sense of what she ought to do are in harmony. In contrast, people who are merely self-controlled must overcome desires prompting them to do the opposite of what they consider best (NE, VII.9.1151b32–1152a3). Thus self-control requires contrary desires against which to contend, while genuine virtue precludes them. In light of this, it seems clear why courage is a problematic virtue. After all, doesn't the courageous person have to *overcome* his fear, a condition thereby resembling self-control more than genuine virtue? How is courage even possible, then, considering Aristotle's claim that courage can be displayed only in the face of legitimately fearful things (e.g. NE, III.6.1115a24–35) and that courageous people do indeed feel fear in the face of those things?[19]

---

here, since the agent's good intent might offer something like a buffer against regret even in the face of failure. But Williams is wary of such a view, questioning the idea that 'a rational individual is always to act so that he need never blame himself no matter how things finally transpire' (Williams 1981, 34). For Williams, the contingency of our grounding projects – their dependence on conditions of luck – means that we cannot guarantee in advance that our gambles will succeed, and when they do not the destruction of these grounding projects can – and should – produce blame and regret. Indeed, the fact that the risk of such blame and regret cannot be fully avoided (no matter how good one's intentions) is constitutive of the danger that the courageous person must face.

[19] In the *Eudemian Ethics*, Book III, 1228b, Aristotle says quite explicitly that brave people feel little to no fear. Further along, however, he suggests that the courageous feel the level of fear that is perfectly appropriate to the degree of danger posed to them: 'the coward thinks things not formidable formidable and things slightly formidable extremely formidable, and the daring man on the contrary thinks formidable things perfectly safe and extremely formidable things only slightly formidable, to the brave man on the other hand things seem exactly what they are' (2011, III 1229b 23–28).

Though Aristotle himself appears to be somewhat conflicted on this point, our primary purpose here is to understand courage, not Aristotle, so we can simply ask ourselves: Is the courageous person always battling fear, or has she achieved a relationship to fear in which it is present, but not as something needing to be fought or perpetually overcome? It seems that the latter is the more appropriate way of understanding courage – and, conveniently enough, this is also consistent with (much of) Aristotle's account.

We can understand this point when we characterize the passion of fear correctly. It is not best understood as a brute, animal-like force that must be eradicated or crushed if one is to act courageously. Rather, we can conceive of fear as displaying a kind of wisdom; when it manifests in the appropriate form it can help to focus one's perception on what is morally salient, not merely inhibit one's ability to act on such a perception. Indeed, without fear one might not fully recognize the import of the choice at hand. Fear is an emotion that communicates that one is facing a moment of crisis. The brave person is legitimately fearful of terrible things and therefore takes reasonable precautions to avoid them, at least when nothing noble is at stake requiring that they not be avoided.[20] If one is entirely lacking fear in a situation of acute existential danger, then one will be unable to recognize the import of the situation or act appropriately.[21] If one has too much fear, however, one will be unable to act on what is demanded. Thus the presence of fear – when it is neither deficient nor excessive – helps the courageous person to recognize the situation as a decision point demanding choice, without overwhelming and paralyzing her capacity to choose or act on that choice.

The Noble Choice

We have seen that courage arises as a possibility in the face of a battle between two possible ways of being. It involves a willingness to endure the suffering and fear associated with the choice of being one's better self. Such a characterization prompts us to turn, finally, to the question of what it can mean to have 'better' and 'lesser' selves. Throughout the chapter so far we

---

[20] See Aristotle 2011, 1229a7–9. In the *Rhetoric*, Aristotle suggests that 'fear sets us thinking what can be done' (1984a, II 5. 1381a27–8). See also Irwin 1986, 219.

[21] As Leighton 1988 puts it: 'fear serves as a channel of information, information particularly pertinent to our well-being, and information that is particularly pressing at the moment ... it provides the motivation, stimulates the thinking, and engages us in the action we need in order to deal with the circumstances of which it warns' (94). See also Gay 1988, 259.

have seen that the courageous person is the person who chooses the right way to be in the face of a crisis that threatens her sense of self. But what makes one's choice the right one? Aristotle argues that a defining feature of courage must be the choice of the noble for the sake of the noble. In other words, the action must be motivated by a recognition of the act's appropriateness, not by other benefits that may accrue as a result of that good act. Mere avoidance of pain, for example, no matter what courageous-seeming actions it happens to trigger, cannot be the motivation appropriate to the courageous person.[22] It is for this reason that Aristotle claims that the political act can most closely approximate the genuine courage he reserves for the battlefield, since a political act can involve facing the danger of legal penalties or reproaches for the sake of a noble object. The politically courageous seek to avoid disgrace or ignobility, not pain. Interestingly, Aristotle suggests that the most terrifying and terrible threat that one faces is not death as such but *shameful* death (*NE*, III.8 1116b20–25). Facing death on the battlefield is the exemplary arena for courage, then, because it is a venue in which one faces not just physical pain and death but conditions of choice that will be absolutely definitive for establishing whether one has conducted oneself with honour or dishonour. Cowards fear death more than disgrace (*NE*, III.6.1116b22–23), whereas the courageous fear disgrace even above death.[23] Thus despite the fact that Aristotle's emphasis on facing death in battle seems to prioritize the fear and suffering associated with *perishing*, in fact the choice to make death in battle the exemplary arena for courage is more existentially fraught than it initially appears, since the threat of *shameful* death unifies existential and physical death – it is the threat of losing the self that one has struggled to be such that there will be no opportunities to recover and begin again. Shameful death is the irrevocable failure to be the self one ought to have been, and the courageous person fears this above all.[24]

---

[22] Socrates makes this point in the *Phaedo* (68d). The emphasis on knowing what nobility demands and being willing and able to suffer through what is required to promote it captures Plato's sense of courage in the *Laches*. There Socrates suggests that courage involves both knowing what is good and what is evil and being able to endure what is necessary for the sake of the former. Thus what differentiates courage from wisdom (knowledge of good and evil) is the notion of endurance (192d). For discussion of this point, see Devereux 1992: 'The view suggested by Nicias (195b–186b) – and apparently endorsed by Socrates – is that a courageous person must know when a risk is worth taking or when it is worthwhile enduring, and this presupposes a deep understanding of what is of value in human life – that is, knowledge of good and evil' (778).

[23] In less shame-based cultures we can also think of fear of a meaningless or insignificant life.

[24] This point returns us to a claim made out the outset – namely, that fear of physical death is grounded on fear of existential death. One might be tempted to object that when viewed through the lens of evolutionary biology, such a claim cannot be true. But in many hunter-gatherer groups the failure to

Acting for the noble is an expression of the virtuous agent's ongoing commitment to excellence. It refers to a condition in which one attempts to live up to certain standards of excellence, seeing one's actions in light of their success or failure at instantiating those norms. As we have seen throughout the book, there are three different classes of such standards: the first-person, second-person, and third-person normative domains. As a result of this normative multiplicity, there are different forms that courageously 'acting for the sake of the noble' can take. In the first-person form, one perseveres in the face of pain and danger – risking the loss of the safety and security of an existing way of being – for the sake of a more fully realized self, a life that is more in keeping with one's potential. There is a great deal of literature celebrating such a stance. One thinks of Nietzsche, for example, and his claim that 'virtue is the will to go under and an arrow of longing' for 'the other shore' (1995, 15). In general we believe that such a disposition is praiseworthy, as Paul Tillich puts it, because 'in the act of courage the most essential part of our being prevails against the less essential' (2000, 5).

One can imagine a case, for example, of someone who chooses to sacrifice the ease and comfort of her current life as an accountant to pursue what she takes to be her higher calling as a novelist. In such a case the agent risks who she has been for the sake of what she can be, and we admire such a choice as courageous insofar as we believe that the self she can be is more valuable than the self that she has been – whether because the resulting activity is itself more valuable or because we take the fact of self-realization itself to be intrinsically valuable. This first-person mode of acting for the sake of the noble involves the affirmation of one's essential nature, if not in terms of the concept of an inner *telos*, at least in terms of the value of self-direction. As Tillich puts it, such cases include 'the possible and, in some cases, the unavoidable sacrifice of elements which also belong to one's being but which, if not sacrificed, would prevent us from reaching our actual fulfillment' (2000, 4–5). What makes this self-affirmation specifically *courageous* is the fact that it comes in the form of sacrifice and risk in conditions of crisis.

We can think here of the notion of the heroic and its tight connection with the virtue of courage. The heroic involves the creation of a better future through the supercession of the past and, in particular, a past version of oneself that is taken to be unequal to the task of bringing

---

courageously face death during the hunt or tribal warfare was punishable by social ostracism – a punishment equivalent to both physical and existential death.

about that future. Most hero narratives involve not only the performance of great deeds but also the story of transformation by which the hero becomes the person capable of such great deeds. For this event of self-overcoming to be legitimately characterized as heroic or courageous, however, the yearned-for future must in fact be better than what has come before.

Such talk of heroes might prompt one to wonder whether this kind of courage – or indeed, my entire account of courage – is fundamentally narcissistic. Does this characterization of the courageous agent portray her as overly concerned with the self that *she* will be, with the life she can realize for *herself* in making the courageous choice? As Callan (1993) points out, courage involves a kind of self-enlarging that seems inconsistent with virtues like patience. Is it right to say that the courageous agent's choices can be best understood as responses to the question 'Who shall *I* be?'

Well, yes and no. We have seen that it is important to avoid falling into the popular but misguided tendency to draw a sharp distinction between egoistic and altruistic motivations. Every choice is necessarily formally egoistic insofar as it is something for which each agent alone must answer. Responsibility for how I comport myself in my struggle to be cannot be shared or passed along but is ultimately always my own. Even if the project I endorse is one of radical altruism, it is nevertheless *I* who must endorse it and implement it in my life. Human beings are entrusted with their own lives and turn to the world to offer them guidance in their struggle to be in the world well. Our orientation toward such standards is rooted in our care for succeeding at being the selves that we are. This does not mean, however, that we cannot legitimately be motivated by other-directed desires. The struggle to be one's best self is always constrained and measured by claims 'external' to it – since to be a self is to be in the world with others. It is for this reason that the other categories of nobility are necessary for understanding courage – namely, second-person modes of normative responsiveness, whereby we respond fully to the claims of love and morality made on us by particular others, and third-person modes of excellence, whereby we answer to the claims made on us by the community and its intersubjective values. Thus there are many cases in which one might courageously face danger and loss for the sake of another person or for the sake of the community and its ideals. I might defend my brother Neil because I feel and respond to the moral claims intrinsic to that loving relationship. Alternatively, I might risk ostracism or jail for the sake of a vision of a more just society. To suggest that the struggle to be one's best self is inconsistent with meeting obligations external to self-interest is to misunderstand the existential project of being in the world well: to successfully answer the question 'Who am I?' demands that I recognize that my being is embedded and expressed in the worldly projects and relationships that I share with others.

One might object, however, that such a characterization is still too focused on the self. After all, it seems to suggest that the existential crisis establishing conditions where courage is appropriate must always be such that I experience a threat to *myself*. But many courageous agents have no thought for the self at all – rather, they are entirely focused on the threat to the other person. Thus to consider how the situation reflects on *my* identity is to have one thought too many. Rather, the second- or third-person claim is experienced *as* an immediate claim without the need for deliberation or for explicit reference to one's own identity.

This is surely correct. Nevertheless, even in the most other-focused experience there is a sense that *I* must answer for this situation, and this is what it means to experience oneself as being at stake in all classes of normative claim. Though it is clear that the distress of the other person is a fully sufficient motivator in many cases of courage, the courageous person's response to this kind of claim is 'What can *I* do?' or, in Lévinas' terms: 'Here I am.' The object is the other's need, but this need is nevertheless always experienced from the position of an agency being called on to act and to answer for how it chooses to do so. Thus the courageous agent might say: 'I could not have lived with myself if I hadn't done something.' Such a stance points to the deep imbrication of the first-person, second-person, and third-person normative arenas. Though it is often the other person's need that establishes the crisis that calls for courage, it is nevertheless the self at stake in its being in the world that experiences itself as called on to take responsibility for answering that call.

Recall Rosa Parks. In such a case of courage we can understand what she is doing as a response to the overlapping moral claims being made on her – to respect herself, to defend others who are also being abused by such conditions, and to fight for a vision of a better society. In every instance of courage one risks the self one has been for the sake of what is noble. The normative measures governing what counts as noble are not up to me – they do not all fall within the auspices of my autonomous choice. Rather, their distinguishing feature is that I experience myself as *claimed* by them – an event of obligation in which, nevertheless, I alone can answer for myself and my interpretation of what I take those claims to demand.

One might object, at this point, that this talk of existential identity and 'better selves' overlooks the obvious and paradigmatic cases of courage in which the agent not only faces death but actually *dies* for the sake of the noble. According to my account, courage is the ability to choose one's best possible self in conditions of crisis, a best self whose excellence is measured in terms of the normative domains of self-becoming, other-responsiveness, and community-creation. Can such an account accommodate cases in which the courageous person *dies* for the sake of the noble?

To answer this, we must return to the distinction between existential death and physical demise. Though we have spoken throughout of cases where one dies *existentially* while continuing to live in the *biological* sense, fatal cases of courage reverse this structure. In other words, to die for the sake of the noble means striving for an existential life that transcends one's demise. Such cases require an agent to see herself as continuing on in the avatar of the relationship, value, or community for which she has sacrificed herself. To die for a cause is to see oneself as transcending the bounds of one's physical life. Such an understanding makes sense only if we decouple the concepts of existential life and death from physical life and death. To die for a cause is to give up one's mortal life for the sake of a way of being in the world that is taken to be of such excellence that it cannot be allowed to pass out of existence, even at the cost of one's very life:

> I show you the death that consummates – a spur and a promise to the survivors. He that consummates his life dies his death victoriously, surrounded by those who hope and promise. (Nietzsche 1995, 71–72)

Conclusion

Aristotle defines humanity's characteristic activity as 'an activity of the soul in accordance with reason' (*NE*, I.7.1098a10–11). I have argued that at its heart practical reason is about grasping and integrating all of the competing considerations that count in favour of an action or belief – the reasons – that claim us in the project of being in the world well. This normative condition is tripartite: the norms governing us fall into three different classes, all of which provide different kinds of reason for belief and action. We experience ourselves as governed by a plurality of 'oughts' that cannot be reduced to each other or to a non-normative natural condition without remainder but rather address us with irreducible and unavoidable normative claims. Practical reason is tasked with negotiating this normative complexity well.

The first-person normative domain refers to imperatives governing the possibility of being one's best self – both in terms of the formal constraints intrinsic to agency as such and in terms of the substantive and idiosyncratic ways that each individual understands herself to fit with the world: her unique style of being. The second-person normative domain refers to the way in which individual others make claims that call into question one's tendency to view the world strictly through the lens of one's own projects and preferences. On this second-person stance the agent recognizes the claims arising from the other person's projects and preferences as reasons. Finally, the third-person normative domain refers to the capacity to experience self and others as partners in a community of equals. It is the stance through which we each experience ourselves as claimed by the project of shared world-building. The third-person normative stance ultimately gives rise to projects of science and philosophy through which we attempt to understand and create this shared human existence.

The complexity that this plurality introduces has prompted many accounts to try to achieve simplicity by granting one perspective priority and do so in a way that obscures the necessary self-world unity characteristic of human life. For example, we have seen that the temptations of the third-person perspective – the appealing simplicity and neatness of the general, universal accounts it provides – can prompt us to forget the existential conditions for its possibility – namely, a first-person commitment to the practical project of living well and a second-person recognition of others as interlocutors and co-deliberators in this project. Similarly, the first-person perspective's emphasis on the self qua individual is at the root of subjectivist approaches to flourishing, which misrepresent that perspective by taking it as evidence for the fundamental independence of self from world. But flourishing cannot be reduced to an experiential state of the solitary subject or to some set of facts about humans understood as worldly objects with no necessary reference to the complex lived agency of the self that exists *as* such an object.

Each normative perspective reveals us to be embedded in the world in a way that challenges this 'subjective' versus 'objective' dichotomy: each perspective represents a different way in which agents are called to live their responsibility for who they will be by responding well to worldly criteria of success and failure. Each of these three normative domains must be understood as a way to live out the kind of self-world fit characteristic of flourishing – components of living in the world well that do not stand in an additive and external relationship to each other but are profoundly interdependent moments of life excellently lived. Each perspective is a way of seeing and responding to the fundamental project at stake in all of them: being in the world well.

If we understand practical reason in terms of this fundamental way of being – as a striving to be who we are that is responsive to these classes of normative constraint imposed on us by our embeddedness in a world that both limits and enables us to be – the question of whether we 'ought' to be this way does not meaningfully apply. Human life occurs under the dominion of the normative. One cannot but be gripped by the value of trying to respond well to the normative claims that allow us to answer the fundamental question: Who am I? A concern for the normative – a commitment to the project of succeeding at being in the world – is constitutive of being a person. One might be incompetent at knowing what this requires or bad at being able to implement it, but one cannot be entirely unmoved – even a deep depression that masquerades as indifference is belied by the agent's suffering. Not to care about the difference between better and worse lives – to be utterly indifferent to reasons that prompt us to choose one way rather than another – is to be outside the space of the human. Though we must often deliberate about how to respond to these normative claims as they manifest in particular situations or particular lives, their demandingness – our recognition of the general authority of these normative domains to shape and constrain our choices – is not itself a deliverance of deliberation or a matter of choice.

Recognizing this limits what we can hope for in any philosophical attempt to provide an account of human flourishing. Such an account cannot step completely outside our existing moral framework and assess it from a neutral perspective such that we could convince those outside this moral terrain to enter it. But the very desire for such an account indicates a misunderstanding of what ethics is. It is not an external theoretical view of human striving that could convince those not already engaged to enter the fray. Rather, it is a way to think about the practical problems and conditions that affect those of us who are already committed to the project of trying to be in the world well.

The consequence of the normative plurality to which we are condemned is that flourishing – doing a good job at being a person in the world – is realized not by following a specific decision procedure or fitting oneself into a cleanly demarcated category but by ongoingly negotiating this condition of irrevocable tension without recourse to a stance from which a hierarchy could be established among these normative sources. Insisting on always prioritizing others over the self, for example, denies the legitimate role that pleasure and self-development play in each person's life, just as insisting that people be treated as equal and interchangeable rational units can obscure the importance of the specificity of human relationships. Instead, flourishing demands ongoing negotiation work in which we strive to meet the demands operative within each normative domain in a way that does not compromise our ability to do so in the others. The lack of an ultimate metric for resolving this normative tension means that flourishing is a complicated and messy project whose success can be recognized only in the shape of a life as a whole. Only then can we assess whether the different kinds of normative claim are being given appropriate weight and proportion in someone's life.

As we have seen, the virtues are excellences of character that manifest as a set of interrelated beliefs, affective orientations, and behavioural tendencies, all of which help people to do this negotiation work. They are the stances through which we respond adequately to the three normative terrains and, in particular, the way that we do so in the face of particular existential challenges. Such virtuous problem-solving does not mean these existential challenges are removed or dissolved, but rather that through the virtues we cope well with irrevocable existential complications to our ability to respond to the claims posed by self, other, and shared world. We saw this in the case of justice, for example, which refers to both a global character state in which all three normative terrains are being given their due and to a particular virtue in which specific competing claims to goods are given their due despite conditions of scarcity. Similarly, we examined the ways in which patience, modesty, and courage are also problem-solving stances that protect agents from being derailed in their efforts to respond well to the goods that claim them.

Each of us is not alone in these efforts to be good at being human. We receive guidance from the moral exemplars whom we find ourselves committed to emulating. We love and admire certain patterns of being in the world – styles of response to the normative terrain we are all traversing – and we model ourselves after them. In so doing we come to experience ourselves in our potential for self-becoming and we develop essential deliberative skills that arise out of critical comparisons among competing visions of the good life.

Flourishing is living an excellent life. But there are multiple domains of human excellence – the excellence of becoming the best self that one can be, the excellence of answering fully to the legitimate claims of others, and the excellence of establishing and maintaining the objective standards and institutions that enable us to share the world. Each of us has the capacity to see the world not merely from the constraints of her own projects, but also in terms of the individual others we encounter and the structures by which we negotiate our place as one among many in the world. When we respond well to the claims that arise from this normative plurality, we accomplish a life of human excellence.

Bibliography

Ackrill, J. L. 1980. 'Aristotle on Eudaimonia'. In A. Rorty, ed., *Essays on Aristotle's Ethics*. Los Angeles: University of California Press, 15–34.
Adams, R. 2006. *A Theory of Virtue*. Oxford: Oxford University Press.
Adorno, T. 1991. *Minima Moralia: Reflections from Damaged Life*, trans. E. F. N. Jephcott. London: Verso.
Algoe, S. B., and Haidt, J. 2009. 'Witnessing Excellence in Action: The "Other Praising" Emotions of Elevation, Gratitude, and Admiration'. *Journal of Positive Psychology* 4: 105–127.
Amundson, R. 2000. 'Against Normal Function'. *Studies in History and Philosophy of Science Part C* 31 (1): 33–53.
Angier, T. 2015a. 'Happiness: Overcoming the Skill Model'. *International Philosophical Quarterly* 55: 5–23.
  2015b. 'Dissent on Core Beliefs in Natural Law'. In S. Chambers and P. Nosco, eds., *Dissent on Core Beliefs: Religious and Secular Perspectives*. Cambridge: Cambridge University Press, 53–75.
  2012. *Techne in Aristotle's Ethics: Crafting the Moral Life*. London: Continuum Publishing.
Annas, J. 2013. 'Being Virtuous and Doing the Right Thing'. In R. Shafer-Landau, ed., *Ethical Theory: An Anthology*. Oxford: Wiley Blackwell, 676–685.
  2011. *Intelligent Virtue*. Oxford: Oxford University Press.
  2003. 'The Structure of Virtue'. In M. DePaul and L. Zagzebski, eds., *Intellectual Virtue*. Oxford: Clarendon, 15–33.
  2002. 'My Station and Its Duties: Ideals and the Social Embeddedness of Virtue'. *Proceedings of the Aristotelian Society* 109–123.
  1995a. *The Morality of Happiness*. Oxford: Oxford University Press.
  1995b. 'Virtue as a Skill'. *International Journal of Philosophical Studies* 3: 227–243.
Arendt, H. 1998. *The Human Condition*. Chicago, IL: University of Chicago Press.
Aristotle. 2011. *Eudemian Ethics*, trans. A. Kenny. Oxford: Oxford University Press.
  2000. *Nicomachean Ethics*, R. Crisp, ed., trans. Cambridge: Cambridge University Press.

1998. *Poetics*, trans. S. Halliwell. Chicago, IL: University of Chicago Press.
1984a. 'Rhetoric'. In W. R. Roberts, ed., trans., *The Complete Works of Aristotle*, vol. 2. Princeton, NJ: Princeton University Press, 2152–2269.
1984b. 'Politics'. In B. Jowett, ed., trans., *The Complete Works of Aristotle*, vol. 2. Princeton, NJ: Princeton University Press, 1986–2129.
Arneson, R. J. 1999. 'Human Flourishing versus Desire Satisfaction'. *Social Philosophy and Policy* 16: 113–142.
Badhwar, N. K. 1996. 'The Limited Unity of Virtue'. *Nous* 30: 306–329.
Bandura, A. 1963. *Social Learning and Personality Development*. New York: Holt, Rinehart & Winston.
Baril, A. 2014. 'Eudaimonia in Contemporary Virtue Ethics'. In S. Van Hooft, ed., *The Handbook of Virtue Ethics*. New York: Acumen, 17–27.
Beauvoir, S. 1976. *The Ethics of Ambiguity*, trans. B. Frechtman. New York: Kensington Publishing.
1952. *The Second Sex*, trans. H. M. Parshley. New York: Random House.
Benhabib, S. 2002. *The Claims of Culture*. Princeton, NJ: Princeton University Press.
Ben-Ze'ev, A. 2003. 'Free Will and the Mystery of Modesty'. *American Philosophical Quarterly* 40: 105–117.
1990. 'The Virtue of Modesty'. *American Philosophical Quarterly* 30: 235–246.
Berlin, I. 1999. *The Roots of Romanticism*, H. Hardy, ed. London: Chatto & Windus.
Blattner, W. D. 1999. *Heidegger's Temporal Idealism*. Cambridge: Cambridge University Press.
Blum, L. A. 1988. 'Moral Exemplars: Reflections on Schindler, the Trocmes, and Others'. *Midwest Studies in Philosophy* 13: 196–221.
Bommarito, N. 2014. 'Patience and Perspective'. *Philosophy East and West* 64: 269–286.
Bostock, D. 2000. *Aristotle's Ethics*. Oxford: Oxford University Press.
Bowlby, J. 1988. *A Secure Base: Clinical Applications of Attachment Theory*. London: Routledge.
Brandom, R. 2002. 'Non-Inferential Knowledge, Perceptual Experience, and Secondary Qualities: Placing McDowell's Empiricism'. In N. Smith, ed., *Reading McDowell: On Mind and World*. London: Routledge, 92–105.
Brandt, R. B. 1998. *A Theory of the Good and the Right*. Amherst, NY: Prometheus. Books.
1996. *Fact, Values, and Morality*. Cambridge: Cambridge University Press.
Bratman, M. 2007. *Structures of Agency*. Oxford: Oxford University Press.
Brennan, J. 2007. 'Modesty without Illusion'. *Philosophy and Phenomenological Research* 75: 111–128.
Burch, M. 2010. 'Death and Deliberation: Overcoming the Decisionism Critique of Heidegger's Practical Philosophy'. *Inquiry* 53: 211–234.
Burnyeat, M. F. 1980. 'Aristotle on Learning to Be Good'. In A. O. Rorty, ed., *Essays on Aristotle's Ethics*. Oakland: University of California Press, 69–92.

Bibliography

Callan, E. 1993. 'Patience and Courage'. *Philosophy* 68: 523–539.
Carel, H. 2016. 'Virtue without Excellence, Excellence without Health'. *Aristotelian Society Supplementary Volume* 90 (1): 237–253.
Carr, D. 2003. 'Character and Moral Choice in the Cultivation of Virtue'. *Philosophy* 78: 219–232.
Chang, R. 2015. *Making Comparisons Count*. London: Routledge.
Chappell, T. 2012. 'Varieties of Knowledge in Plato and Aristotle'. *Topoi* 31: 175–190.
  2006. 'The Variety of Life and the Unity of Practical Wisdom'. In T. Chappell, ed., *Values and Virtues: Aristotelianism in Contemporary Ethics*. Oxford: Oxford University Press, 136–157.
Chappell, T., and Oderberg, D. 2004. *Human Values*. New York: Palgrave Macmillan.
Cohen, A. J. 2004. 'What Toleration Is'. *Ethics* 115: 68–95.
Cohen, G. A. 1991. 'Incentives, Inequality, and Community'. Tanner Lectures on Human Values, Stanford University. Available at http://tannerlectures.utah.edu/_documents/a-to-z/c/cohen92.pdf.
Conant, J. 2010. 'Nietzsche's Perfectionism: A Reading of Schopenhauer as Educator'. In R. Schacht, ed., *Nietzsche's Postmoralism: Essays on Nietzsche's Prelude to Philosophy's Future*. Cambridge: Cambridge University Press, 181–257.
Cooper, D. 2002. *The Measure of Things*. Oxford: Oxford University Press.
Cooper, J. M. 1998. 'The Unity of Virtue'. *Social Philosophy and Policy* 15: 233–274.
Coplan, A. 2010. 'Feeling without Thinking: Lessons from the Ancients on Emotion and Virtue-Acquisition'. *Metaphilosophy* 41: 132–151.
Crisp, R. 2015. 'A Third Method of Ethics?' *Philosophy and Phenomenological Research* 90: 257–273.
Crittenden, P. 1999. 'Justice, Care and Other Virtues: A Critique of Kohlberg's Theory of Moral Development'. In D. Carr and J. Steutel, eds., *Virtue Ethics and Moral Education*. London: Routledge, 173–188.
Crowell, S. 2017. 'Exemplary Necessity: Heidegger, Pragmatism, and Reason'. In O. Svec and J. Capek, eds., *Pragmatic Perspectives in Phenomenology* London: Routledge, 242–256.
  2013. *Normativity and Phenomenology in Husserl and Heidegger*. Cambridge: Cambridge University Press.
  2012. 'Why Is Ethics First Philosophy? Lévinas in Phenomenological Context'. *European Journal of Philosophy* 23: 564–588.
  1998. 'There *Is* No Other: Notes on the Logical Place of a Concept'. *Paideuma: Mitteilung zur Kulturkunde* 44: 13–29.
Curren, R. 1999. 'Cultivating the Intellectual and Moral Virtues'. In D. Carr and J. Steutel, eds.. *Virtue Ethics and Moral Education*. London: Routledge, 69–83.
Curzer, H. 2001. 'To Become Good'. Available at www.bu.edu/wcp/Papers/Anci/AnciCurz.htm.

Dahlstrom, D. 1995. 'Heidegger's Concept of Temporality: Reflections on a Recent Criticism'. *Review of Metaphysics* 49: 95–115.
Darwall, S. 2006. *The Second-Person Standpoint: Morality, Respect, and Accountability*. Cambridge, MA: Harvard University Press.
 2004. 'Respect and the Second-Person Standpoint'. *Proceedings and Addresses of the APA* 78: 43–59.
Daston, L. 1992. 'Objectivity and the Escape from Perspective'. *Social Studies of Science* 22: 597–618.
Devereux, D. T. 1992. 'The Unity of the Virtues in Plato's Protagoras and Laches'. *Philosophical Review* 101: 765–789.
Diamond, C. 1997. 'Moral Differences and Distances: Some Questions'. In L. Alanen, S. Heinama, and T. Wallgren, eds., *Commonality and Particularity in Ethics*. New York: Palgrave Macmillan, 197–215.
Diener, E., Suh, E. M., Lucas, R. E., and Smith, H. L. 1999. 'Subjective Well Being: Three Decades of Progress'. *Psychological Bulletin* 125: 276–302.
Dilthey, W. 2002. *Selected Works*, vol. 3: *The Formation of the Historical World in the Human Sciences*, R. A. Makkreel and F. Rodi, eds. Princeton, NJ: Princeton University Press.
Doring, S. 2007. 'Seeing What to Do: Affective Perception and Rational Motivation'. *Dialectica* 61 (3): 363–394.
Doris, J. M. 2002. *Lack of Character: Personality and Moral Behaviour*. Cambridge: Cambridge University Press.
Dreyfus, H. 2000. 'Could Anything Be More Intelligible than Everyday Intelligibility? Reinterpreting Division I of *Being and Time*'. In J. Faulconer and M. Wrathall, eds., *Appropriating Heidegger*. Cambridge: Cambridge University Press, 155–174.
Dreyfus, H., and Dreyfus, S. 1991. 'Towards a Phenomenology of Ethical Expertise'. *Human Studies* 14: 229–250.
Driver, J. 2005. 'Moralism'. *Journal of Applied Philosophy* 22: 137–151.
 1999. 'Modesty and Ignorance'. *Ethics* 109: 827–834.
 1989. 'The Virtues of Ignorance'. *Journal of Philosophy* 86: 373–384.
Drummond, J. 2016. 'Time and the "Antinomies" of Deliberation'. In R. Altschuler and M. Sigrist, eds., *Time and the Philosophy of Action*. New York: Routlege, 175–188.
 2002. 'Aristotelianism and Phenomenology'. In J. J. Drummond and L. Embree, eds., *Phenomenological Approaches to Moral Philosophy: A Handbook*. Dordrecht: Kluwer Academic, 15–45.
Eliot, T. S. 1920. 'The Love Song of J. Alfred Prufrock'. In *Prufrock, and Other Observations*. New York: A. A. Knopf.
Ellis, H. 1929. *Studies in the Psychology of Sex*, vol. 1. Philadelphia: University of Pennsylvania Press.
Enoch, D. 2006. 'Agency, Shmagency: Why Normativity Won't Come from What Is Constitutive of Action'. *Philosophical Review* 115: 169–198.
Farnham, D. 2006. 'A Good Kind of Egoism'. *Journal of Value Inquiry* 40: 433–450.

Fichte, J. G. 2005. *The System of Ethics*, D. Breazeale and G. Zöller, eds. Cambridge: Cambridge University Press.
Finnigan, B. 2015. 'Phronēsis in Aristotle: Reconciling Deliberation with Spontaneity'. *Philosophy and Phenomenological Research* 91: 674–697.
Flanagan, O. 1991. *Varieties of Moral Personality*. Cambridge, MA: Harvard University Press.
  1990. 'Virtue and Ignorance'. *Journal of Philosophy* 87: 420–428.
Foot, P. 2003. *Moral Dilemmas*. Oxford: Oxford University Press.
  2002. *Virtues and Vices*. Oxford: Oxford University Press.
  2001. *Natural Goodness*. Oxford: Clarendon Press.
Forman, D. 2008. 'Autonomy as Second Nature: On McDowell's Aristotelian Naturalism'. *Inquiry* 51: 563–580.
Fossheim, H. J. 2006. 'Habituation as *Mimesis*'. In T. Chapell, ed., *Values and Virtues*. Oxford: Oxford University Press, 105–117.
Frankfurt, H. 1998. *The Importance of What We Care About*. Cambridge: Cambridge University Press.
Freeland, C. 2010. *Feminist Interpretations of Aristotle*. University Park, PA: Penn State University Press.
Freyenhagen, F. 2013. *Adorno's Practical Philosophy: Living Less Wrongly*. Cambridge: Cambridge University Press.
Friedman, M. 1986. 'Autonomy and the Split-Level Self'. *Southern Journal of Philosophy* 24: 19–35.
Garrels, S. R. 2006. 'Imitation, Mirror Neurons, and Mimetic Desire: Convergence between the Mimetic Theory of René Girard and Empirical Research on Imitation'. *Contagion: Journal of Violence, Mimesis, and Culture* 13: 47–86.
Gay, R. 1988. 'Courage and Thumos'. *Philosophy* 63: 255–265.
Gilligan, C. 1982. *In a Different Voice: Psychological Theory and Women's Development*. Cambridge, MA: Harvard University Press.
Girard, R. 2004. 'Violence and Religion: Cause or Effect?' *Hedgehog Review* 6: 8–13.
Goldie, Peter. 2007. 'Seeing What Is the Kind Thing to Do: Perception and Emotion in Morality'. *Dialectica* 61 (3): 347–361.
Goldman, A. 1993. 'Ethics and Cognitive Science'. *Ethics* 103: 337–360.
Griffin, J. 1986. *Well-Being: Its Meaning, Measurement and Moral Importance*. Oxford: Oxford University Press.
Haidt, J. 2003. 'Elevation and the Positive Psychology of Morality'. In C. L. M. Keyes and J. Haidt, eds., *Flourishing: Positive Psychology and the Life Well-Lived*. Washington, DC: American Psychological Association, 275–289.
  2001. 'The Emotional Dog and the Rational Tail: A Social Intuitionist Approach to Moral Judgment'. *Psychological Review* 108: 814–834.
Haldane, J. 2009. *Practical Philosophy*. Exeter: Imprint Academic.
Haugeland, J. 2013. *Dasein Disclosed: John Haugeland's Heidegger*, J. Rouse, ed. Cambridge, MA.: Harvard University Press.
  1998. *Having Thought: Essays in the Metaphysics of Mind*. Cambridge, MA.: Harvard University Press.

Haybron, D. 2008. 'Happiness, the Self, and Human Flourishing'. *Utilitas* 20: 21–49.
  2007. 'Well-Being and Virtue'. *Journal of Ethics and Social Philosophy* 2: 1–24.
Hegel, G. W. F. 1991. *Elements of the Philosophy of Right*. A. W. Wood, ed. Cambridge: Cambridge University Press.
Heidegger, M. 2003. *Plato's Sophist*, R. Rojcewicz and A. Schuwer, trans. Bloomington: Indiana University Press.
  2002. 'Anaximander's Saying'. In J. Young and K. Haynes, eds., trans., *Martin Heidegger: Off the Beaten Track*. Cambridge: Cambridge University Press, 242–281.
  2001. *The Zollikon Seminars*, F. Mayr and R. Askay, trans., M. Boss, ed. Evanston, IL: Northwestern University Press.
  2000. *Introduction to Metaphysics*, G. Fried and R. Polt, eds. New Haven, CT: Yale University Press.
  1985. *Being and Time*, J. Macquarrie and E. Robinson, trans. Oxford: Blackwell.
  1984. *The Metaphysical Foundations of Logic*, M. Heim, trans. Bloomington: Indiana University Press.
  1982. *The Basic Problems of Phenomenology*, A. Hofstadter, trans. Bloomington: Indiana University Press.
Herder, J. G. 2002. *On the Cognition and the Sensation of the Human Soul (1778)*. Cambridge: Cambridge University Press.
Hurka, T. 2001. *Virtue, Vice, and Value*. Oxford: Oxford University Press.
  1999. 'The Three Faces of Flourishing'. *Social Philosophy and Policy* 16: 44–71.
Hursthouse, R. 1999. *On Virtue Ethics*. Oxford: Oxford University Press.
  1988. 'Moral Habituation: A Review of Troels Engberg-Pedersen, *Aristotle's Theory of Moral Insight*'. *Oxford Studies in Ancient Philosophy* 6: 201–219.
Husserl, E. 1999. *Cartesian Meditations*, D. Cairns, trans. Dordrecht: Kluwer Academic Publishers.
  1989. *Ideas Pertaining to a Pure Phenomenology and to a Phenomenological Philosophy: Second Book*, R. Rojcewicz and F. Kersten, trans. Dordrecht: Kluwer Academic.
  1970. *The Crisis of European Sciences and Transcendental Phenomenology: An Introduction to Phenomenological Philosophy*, D. Carr, ed., trans. Evanston, IL: Northwestern University Press.
Hutto, D. D., and Herschbach, M. 2011. 'Editorial: Social Cognition: Mindreading and Alternatives'. *Review of Philosophy and Psychology* 2: 375–395.
Irwin, T. H. 1997. 'Practical Reason Divided: Aquinas and His Critics'. In G. Cullity and B. Gaut, eds., *Ethics and Practical Reason*. Oxford: Clarendon Press, 189–214.
  1988. 'Disunity in the Aristotelian Virtues'. *Oxford Studies in Ancient Philosophy*, supp. vol., 62–72.
  1986. 'Stoic and Aristotelian Conceptions of Happiness'. In M. Scholfield and G. Striker, eds., *The Norms of Nature: Studies in Hellenistic Ethics*. Cambridge: Cambridge University Press.

Jacobson, D. 2005. 'Seeing by Feeling: Virtues, Skills, and Moral Perception'. *Ethical Theory and Moral Practice* 8: 387–409.
Jollimore, T. 2011. *Love's Vision*. Princeton, NJ: Princeton University Press.
Kahneman, D. 2011. *Thinking, Fast and Slow*. New York: Farrar, Straus and Giroux.
Kainz, H. P. 2004. *Natural Law: An Introduction and Re-Examination*. Chicago, IL: Open Court.
Kamtekar, R. 2004. 'Situationism and Virtue Ethics on the Content of our Character'. *Ethics* 114: 458–491.
Kant, I. 2000. *Critique of the Power of Judgment*, P. Guyer, ed., P. Guyer and E. Matthews, trans. Cambridge: Cambridge University Press.
  1997. *Groundwork of the Metaphysics of Morals*, M. Gregor, trans. Cambridge: Cambridge University Press.
  1996. *The Metaphysics of Morals*, M. Gregor and R. J. Sullivan, trans. Cambridge: Cambridge University Press.
  1965. *Critique of Pure Reason*, N. K. Smith, trans. New York: St. Martin's Press.
  1900. *On Education* [*Über Pädagogik* 1803]. A. Churton, trans. Boston: D.C. Available at http://oll.libertyfund.org/titles/356#Kant_0235_164.
Kaster, R. A. 2002. 'The Taxonomy of Patience, or When Is Patientia Not a Virtue?' *Classical Philology* 97: 133–144.
Kawall, J. 2009. 'In Defense of the Primacy of the Virtues'. *Journal of Ethics and Social Philosophy* 3: 1–21.
Kaye, K. 1982. *The Mental and Social Life of Babies: How Parents Create Persons*. Chicago, IL: University of Chicago Press.
Kisiel, T. 1993. *The Genesis of Heidegger's Being and Time*. Berkeley: University of California Press.
Kohlberg, L. 1981. *The Philosophy of Moral Development: Moral Stages and the Idea of Justice*. New York: Harper & Row.
Kompridis, N. 2011. *Critique and Disclosure: Critical Theory between Past and Future*. Boston: MIT Press.
Korsgaard, C. 2009. *Self-Constitution: Agency, Identity, and Integrity*. Oxford: Oxford University Press.
  2008. *The Constitution of Agency*. Oxford: Oxford University Press.
  1996. *Sources of Normativity*. Cambridge: Cambridge University Press.
Koukal, D. 2001. 'The Rhetorical Impulse in Husserl's Phenomenology'. *Continental Philosophy Review* 34: 21–43.
Kristjánsson, K. 2006. 'Emulation and the Use of Role Models in Moral Education'. *Journal of Moral Education* 35: 37–49.
Kupfer, J. 2007. 'When Waiting Is Weightless: The Virtue of Patience'. *Journal of Value Inquiry* 41: 265–280.
Lear, J. 2006. *Radical Hope: Ethics in the Face of Cultural Devastation*. Cambridge, MA: Harvard University Press.
LeBar, M. 2014. 'The Virtue of Justice Revisited'. In S. van Hooft, ed., *The Handbook of Virtue Ethics*. New York: Acumen, 265–275.

2009. 'Virtue Ethics and Deontic Constraints'. *Ethics* 119: 642–671.
2005. 'Eudaimonist Autonomy'. *American Philosophical Quarterly* 42: 171–183.
2004. 'Good for You'. *Pacific Philosophical Quarterly* 85: 195–217.
Leighton, S. R. 1988. 'Aristotle's Courageous Passions'. *Phronēsis* 33: 76–99.
Lévinas, E. 2007. *Totality and Infinity*, A. Lingis, trans. Pittsburgh, PA: Duquesne University Press.
Lipscomb, T. J., Larrieu, J. A., McAllister, H. A., and Bregman, N. J. 1982. 'Modeling and Children's Generosity: A Developmental Perspective'. *Merrill-Palmer Quarterly* 28: 275–282.
Lockwood, P., and Kunda, Z. 1997. 'Superstars and Me: Predicting the Impact of Role Models on the Self'. *Journal of Personality and Social Psychology* 73: 91–103.
Louden, R. B. 1992. 'Go-Carts of Judgment: Exemplars in Kantian Moral Education'. *Archiv für Geschichte der Philosophie* 74: 303–322.
Luthra, Y. 2015. 'Aristotle on Choosing Virtuous Action for Its Own Sake'. *Pacific Philosophical Quarterly* 96: 423–441.
MacIntyre, A. 1999. *Dependent Rational Animals: Why Human Beings Need the Virtues*. Chicago, IL: Open Court.
1984. *After Virtue*. Notre Dame, IN: Notre Dame University Press.
Maxwell, B., and Reichenbach, R. 2005. 'Imitation, Imagination and Re-Appraisal: Educating the Moral Emotions'. *Journal of Moral Education* 34: 291–307.
McDowell, J. 2007. 'What Myth?' *Inquiry* 50: 338–351.
1998. 'Virtue and Reason'. In *Mind, Value, and Reality*. Cambridge, MA: Harvard University Press.
1980. 'The Role of Eudaimonia in Aristotle's Ethics'. Reprinted in *Essays on Aristotle's Ethics*, A. O. Rorty, ed. Berkeley: University of California Press, 359–76.
McGregor, I., and Little, B. R. 1998. 'Personal Projects, Happiness, and Meaning: On Doing Well and Being Yourself'. *Journal of Personality and Social Psychology* 74: 494–512.
McMullin, I. 2013. *Time and the Shared World*. Evanston, IL: Northwestern University Press.
2010. 'A Modest Proposal: Accounting for the Virtuousness of Modesty'. *Philosophical Quarterly* 60: 783–807.
McNeill, W. 1999. *The Glance of the Eye: Heidegger, Aristotle, and the Ends of Theory*. Albany: State University of New York Press.
Meltzoff, A., and Decety, J. 2003. 'What Imitation Tells Us about Social Cognition: A Rapprochement between Developmental Psychology and Cognitive Neuroscience'. *Philosophical Transactions of the Royal Society B: Biological Sciences* 358: 491–500.
Meltzoff, A., and Moore, K. 1989. 'Imitation in Newborn Infants: Exploring the Range of Gestures Imitated and the Underlying Mechanisms'. *Developmental Psychology* 25: 954–962.

1983. 'Newborn Infants Imitate Adult Facial Gestures'. *Child Development* 54: 702–709.

1977. 'Imitation of Facial and Manual Gestures by Human Neonates'. *Science* 198: 75–78.

Mensch, J. 2015. *Lévinas's Existential Analytic: A Commentary*. Evanston, IL: Northwestern University Press.

Miller, F. D. 1997. *Nature, Justice, and Rights in Aristotle's 'Politics'*. Oxford: Clarendon Press.

Miller, R. L., Brickman, P., and Bolen, D. 1975. 'Attribution versus Persuasion as a Means for Modifying Behaviour'. *Journal of Personality and Social Psychology* 31: 430–441.

Miller, W. I. 2002. *The Mystery of Courage*. Cambridge, MA: Harvard University Press.

Moberg, D. J. 2000. 'Role Models and Moral Exemplars: How Do Employees Acquire Virtues by Observing Others?' *Business Ethics Quarterly* 10: 675–696.

Myers, D. G., and Diener, E. 1995. 'Who Is Happy?' *Psychological Science* 6: 10–19.

Nagel, T. 1979. *Mortal Questions*. Cambridge: Cambridge University Press.

Natali, C. 2001. *The Wisdom of Aristotle*, G. Parks, trans. Albany, NY: SUNY Press.

Nehamas, A. 1985. *Nietzsche: Life as Literature*. Cambridge, MA: Harvard University Press.

Nietzsche, F. 2001. *The Gay Science*, B. Williams, ed., J. Nauckhoff and A. Del Caro, trans. Cambridge: Cambridge University Press.

1997. 'Schopenhauer as Educator'. In D. Breazeale, ed., and R. J. Hollingdale, trans., *Untimely Meditations*. Cambridge: Cambridge University Press, 125–194.

1996. *Human, All Too Human: A Book for Free Spirits*, R. J. Hollingdale, trans. Cambridge: Cambridge University Press.

1995. *Thus Spoke Zarathustra*, W. Kaufmann, trans. New York: Modern Library.

1989a. *Beyond Good and Evil: Prelude to a Philosophy of the Future*, W. Kaufmann, trans. New York: Vintage Books.

1989b. *On the Genealogy of Morals*, W. Kaufmann, trans. New York: Vintage Books.

Noddings, N. 1984. *Caring: A Feminine Approach to Ethics and Moral Education*. Berkeley: University of California Press.

Noë, A. 2006. *Action in Perception*. Cambridge, MA: MIT Press.

Nozick, R. 1974. *Anarchy, State, and Utopia*. New York: Basic Books.

Nussbaum, M. 1999. 'Virtue Ethics: A Misleading Category?' *Journal of Ethics* 3: 163–201.

1993. 'Non-Relative Virtues: An Aristotelian Approach'. In A. Sen and M. Nussbaum, eds., 1993, *The Quality of Life*. Oxford: Clarendon Press, 242–269.

1990. *Love's Knowledge*. Oxford: Oxford University Press.
1986. *The Fragility of Goodness*. Cambridge: Cambridge University Press.
Nuyen, A. T. 1998. 'Just Modesty'. *American Philosophical Quarterly* 35: 101–109.
Olberding, Amy. 2012. *Moral Exemplars in the Analects: The Good Person Is That*. New York: Routledge.
O'Neill, O. 1986. 'The Power of Example'. *Philosophy* 61 (235): 5–29.
Parfit, D. 1984. *Reasons and Persons*. Oxford: Oxford University Press.
Park, J. J. 2013. 'Prototypes, Exemplars, and Theoretical and Applied Ethics'. *Neuroethics* 6: 237–247.
Pfeifer, J. H., Iacoboni, M., Mazziotta, J. C., and Dapretto, M. 2008. 'Mirroring Others' Emotions Relates to Empathy and Interpersonal Competence in Children'. *Neuroimage* 39: 2076–2085.
Phillips, D. Z. 1965. 'Does It Pay to Be Good?' *Proceedings of the Aristotelian Society* 45–60.
Pianalto, M. 2016a. *On Patience: Reclaiming a Foundational Virtue*. London: Lexington Books.
2016b. 'Nietzschean Patience'. *Journal of Value Inquiry* 50: 141–152.
2014. 'In Defense of Patience'. In D. R. Gordon and D. B. Suits, eds., *Epictetus: His Continuing Influence and Contemporary Relevance*. Rochester, NY: RIT Press, 89–104.
2012. 'Moral Courage and Facing Others'. *International Journal of Philosophical Studies* 20: 165–184.
Plato. 1993. *Republic*, R. Waterfield, trans. Oxford: Oxford University Press.
Presbie, R. J., and Coiteux, P. F. 1971. 'Learning to Be Generous or Stingy: Imitation of Sharing Behaviour as a Function of Model Generosity and Vicarious Reinforcement'. *Child Development* 42: 1033–1038.
Railton, P. 1986. 'Facts and Values'. *Philosophical Topics* 14: 5–31.
Raphael, D. D. 1988. 'The Intolerable'. In S. Mendus, ed., *Justifying Toleration: Conceptual and Historical Perspectives*. Cambridge: Cambridge University Press, 137–153.
Rasmussen, D. B. 1999. 'Human Flourishing and the Appeal to Human Nature'. *Social Philosophy and Policy* 16: 1–43.
Ratcliffe, M. 2012. 'Phenomenology as a Form of Empathy'. *Inquiry* 55: 473–495.
Rawls, J. 1999. *A Theory of Justice*. Cambridge, MA: Harvard University Press.
Raz, J. 1986. *The Morality of Freedom*. Oxford: Clarendon Press.
Richards, N. 1988. 'Is Humility a Virtue?' *American Philosophical Quarterly* 25: 253–259.
Ridge, M. 2000. 'Modesty as a Virtue'. *American Philosophical Quarterly* 37: 269–283.
Rodgers, T. J., and Warmke, B. 2015. 'Situationism versus Situationism'. *Ethical Theory and Moral Practice*. 18 (1): 9–26.
Rorty, A. O. 1986. 'The Two Faces of Courage'. *Philosophy* 61: 151–171.
Ross, W. D. 1995. *Aristotle*. New York: Routledge.

Rudd, A. 2008. 'Kierkegaard on Patience and the Temporality of the Self: The Virtues of a Being in Time'. *Journal of Religious Ethics* 36: 491–509.
Russell, D. C. 2014. 'Aristotle on Cultivating Virtue'. In N. E. Snow, ed., *Cultivating Virtue: Perspectives from Philosophy, Theology, and Psychology*. Oxford: Oxford University Press.
  2009. *Practical Intelligence and the Virtues*. Oxford: Oxford University Press.
  2008. 'Agent-Based Virtue Ethics and the Fundamentality of Virtue'. *American Philosophical Quarterly* 45: 329–347.
Ryan, R. M., and Deci, E. L. 2000. 'Self-Determination Theory and the Facilitation of Intrinsic Motivation, Social Development, and Well-Being'. *American Psychologist* 55: 68–78.
Sanderse, W. 2013. 'The Meaning of Role Modelling in Moral and Character Education'. *Journal of Moral Education* 42: 28–42.
Sartre, J.-P. 1992. *Being and Nothingness*, H. E. Barnes, trans. New York: Washington Square Press.
Scanlon, T. 1993. 'Value, Desire, and Quality of Life'. In M. C. Nussbaum and A. Sen, eds., *The Quality of Life*. Oxford: Clarendon Press, 185–200.
Schechtman, M. 2004. 'Self-Expression and Self-Control'. *Ratio* 17: 409–427.
  1996. *The Constitution of Selves*. Ithaca, NY: Cornell University Press.
Scheler, M. 1987. 'Exemplars of Persons and Leaders'. In M. S. Frings, ed., *Person and Self-Value*. Dordrecht: Martinus Nijhoff, 127–198.
  1973. *Formalism in Ethics and Non-Formal Ethics of Values*. Evanston, IL: Northwestern University Press.
Schmidtz, D., and Thrasher, J. 2014. 'The Virtues of Justice'. In K. Timpe and C. A. Boyd, eds., *Virtues and Their Vices*. Oxford: Oxford University Press, 59–74.
Schopenhauer. A. 1995. *The Wisdom of Life and Counsels and Maxims*, T. Bailey Saunders, trans. New York: Prometheus Books.
Schueler, G. F. 1999. 'Why IS Modesty a Virtue?' *Ethics* 109: 835–841.
  1997. 'Why Modesty Is a Virtue'. *Ethics* 107: 467–485.
Sen, A. 1987. *On Ethics and Economics*. Oxford: Basil Blackwell.
Sher, G. 1998. 'Ethics, Character, and Action'. *Social Philosophy and Policy* 15: 1–17.
Sherman, N. 1999. 'Character Development and Aristotelian Virtue'. In D. Carr and J. Steutel, eds., *Virtue Ethics and Moral Education*. London: Routledge, 35–49.
  1989. *The Fabric of Character*. Oxford: Oxford University Press.
Siegel, H. 2017. *Education's Epistemology: Rationality, Diversity, and Critical Thinking*. Oxford: Oxford University Press.
Skog, O. 2001. 'Theorizing about Patience Formation: The Necessity of Conceptual Distinctions'. *Economics and Philosophy* 17: 207–219.
Slote, M. 2001. *Morals from Motives*. Oxford: Oxford University Press.
  1999. 'Caring vs. the Philosophers'. *Philosophy of Education* 25–35.
  1998. 'The Justice of Caring'. *Social Philosophy and Policy* 15: 171–195.

1993. 'Virtue Ethics and Democratic Values'. *Journal of Social Philosophy* 24: 5–37.
    1992. *From Morality to Virtue*. Oxford: Oxford University Press.
Smilansky, S. 2003. 'Free Will and the Mystery of Modesty'. *American Philosophical Quarterly* 40: 105–117.
Smith, A. 1976 [1759]. *The Theory of Moral Sentiments*, D. D. Raphael and A. L. Macfie, eds. Indianapolis, IN: Liberty Fund.
Smith, N. D. 2008. 'Modesty: A Contextual Account'. *Proceedings and Addresses of the American Philosophy Association* 82: 23–45.
Smith, W. H. 2012. *The Sources of Moral Normativity*. London: Routledge.
Snow, N. E. 2008. 'Virtue and Flourishing'. *Journal of Social Philosophy* 39: 225–245.
Solomon, D. 1988. 'Internal Objections to Virtue Ethics'. *Midwest Studies in Philosophy* 13: 428–441.
Spiecker, B. 1999. 'Habituation and Training in Early Moral Upbringing'. In D. Carr and J. Steutel, eds., *Virtue Ethics and Moral Education*. London: Routledge, 217–230.
Sreenivasan, G. 2009. 'Disunity of Virtue'. *Journal of Ethics* 13: 195–212.
Statman, D. 1992. 'Modesty, Pride and Realistic Self-Assessment'. *Philosophical Quarterly* 42: 420–438.
Stichter, M. 2007. 'Ethical Expertise: The Skill Model of Virtue'. *Ethical Theory and Moral Practice* 10: 183–194.
Stocker, M. 1976. 'The Schizophrenia of Modern Ethical Theories'. *Journal of Philosophy* 73: 453–466.
Sumner, L. W. 1996. *Welfare, Happiness, and Ethics*. Oxford: Oxford University Press.
Swanton, C. 2003. *Virtue Ethics: A Pluralistic View*. Oxford: Oxford University Press.
    1997. 'Virtue Ethics and the Problem of Indirection'. *Utilitas* 9: 167–181.
Tavani, H. 2007. 'Moral Arrogance'. *Metaphilosophy* 38 (4): 365–419.
Taylor, C. 1997. 'Leading a Life'. In Ruth Chang, ed., *Incommensurability, Incomparability, and Practical Reasoning*. Cambridge, MA: Harvard University Press, 170–183.
Tessman, L. 2015. *Moral Failure: On the Impossible Demands of Morality*. New York. Oxford University Press.
    2005. *Burdened Virtues: Virtue Ethics for Liberatory Struggles*. New York: Oxford University Press.
Thomson, I. 2009. 'Rethinking Lévinas on Heidegger on Death'. *Harvard Review of Philosophy* 16: 23–43.
Tiberius, V., and Walker, J. D. 1998. 'Arrogance'. *American Philosophical Quarterly* 35 (4): 379–390.
Tillich, P. 2000. *The Courage to Be*. New Haven, CT: Yale Nota Bene Press.
Trevarthen, C., Kokkinaki, T., and Fiamenghi, G. Jr. 1999. 'What Infants' Imitations Communicate: With Mothers, with Fathers, with Peers'. In

J. Nadel and G. Butterworth, eds., *Imitation in Infancy*. Cambridge: Cambridge University Press, 9–35.

Upton, C. 2013. 'What Virtues Are There?' In S. van Hooft, ed., *The Handbook of Virtue Ethics*. New York: Acumen, 165–176.

Van Buren, J. 1994. *The Young Heidegger: Rumor of the Hidden King*. Bloomington: Indiana University Press.

Van Hooft, S. 2014. 'Virtue and Identity'. In S. van Hooft, ed., *The Handbook of Virtue Ethics*. New York: Acumen, 153–163.

Vasiliou, I. 1996. 'The Role of Good Upbringing in Aristotle's Ethics'. *Philosophy and Phenomenological Research* 56: 771–797.

Velleman, J. D. 2015. 'Time for Action'. In R. Altschuler and M. Sigrist, eds., *Time and the Philosophy of Action*. New York: Routledge, 161–174.

2006. *Self to Self*. Cambridge: Cambridge University Press.

2002. 'Motivation by Ideal'. *Philosophical Explorations* 5: 89–103.

1988. 'Brandt's Definition of "Good"'. *Philosophical Review* 97: 353–371.

Vianello, M., Galliani, E. M., and Haidt, J. 2010. 'Elevation at Work: The Effects of Leaders' Moral Excellence'. *Journal of Positive Psychology* 5: 390–411.

Ward, K. 2008. *Augenblick: The Concept of the 'Decisive Moment' in 19th and 20th Century Western Philosophy*. Hampshire: Ashgate.

Warren, R. P. 1972. 'A Dearth of Heroes'. *American Heritage* 23: 4–7.

Waterman, A. S. 1993. 'Two Conceptions of Happiness: Contrasts of Personal Expressiveness (Eudaimonia) and Hedonic Enjoyment'. *Journal of Personality and Social Psychology* 64: 678–691.

Watson, G. 2003. 'On the Primacy of Character'. In S. Darwall, ed., *Virtue Ethics*. Oxford: Blackwell, 229–250.

1984. 'Virtues in Excess'. *Philosophical Studies* 46: 57–74.

Weber, M. 1949 [1904]. '"Objectivity" in Social Science and Social Policy'. In E. Shils and H. Finch, eds., *The Methodology of the Social Sciences*. New York: Free Press.

Whiting, J. 1988. 'Aristotle's Function Argument: A Defense'. *Ancient Philosophy* 8: 33–48.

Wiggins, D. 2004. 'Neo-Aristotelian Reflections on Justice'. *Mind* 113: 447–512.

1975. 'Deliberation and Practical Reason'. *Proceedings of the Aristotelian Society* 76: 29–51.

Williams, B. 1996. 'Toleration: An Impossible Virtue'. In *Toleration: An Elusive Virtue*. Princeton, NJ: Princeton University Press, 18–27.

1985. *Ethics and the Limits of Philosophy*. Cambridge, MA: Harvard University Press.

1981. *Moral Luck: Philosophical Papers 1973–1980*. Cambridge: Cambridge University Press.

1976. *Problems of the Self*. Cambridge: Cambridge University Press.

1972. *Morality: An Introduction to Ethics*. Cambridge: Cambridge University Press.

Wohlschlager, A., and Bekkering, H. 2002. 'The Role of Objects in Imitation'. In M. Stamenov and V. Gallese, eds., *Mirror Neurons and the Evolution of Brain and Language*. Amsterdam: John Benjamins, 101–114.
Wolf, S. 2007. 'Moral Psychology and the Unity of the Virtues'. *Ratio* 20: 145–167.
Wrathall, M. 2015. 'Autonomy, Authenticity, and the Self'. In D. McManus, ed., *Heidegger, Authenticity, and the Self: Themes from Division Two of Being and Time*. New York: Routledge, 193–214.
Young, C. 2009. 'Courage'. In G. Anagnostopoulos, ed., *A Companion to Aristotle*. Oxford: Blackwell.
Zagzebski, L. 2017. *Exemplarist Moral Theory*. Oxford: Oxford University Press.
    2013. 'Moral Exemplars in Theory and Practice'. *Theory and Research in Education* 11: 193–206.
    2010. 'Exemplarist Virtue Theory'. *Metaphilosophy* 41: 41–57.
    2006. 'The Admirable Life and the Desirable Life'. In T. Chappell, ed., *Values and Virtues: Aristotelianism in Contemporary Ethics*. Oxford: Oxford University Press, 53–66.
Zahavi, D. 2001. *Husserl and Transcendental Intersubjectivity*, E. A. Behnke, trans. Athens: Ohio University Press
    1999. *Self-Awareness and Alterity*. Evanston, IL: Northwestern University Press.

Index

action
   fluid, 132–137, 140, 145, 147–148, 150;
      See also agency, practical; critical
      comparison; moral perception; *phronēsis*
      (practical intelligence); reason, practical
   intentional structure of, 20
   norm-governed, 16, 18–19
   unity of, 17; *See also* moral evaluation, action
      as object of; flourishing, as normative
      balance; right action
action-guidingness. *See* excellence; flourishing, as
   living excellently; moral evaluation, action
   as object of; moral exemplars; virtue
   ethics, right action; virtues
aesthetic judgment. *See* Kant, Immanuel
agency, 3, 31, 35, 40, 43, 46, 78, 133, 145, 158,
      174–175
   and autonomy, 40, 45, 122, 127, 132
   and deliberation, 44, 132
   and habituation, 130
   intentional structure of, 16, 18
   and intentionality, 16, 116
   limited nature of, 172
   and moral luck, 12
   norm-responsive, 9, 146, 148
   and patience, 156–157, 160, 164
   phenomenology of, 15, 33, 66, 77, 79, 125,
      133–150, 167, 173; *See also* attunement;
      Heidegger, Martin
   practical, 15, 40, 77, 134, 136
   temporal, 12, 14–15, 18–19, 21, 31, 41, 46,
      156, 161, 173; *See also* finitude, as
      temporal dispersal
altruism, 30, 65, 220
Annas, Julia, 12, 30, 92, 110, 122, 131, 136–137
anxiety
   existential, 147, 204
   and foreclosure of possibilities, 155
arête (virtue), 71, 74. *See also* Socrates; virtues
Aristotle, 98, 113, 155, 175
   on agency, 92
   on confidence, 213–216
   on courage, 10, 202, 205, 207, 213–214, 216,
      218
   on deliberation, 132
   on the emotions, 119
   on *ergon* (function), 26–27, 33
   on *eudaimonia*, 77–79; *See also eudaimonia*
   on fear, 213–217
   on friendship, 42, 143
   on the good, 130
   on the good life, 31
   on habituation, 118–121, 129
   on honour, 218
   on hope, 214
   on justice, 79, 100
   on *mimesis*, 114, 125
   Nicomachean Ethics, 41–42, 79, 83, 87,
      89–93, 118–120, 130–131, 139
   on the noble, 33, 42, 121, 130, 139, 218–219
   on *phronēsis* (practical intelligence), 89–93,
      107, 122, 131, 150
   on pleasure, 121
   on practical reason, 33, 223
   on rashness, 213–216
   on self-love, 41–43
   on the soul, 33, 130, 223
   on temperance, 69
arrogance, 194–195
attunement, 35–36, 70, 201. *See also* agency,
   phenomenology of; Heidegger, Martin
Augenblick (moment of vision), 211–212
authenticity, 212
   and courage, 212; *See also* courage
autonomy, 40, 45, 121–122, 127, 132, 158.
   See also agency; Korsgaard, Christine

bad faith. *See also* arrogance; perfectionism
   in self-understanding, 1, 7, 193–199
   in virtue ethics, 1, 8, 66, 196–199
being in the world, 7–8, 33, 36–38, 50, 64–65, 74,
   76, 78–79, 85, 108–110, 113, 115, 118,

241

Index

142, 150, 163, 221–222, 226; *See also* flourishing, as normative responsivity
as care, 36, 45, 78, 93, 97, 223–224; *See also* Heidegger, Martin
Bentham, Jeremy, 24
Bommarito, Nicholas, 159, 161–165, 168–169
Bratman, Michael, 19, 46, 134
Buddhism, 161, 165, 176

care. *See* being in the world, as care
  ethics of, 55
Chang, Ruth, 94–98
character, 12–14, 18, 73; *See also* excellence; flourishing; virtues
  dispositionalist account of, 16, 18
  and habituation, 14, 143, 162, 173
  as modes of responsivity, 16
charity, virtue of, 28
community, 3, 8, 56, 58–59, 61, 64, 84, 94–95, 98, 100, 103, 114, 128, 144, 148, 150, 158–160, 170, 174, 176, 220, 222–223. *See also* flourishing, third-personal dimension of; Kant, Immanuel; normative claim(s), third-personal
confidence, 213–216
consciousness, 6
consequentialism, 116
courage, 10, 17, 22, 86–87, 89, 96, 147, 202–222; *See also* virtues
  as choosing one's better self, 10, 214, 218–220, 222
  and confidence, 213–218
  and fear, 213–218
  as masculine virtue, 209
  and normative balance, 213, 215, 217, 221
  as problem-solving stance, 70, 203, 205–207, 209–210, 212–213, 219, 221, 226
  and self-control, 216
Crisp, Roger, 27
critical comparison, 9, 24, 35, 49, 94–98, 107–109, 113, 136–150, 226. *See also* flourishing, as normative responsivity; moral perception; reason, practical; normative claim(s), competing; virtues, as problem-solving stances
critical distance, 132–133, 136–150. *See also* critical comparison; deliberation; habituation; moral exemplars; moral perception; normative responsivity
Crowell, Steven, 6, 52, 133, 146

Darwall, Stephen, 50–56, 187
death, 147, 167, 186
  existential, 147, 203–209, 212, 218, 222
  physical, 202, 205, 218, 222

for the sake of the noble, 222
deliberation, 24, 90, 125–128, 131–132, 136–145, 148, 150, 213, 224, 226; *See also* critical comparison; habituation; moral exemplars; moral perception; normative responsivity
  and courage, 221
  as distinguishing human feature, 132
  and moral perception, 10, 131, 136–144
deontic constraints, 5, 82, 99–101. *See also* rights, concept of
deontology, 65, 116
  Kantian, 4
  as third-personal stance, 4
dispositionism. *See* character
Driver, Julia, 178–180, 182–183, 196, 210

egoism, motivational, 75–77, 79, 220–222
embodiment, as defining human feature, 72
emotions, 91–92, 112, 119, 127, 129–130
endurance, 216
Enlightenment, the, 62
ergon (function), 35
eudaimonia, 22, 27, 29–30, 75–79, 105, 109. *See also* excellence; flourishing
excellence. *See also* flourishing
  of character, 68, 80, 88, 92, 112, 119, 128, 131, 143, 148, 199–200, 202, 208, 212, 219, 225
  as habituation, 15, 92, 143, 216
  second-personal modes of, 221
  third-personal modes of, 188
excellent life. *See* Aristotle; flourishing; moral evaluation, life as object of
existentialism. *See* phenomenology, existential

fear, 213–217
finitude
  as defining human feature, 72, 106, 176
  and patience, 152, 155, 175
  as temporal dispersal, 10, 12, 15, 152, 156, 167, 171, 173, 175; *See also* time, phenomenology of
  temporal scarcity, 10, 69–70, 152–158, 171–173, 175, 204
finitude, radical. *See* death, existential
flourishing, 165; *See also* critical comparison; excellence; moral perception; *phronēsis* (practical intelligence); reason, practical; virtues
  Aristotelian account of, 26
  challenges to, 69–70, 72–73, 80, 88, 91, 151–152, 156
  first-personal dimension of, 1–2, 4, 8, 23, 28–29, 40–50, 76, 98, 109–128, 158

Index

hybrid views, 24, 28
impossibility of, 98, 101–106, 130
as incomplete project, 70, 108, 125, 142
as living excellently, 1, 4–5, 14, 22, 30, 35, 38–39, 43, 63, 70, 88, 223–226
and moral exemplars, *See also* moral exemplars
as normative balance, 3–5, 8–9, 20, 33, 35–39, 41, 45, 64–65, 69, 71, 73, 76, 79, 81–82, 98, 101, 119, 148, 160, 224–225
as normative responsivity, 1, 3, 14, 18, 35–36, 38, 41, 46, 51, 56, 63–64, 68–70, 72, 76, 78–79, 87–88, 98, 109, 150, 200, 213, 220, 224
objectivist accounts of, 8, 25–31, 37, 65
naturalism, 26, 29, 34–35, 72
phenomenology of, 19, 35, 82, 123, 129, 133, 212
second-personal dimension of, 2, 4, 50–56, 76
as self-world fit, 1, 9, 32–33, 35–37, 39, 47–48, 68, 72, 76, 78, 148, 223
subjectivist accounts of, 7–8, 23–25, 28, 30–31, 35, 37, 224
hedonism, 23–24
third-personal dimension of, 1–2, 4, 8, 31, 42, 56–65, 76, 105, 128, 144
world-embedded, 32–33, 36, 50, 58, 63, 72, 224
fluid action. *See* action, fluid
Foot, Philippa, 26, 83
forgiveness, 172
fortitude, 207–208
freedom, 50, 147, 195–198. *See also* bad faith, in self-understanding
friendship, 95, 118. *See also* Aristotle; self-becoming; virtues

generosity, 84, 86, 158
good, the, 17, 23, 26, 35, 170
Aristotle on, 130
good life, the, 30, 140, 142, 226; *See also* excellence; flourishing; virtues
Aristotelian, 31
goods, 77–78, 95, 151
knowledge, 77–78
pleasure, 77–78
plurality of. *See* Aristotle; normative claim(s), plurality of

habituation, 9, 108–109, 118–125, 129–130, 149–150; *See also* critical comparison; critical distance; deliberation; moral perception; normative responsivity
Aristotle on, 118–122, 129
moral exemplars and, 118–125, 129
self-becoming and, 109, 118–125, 129

Haybron, Daniel, 30
hedonism. *See* flourishing, subjectivist accounts of
Hegel, Georg Wilhelm Friedrich, 62
Heidegger, Martin, 7, 20, 131, 139, 146–147, 204, 210–213; *See also* agency, phenomenology of; attunement
on death, 203, 205
on lived time, 15
Herder, Johann Gottfried, 43
honesty, 49, 86, 88–89, 112
honour, Aristotle on, 218
Hurka, Thomas, 75–78
Hursthouse, Rosalind, 28, 127, 131
on V-rules, 111–114
Husserl, Edmund, 6–7, 57–61, 78
on objectivity, 57–58
on perspectival incompleteness, 59
on scientific understanding, 57–59
on solipsism, 57–58

identity, 10, 22; *See also* self, the
existential awareness of, 212, 221–222
grounding, 205–208, 210, 213, 216
peripheral, 210
and self-becoming, 42–43, 50
and self-creation, 43–50
and stable traits, 13
imagination, role in self-becoming, 125, 191
impatience, 152, 167, 174–176
and anxiety, 155, 173
as foreclosure of possibilities, 154, 173
as moralism, 171
and perfectionism, 171
as self-privileging, 155
as temporal orientation, 154, 171
incommensurability, 9
incommensurable normative claims, 6, 9, 65, 93–98
individuality. *See* flourishing, first-personal dimension of
injustice, 83
integrity, 100
intentionality, 6–7, 15–16
intersubjectivity. *See* flourishing, third-personal dimension of

justice, 4, 9, 22, 31, 55, 62, 73–87, 89, 92; *See also* deontic constraints; rights, concept of; virtues
as global virtue, 4, 9–10, 74, 79–84, 91, 100–102, 226
institutional, 74, 79
second-personal dimension of, 82–83
self-directed, 83–85, 98–100
as specific virtue, 10, 74, 79–80, 83, 98–99, 226

Index

Kant, Immanuel, 44, 132
   on moral exemplars, 116, 122
   on moral judgement, 122
   on *sensus communis*, 60–64
Kierkegaard, Søren, 67, 146, 161, 167–168, 176, 211
Korsgaard, Christine, 13, 19, 27, 34, 40–41, 43, 132–134, 149

Lévinas, Emmanuel, 51–56, 131, 221
   on asymmetry, 51, 53
   on the face-to-face, 52–55
   on freedom, 52, 54
love
   Aristotle, on self-, 41–43
   mimetic, and moral exemplars, 114–118, 129, 138, 141

McDowell, John, 130–131
metaphysics, 176
Mill, John Stuart, 24. *See also* flourishing, subjectivist accounts of
mimesis (imitation), 108–109, 123, 141. *See also* moral exemplars, and mimetic love
   Aristotle on, 114, 125
modesty, 10, 22, 181; *See also* virtues
   and arrogance, 181–182, 184, 186, 189–190, 193–196, 199
   egalitarian view, 185–197
   false, 179, 184, 186, 198
   as feminine virtue, 181
   first-personal dimension of, 182–184, 190
   as ignorance of self-worth, 179
   as normative balance, 178, 187, 189–190, 192, 196, 199–201
   phenomenology of, 180, 182, 186, 193
   as problem-solving stance, 70, 178, 185, 201, 226
   second-personal dimension of, 180–184, 187, 192, 200
   and self-abnegation, 182, 190, 197
   and self-deprecation, 179
   third-personal dimension of, 10, 183, 185, 187, 190
moral evaluation. *See* critical comparison; deliberation; flourishing; habituation; moral perception; normative claim(s); normative responsivity
   action as object of, 4, 12–14, 16–17, 19–20, 81, 111; *See also* Sher, George
   character as object of, 12–13, 16, 18–19, 21
   life as object of, 1, 8–9, 12–13, 17, 19–21, 76, 81, 112, 115–117, 139, 143
   phenomenology of, 131
moral exemplars, 9, 45, 82, 108–118, 121–125, 141, 143; *See also* flourishing; normative responsivity

bad, 9, 129, 132, 145
   and critical distance, 10, 136–150
   and deliberation, 125–128, 136–144
   and habituation, 118–125, 129
   and mimetic love, 114–118, 129, 138, 141–142
   and narrativity, 145
   and normative balance, 170
   and perspectival balancing, 5
moral luck, 12, 80, 101, 104, 106, 215. *See also* agency and moral luck; flourishing; virtue ethics
moral perception, 10, 130–131, 134–136, 151, 217. *See also* critical comparison; deliberation; flourishing, as normative responsivity; habituation; moral exemplars; *phronēsis* (practical intelligence); reason, practical; virtues
moral theory, 63
mortality. *See* finitude, temporal scarcity

narcissism, 220. *See also* egoism, motivational
narrativity
   patience and, 169
   and the self, 45
   self-becoming and, 118, 143
naturalism, 1, 26, 29, 34–35, 72. *See also* flourishing, objectivist accounts of; virtue ethics
Nietzsche, Friedrich, 47, 49, 67, 207, 222
   on self-becoming, 47–48
   on self-overcoming, 211
   on virtue, 219
noble, the, 205, 210, 217, 222. *See also* Aristotle
normative balance. *See* normative claim(s), balance of
normative claim(s), 2–8, 29
   balance of, 3, 65, 73, 76, 93, 109, 156, 170, 187, 191, 216, 223, 225
   competing, 3–5, 20, 64–66, 73, 79–82, 93, 103, 196, 221, 223, 225
   first-personal, 2–3, 35, 37, 40–47, 50, 82, 100, 104, 223–224
   incommensurable, 6, 9, 65, 93–98
   irreducible, 2–4, 64–65, 70, 93, 149, 159, 223–225
   plurality of, 3, 5, 8–9, 37–38, 64–66, 68, 72, 76, 85, 92, 94, 101–102, 148–149, 151, 196, 199, 201, 219, 223, 225–226
   second-personal, 2–3, 37, 50–56, 66, 94, 100, 122, 220, 222–224
   third-personal, 2–3, 37, 56–64, 78, 100–101, 138–139, 141, 190, 220, 223–224
   world-embedded, 224
normative demand. *See* normative claim(s)

Index

normative perspective. *See* perspective, normative
normative responsivity, 134–136. *See also* critical comparison; critical distance; deliberation; flourishing, as normative responsivity; habituation; moral exemplars; moral perception; *phronēsis* (practical intelligence); reason, practical; virtues
normativity. *See* normative claim(s)
Nozick, Robert, 23

objectivity, 57, 60, 63
   Husserl on, 57–58

patience, 86, 96, 152, 177; *See also* virtues
   as character trait, 160
   contrasted with complacency, 155
   contrasted with endurance, 153, 157
   and entitlement, 175–177
   first-personal dimension of, 156, 159
   and narrativity, 169
   and normative balance, 155, 160, 170, 177
   as orientation to world, 172
   as problem-solving stance, 10, 70, 152, 175, 226
   second-personal dimension of, 10, 153, 155–157, 159, 164
   and self-abnegation, 159
   as self-restraint, 153, 155–158, 160–161, 164, 166, 172–175
   as temporal orientation, 154–155, 158, 160–162, 164–169, 171, 174–175
   third-personal dimension of, 156, 158
   as tolerance, 156–160
perception, 57–60, 78, 117, 130–132, 134–137, 141, 217. *See also* moral perception
perfectionism, 103
   and impatience, 171
perseverance, 207
perspective, normative. *See* normative claim(s), first-personal; normative claim(s), plurality of; normative claim(s), second-personal; normative claim(s), third-personal
phenomenology, existential, 1–2, 5, 7
   first-personal, 6
   and metaphysics, 169
   as method, 2, 6–8, 38, 65–67, 169
   second-personal, 6
   third-personal, 6
phronēsis (practical intelligence), 4, 9, 71, 89–93, 107, 131, 146, 150–151, 159, 211; *See also* Aristotle; critical comparison; flourishing, as normative balance; flourishing, as normative responsivity; reason, practical; virtues, as problem-solving stances
   and deliberation, 91–92
   as moral perception, 134
   as primary virtue, 91
Plato
   on the Forms, 110
   on justice, 74, 91
   Republic, 74, 83
pleasure, 8, 23, 31–32, 38, 42, 61, 69, 78, 109, 120–121, 124, 213–214, 225. *See also* Aristotle, on pleasure; goods, pleasure
   aesthetic, 62

rashness, 214–215. *See also* Aristotle, on courage
Rawls, John, 74
reason, practical, 8, 33–37, 45, 65, 96–97, 122, 132, 134, 223–224; *See also* critical comparison; flourishing, as normative responsivity; moral perception; normative claim(s), competing *phronēsis* (practical intelligence); virtues, as problem-solving stances
   and deliberation, 8, 35–36
   and normative plurality, 8
relativism, 68, 72–73, 144–145. *See also* flourishing, challenges to; virtues, as problem-solving stances
responsibility, 50, 147, 192–195, 198–199, 201, 212, 220, 224
   as 'resoluteness', 212; *See also* Heidegger, Martin
right action, 77, 82, 107
   agent-centered, 9, 112
   consequentialism, 12
   deontology, 12
   and self-control, 13
   Utilitarianism, 5
   world-embedded, 1–2, 64
rights, concept of, 55, 62, 95, 99–101. *See also* deontic constraints; justice
role models. *See* moral exemplars
Romanticism, 43–46, 48–49, 62
Rudd, Anthony, 167–169
Russell, David, 16, 90, 119, 121, 128

Sartre, Jean-Paul, 81
Scheler, Max, 115–116
Schueler, G. F., 179–180, 182, 197
science, 33, 63–64. *See also* Husserl, Edmund, on scientific understanding
Seinkönnen (ability-to-be), 139, 146. *See also* flourishing, as normative responsivity; identity; virtues, as problem-solving stances; virtues, skill model of